6482

IMPORTANT TO ME

IMPORTANT TO ME

PERSONALIA

Pamela Hansford Johnson

MACMILLAN

SBN 333 16559 4

First published 1974 by
MACMILLAN LONDON LIMITED
London and Basingstoke
Associated companies in New York Dublin
Melbourne Johannesburg and Delhi

Printed in Great Britain by
NORTHUMBERLAND PRESS LIMITED
Gateshead

Contents

TO THE YOUNG SOFAERS –
Clive, David Jr and Moira

Introduction

This book is not a straight autobiography, though by its nature it must contain a sizeable amount of autobiographical matter. No novelist should attempt to write his full autobiography – he has written himself and his life into his novels, no matter how much both are disguised. I am conscious of only two direct self-portraits in the whole of my books: but how could I have made the portrait of anyone, *The Unspeakable Skipton* included, without having something of him, however buried, however far from being consciously realised, in myself? Tolstoy said that he had no imagination. Who am I to claim any? Although I could swear that many of my characters are products of imagination pure and simple, I could be wrong. At least some of their backgrounds have been imagined or researched, but farther than that I cannot go.

This, then, is a book of reflections upon things that have been important to me in my life, and some acknowledgment of people who have enhanced it. I am, perhaps, old enough now to write these things with some confidence, without much caring how much I may make a fool of myself. But I cannot write in a starshell burst of orange revelation, about people who are still alive and could be wounded. Certainly not intimately about my children. They are all full-grown. I only hope they will forgive me my shortcomings towards them. They have, of course, been among the great importances. I have often failed them, and I know it. But I only hope, as I say, to be forgiven. It is hard for me to believe in divine forgiveness if one has not the forgiveness of the living. Poor theology, I suppose. It never was my strong point.

1. St Mark's and Mr Russell's

St Mark's Church stands almost at the peak of the Other Battersea Rise. We called it that because we lived on the opposite
one. The Rise sweeps down from Clapham Common (our side)
down to the junction of St John's and Northcote Roads, and up
again to Wandsworth Common, to the West. We lived in
a large brick terrace house bought by my grandfather some
time in the eighties, when it looked out on fields where sheep
might safely graze. But by the time I was born, the railway
had come, and the houses had been built up right over the hills
between it and us. Not pretty, I suppose. But in my childhood
I could create an Arabian Nights fantasy about anything, and
found the smoky sunset between the spires of St Mark's and the
Masonic School magical to contemplate. (Just as I found beauty
in the 1911 turrets of my red-brick school, also between the
two Commons, in Broomwood Road.)

My mother took me faithfully to St Mark's on Sunday
mornings, and never let me out before the sermon. On the
whole, sermon apart, I enjoyed it: I revelled in Broad Church
ritual. The Stanford *Te Deum*! There was a real male choir
in those days, and I would wait breathless for the great basses
to come in with 'the holy company of the apostles praise thee'.
(I think that was where they came in.) And the springlike
unbudding of the Benedicite, which came far too seldom.
There was never a time when all this failed to move me
emotionally: and I often wonder if, today, I go to church so
rarely because I am lazy, or because it comes at unreasonable
hours, or because I cannot bear the often quite irrelevant flood-
ing of emotion which it induces.

My father, on his rare terms of leave from the Gold Coast,
where he was a Civil Servant on the railways, used to assure

my mother that he too would gladly accompany us to St
Mark's, if only they would let him smoke.

He died of a coronary thrombosis when I was eleven, on his
penultimate leave before retirement. But that is another story.

I may say that from those early days, belief was with me:
and I have not changed it, though aware that faith is not
enough. Sometimes I feel, often now, unpopular with the
Lord. I don't wonder at it.

But when I was fifteen, my way of worship was abruptly
changed by my Aunt Kalie (a corruption of her beautiful and
Stendhalian name, Clélia). She began to attend Clapham
Congregational Church, under the ministry of the brilliant,
histrionic George Stanley Russell, and nothing would do for
her but that I must go there too.

The Church was in Grafton Square, in Clapham Old Town,
a bus ride away from us. Mr Russell was a tall, rubicund, rather
portly man with a magnificent voice: and a taste for ceremonial that I failed to find later among other Nonconformist
ministers. (It was, of course, eccentric and contrary to Con-
gregationalist ethos.) Musically, the services were admirable:
Stanford in *A* occasionally, but usually Vaughan Williams. I
was not deprived of my favourite hymns – 'O Worship the
King', 'Immortal, Invisible', etc. – and was really interested
in the sermons, which, though overlong, often took their texts
from Shakespeare and Shaw. The literary and musical societies
were run on a high level: I remember the young John Barbir-
olli and William Primrose giving us recitals, though one of
the latter's was nearly disrupted by a fit of *fou rire* from the
brother of my best friend, who had just discovered that I was
wearing my Wellington boots on the wrong feet.

The differences between Clapham Congregational and St
Mark's were not, at that time, very clear to me: except that
I much approved of extempore prayers, and of the practice of
baptising a child before the whole congregation. (I had been
baptised into the Church of England myself.) I was fourteen

when I was first led to sit under Mr Russell: sixteen when, after a brief course of instruction, I was received as a church member, and took my first Communion: which, as the wine came round in tiny glasses, instead of being taken from a common cup, should have pleased me for hygienic reasons but never did. My mother used scornfully to call it a 'Nippy' service. Nippies were then Lyons' waitresses.

Under the influence of Mr Russell, and Martin Attwater, his handsome, Spanish-looking choir-master, the church burgeoned and in fact became what I can only call 'smart'. It attracted most of the intellectuals of Clapham (there were a good many, in varying degrees) and was always crowded. There was a sizeable homosexual element. I might mention that Martin Attwater gave me piano-lessons, and would rap me over the knuckles in the old-fashioned way, when he felt I had done insufficient practice. This did not at all prevent me from being in love with him: I was always, in a greenstick way, in love with somebody or other, and never went through the normal period of passion for my own sex. I had all the promise of being a tolerable pianist, but gave it up because my fingers were slightly webbed and I could only just stretch an octave.

Much later on, when Mr Russell had been transported to the big Deer Park Church in Toronto – premises extensive and car provided – I found myself increasingly drawn back towards the Church of England. For I had found – and this, I know, is a kind of frivolity, proving that my Nonconformism was not very sincere – that there weren't very many Mr Russells about.

The streak of emotional Calvinism in my make-up was not, so far as I can see, attributed either to Mr Russell or to St Mark's. It is a grim streak, emergent only at times, when I think of William Cowper. The doctrine of the Damned and the Elect is one of the most dreadful ever formulated, but, though I don't believe it, I cannot forget it. It drove Cowper mad. The trouble was that I could never be sure that I was

either, but I think most Calvinists must have felt themselves
Elect or life would have been intolerable. When I think of
religion in the Middle Ages, and then look at medieval paintings where people are heartily enjoying themselves, I cannot
think that they believed, more than sporadically, in their horrible idea of Hell.

But there is some comfort. The Abbé Mugnier – quoted by
George D. Painter in his biography of Marcel Proust – in
answer to a lady's question as to whether he believed in hell,
replied – 'Yes, because it is a dogma of the Church, but I don't
believe there is anyone in it.'

My two elder children were baptised in the Congregational
Church at Staines. My son by my second marriage was
christened (for complicated reasons) at the age of three, walking to the ceremony with much pride and only regretting
that he had not been given a speaking part, in a Church of
England ceremony in Christ's College Chapel, Cambridge, by
Canon Ian Ramsey, later Bishop of Durham, and confirmed in
his school Chapel. Andrew, my eldest son, by my first marriage, refused to be confirmed at all and I had to write the
most difficult letter to his headmaster concerning his 'doubts'.
(He had no doubts.)

All this brings me to my own problem. Years later, when
I had remarried, I attended for a while the excellent Kensington Chapel. But I found it too austere. I was being steadily
drawn back to the Church of England, and I should have
liked to take Communion there. But it seems to me I can't,
unless, at the age of sixty, I am confirmed in that faith. For
some reason, I can't go through with this. Liberal churchmen
have told me that since I was christened into the C. of E. I
should go ahead and take the Sacraments where I choose. But
that, it seems to me, is swindling. Churchmen not so liberal
have more or less agreed with me. So I have become no church-
goer, and guilty at times because of it.

I am always guilty about something. Guilt has been my besetting misfortune, a torment to attack me at the strangest moments.

However in *The Times* text for the day, I have just read this: 'I have swept away your transgressions like a cloud, and your sins like mist: return to me for I have redeemed you.' Isaiah 44:22.

Can this be so?

2. Auschwitz

'As I looked towards the east, high up to the sun, I saw a tower on a hill-top well and truly made: a deep dale beneath with a dungeon in it, with deep ditches and dark ones, dreadful to see. A fair field of folk I found between them, all manner of men, the middling and the rich, working and wandering, as the world asks.'

Langland, *Piers Plowman*
trans. Nevill Coghill.

It was a magnificent, warm, golden day in the late summer of 1967 when Charles, my husband, my younger son Philip, his friend Martin, and our interpreter, set out from Cracow to Auschwitz. (Auschwitz is what the Germans called it: in Polish it is Oswiecim.) The boys were then fifteen. I had said to them, 'This is history: but it is horrible history. Do you want to go?' They said they did. First, we stopped at a farm where we bought flowers to lay eventually upon the monument. We rode on past fair fields of folk, ploughing with ancient implements: it was idyllic for us, but I don't suppose it was for them. They would have preferred to have tractors. But there it was, the bright earth, the men and women in bright colours, the docile oxen before them.

I had steeled myself for what we were going to see: perhaps too rigorously, as it turned out. It was a long drive, but at last we came to the small town of Oswiecim, which is commonplace. But it is near to the camps, which were reached by a single-track railway. What was heard? What smoke seen to ascend? I had reached my peak of political consciousness and activity in the middle thirties: the thirties have haunted me ever since. But the boys? They were both highly intelligent and well-read in modern history, but to them it must necessarily be hearsay. Was the murder of 6,000,000 Jews carried out by what must have been a large and efficient Civil Service, even

conceivable? I remember being awakened to the reality of Naz-
ism in 1934 by, of all places to find it, a photograph in *Time*
magazine, of a girl shaven and placarded, being paraded
through – where? Nuremburg? I can't recall. But I do recall
the vividness of the shock, horror and rage, that human beings
should behave so to each other. They were to behave a million
times worse.

At last we came to the camp itself. Over the entrance was the
risible legend (had one felt like laughing) ARBEIT MACHT
FREI (Work makes Free). It was a tidy settlement, the doing
of an orderly people. God knows they were orderly. There were
neat brick barrack blocks, divided by roads along which trees
were nicely planted. We went into the visitors' hall, which was
no more ominous than the hall of a well-run hospital: an
information desk, pamphlets, seats for the weary or for the
overcome. Now it was hot, at the peak of the day. Next we
went into the first of the exhibition rooms: behind large
plate-glass windows were the huge-piled relics of the murdered: teeth, hair, rags, a few toys. I noticed two little plaits,
a child's plaits, still tied with faded blue ribbon.

And I could not feel. The pain itself had numbed pain. Try
as I would, I could not react: I might have been making a
tour of an engineering works. I could not tell what Charles or
Philip were feeling: their faces showed nothing.

We went on, through room after room, till we came to the
gas-ovens. Martin had, by this time, retired to the open air. The
gas-ovens. We were shown over them by guides, some of them
ex-prisoners here, who exhibited a kind of gusto that was
almost cheerful. I stared at rusted iron: that was all it was, to
me.

At last, that part of the visit was over. We rejoined Martin,
and went to see the gallows on which Hoess, Commandant of
the camp, was hanged. It seemed a very small gallows.

And at once I was flooded by all the emotions that had
repressed themselves. The full horror broke over me, the dying

millions. Charles, Philip and Martin, to whom the dreadful-
ness had been present all the time, were visibly shaken. I don't
know that I was. All this revulsion was inside me.

We got in the car, and bumped over fields – there was no
road then – to the monument to the victims of Auschwitz. It
was the boys who laid the flowers upon it. Extremely hot now,
and the petals shrivelling in the sun.

It was some time later that I learned how their attitudes
differed from mine. Yes, they seemed to think, this must not
be forgotten nor forgiven, *but it was the past*, and it was their
business to remake the future. We could not remain at enmity
with any nation for ever. At any rate the English young –
and not just the young – were deeply moved by Willy Brandt's
grave and audacious gesture when he knelt three years later on
the steps of the Auschwitz monument.

The Russians of my generation, with their twenty million
dead (that may be an understatement) are only now learning
a degree of compulsory forgetting. (Only just.) I think I
expressed, not unfairly, the attitude of the older Russians, who
had experienced the war, in Mamonov's speech regarding the
Germans, at his own table, in my novel, *The Survival of the
Fittest*. What the young Russians think I don't know. I have
had many opportunities to ask them, but somehow I never
have.

Standing looking out across the Polish fields, now glossed
by a sun beginning to set, like a landscape by Samuel Palmer,
I thought of our own war crimes. I have heard the atom bombing of Hiroshima defended often enough: I say that it was
indefensible. It could have been dropped off-shore as a warning, and I dare say would have done harm enough then.
I first heard the news from Frank Phillips, who had just
announced it, when I happened to meet him in the B.B.C.
club after some broadcast of my own. I have never felt more
sick, or more ashamed. And of course, the subsequent bombing of Nagasaki was damnable, and beyond all reason. So

were lesser things, like the militarily useless and wanton bombing of Dresden.

I do not subscribe to the fashionable shibboleth that 'we are
all guilty'. It is an escapist's excuse for not feeling guilty
about anything at all. I shall revert to this subject. I did not
know the atom bomb existed, and had I known, and had I
been older and in any position of power, should have protested
at the plan to drop it with every bit of force at my disposal, as
Szilard and his colleagues did – without result. But the feeling
of shame persists. It will not be forgiven those who were
responsible.

I thought of all this as the boys rose from spreading their
dead flowers on the memorial. At least – and this I took for
my comfort – we had not so much collective guilt for the
cruelty of individual man to individual man. This seems to me
the worst of all, that gleeful (or indifferent) eyes must have
met eyes in terror.

We rode back to Cracow through the sunset, and I do not
think we talked much of what we had experienced that day.
Indeed, as the evening wore on, I believe we ceased to think
about it. 'We forget because we must.'

3. R.K.

Reginald Kenneth Johnson was my father, born in 1874. He was seven years older than my mother.

R.K., as his friends on the Gold Coast came to call him, was born in the tiny Dorset village of Nettlecombe, near Powerstock – no metropolis in itself – into a notably pious family, of which he was, in a sense, the black sheep: his brother Dudley had been preparing for ordination when the First World War came, and he was killed in the trenches. As a young man, R.K. would outrage his mother by such ditties as this:

> David wrote to the Captain of the Host
> My friend, if you'd be savèd,
> Put Uriah in the front of the fire,
> I am, yours truly, David.

But, black sheep as he might be, he was never cast out – he was very fond of his mother, who always had ready for him supplies of cold tea, which he loved.

When I was born in 1912, the Johnson side of the family had left the country and had created a curiously countrified atmosphere about them in a small villa off Broomwood Road, where I was later to go to school. The house was rather fusty, smelling of lavender, biscuits, and something quite indefinable. Grandmother Johnson and Aunt Minnie provided enormous high teas for me and my two cousins: ham, salad, pears and custard, and cream cakes. Outside was a small garden with a laburnum tree. My cousin Kenneth and I used to go and pop the pods. It never occurred to us to eat their contents, which I now know was lucky for us.

R.K. had taken up his job on the Gold Coast, as Chief Storekeeper on the Baro-Kano railway, many years before my birth, and before his marriage to my mother. (The Johnsons were shocked: 'An actress!' but they came to accept her.) He was in love with Africa. His tours of duty were long – I can't remember whether I exaggerate when I say three years – with three months leave in between. But he would only have been home a month before he began to hear what he insisted on describing as 'the call of the Coast', and fret to be getting back, among – so he said – the spicy smells, the parrots, the witch-doctors, and the long evenings on the verandahs with whisky and poker-games. (The last were to be his downfall. Poker was his passion, but he was apparently no dab hand at it.) I think he would have been amused had he known that Philip, his grandson, who made a trip along the length of East Africa at the age of sixteen and returned to Tanzania three years later, had also, in a very different way, heard that call. Why, Philip asks me, had I never gone to Africa? Well, children like myself never did, and women very seldom – certainly not mother. The Gold Coast was known as 'The White Man's Grave', and there were few wives to interrupt the poker schools.

R.K. was one of the old-fashioned type of Colonial administrator: the concept of a wind of change was not one that would have entered his head, though I found out that his junior colleagues, who gave me and my mother much help and comfort after his death, were of a very different mind. They knew that a change was coming – not when – but when it came they would be prepared for it.

He used to cane his 'boys' (his African servants) for flagrant wrongdoing, but claimed, with what seems to me quite unjustifiable optimism, that they never resented this. At all events, he insisted, the 'boys' hardly ever ran away from him, and no one ever put ground-glass in his soup. His younger friends did assure me later that, so far as Colonial administrators went, he was popular. But sometimes I do not like to look Philip's many African friends – and mine – in the face. I hope they will not visit the sins of the fathers upon the children, even unto the third and fourth generations.

What was R.K. like? I hardly remember. I had no time to. But I do recall that when expecting him home on leave, we would stand waiting in the drawing-room window for his appearance on the Rise. And sure enough, he would appear in the sunset – bronzed as a sea captain, bearing some extraordinary gift, such as a Benin mask, and once a canary in a cage, which he had already christened 'Battling Siki', after a prize-fighter of the period.

I think he was a good-looking, though not a handsome, man. My mother always claimed that he resembled the long-gone matinée idol, Lewis Waller, and I suppose, judging from photographs, that this was not altogether without its point. His features were rugged but clear, his upper-lip on the long side, like mine, his thick hair parted in the middle. A little above average height, no more.

What I do recall was his passion for children. Sometimes he would meet me from school; and a Pied Piper's ragtail and bobtail of my friends would go with us all the way, with R.K. filling us up with sweets at every sweetshop we passed. I do not think he ever spoke a cross word to me – though doubtless he did not know me well enough to do so.

When I was seven, my mother gave birth to another child, a girl, my sister. Of course, I had had no warning of the event. It still gives me shame to think how I resented this. I clung to the stairs leading down into the garden, and prayed that I should be glad. Under the hollyhocks, I prayed with fervour. Beryl was an extremely pretty baby (a turn of the screw) and I tried to love her. When she died of marasmus, a wasting disease, at the age of five or six months, I tried, under those same sacramental hollyhocks, to feel sorry. I couldn't. It was the beginning of guilt.

One morning, during R.K.'s final leave – or what was to be his final leave – my mother woke me abruptly. She was wearing a very gaudy jacket (in order not to frighten me, she said later) and told me that my father was not too well, and that I must spend the day with friends.

Of course, he was dead. He had gone to the lavatory (two floors down) in the middle of the night, and had not come back. He was found by my Aunt Kalie, who had been in love with him, though unexpectedly he had proposed to my mother. She recalled to me afterwards, that, on the very night, I had been singing in my bed (at the top of my voice, in the hope of recalling my parents) a Negro spiritual that was all the rage then: 'Sometimes I feel like a motherless child.' This I had adapted to my own purpose. 'Sometimes I feel like a fatherless child, a long way from home, from home, a long way from home.'

After his death, we knew the worst. He had left us nothing but debts. We had had to borrow to bury my sister: now we had to borrow to bury him. The prosperous part of my early life had come to a close.

What did it mean to me, having scarcely known a father? Not what might reasonably be expected. I never went in search of a 'father-figure'. I was seldom especially attracted to men much older than myself, and indeed, my first husband was younger than I.

But a longing is there, or rather, a longing to know what R.K. would have thought, and from what he might have saved me. I do know that he would have borrowed my cigarettes: he was a heavy smoker (sixty a day), my mother also, and so am I, inescapably. Yet I hope still to meet him again, if there is a comprehensible after-life, a meeting-place.

For – and this I do not forget – he was gentle, irreverent, and fun.

4. A Vision of the Marvellous

It is not of that vision that I am at once going to write. First comes a silly thing, something of a horror story, an experience in which I do not believe. I am repelled by the occult: by mediums, séances, ghosts and fortune-tellers. I have been warned what happens on the road to Endor. But this does not mean that I don't enjoy a good ghost story, by M. R. James or Algernon Blackwood.

When I was working at the Central Hanover Bank, I was sent by the manager to take a message to a client staying, for some incomprehensible reason, in Sutherland Avenue. It was a day in early autumn, heavy and humid, with a low ceiling of cloud. With my customary incompetence in matters of travel, I arrived at the wrong end of the Avenue, and had an interminable walk before I found the house. It was large, grey and shabby, and did not look the place that would be chosen by a travelling and presumably well-heeled American. I went up the steps and knocked at the door: no one came. I rang every bell. Finally, I decided that I had better descend to the basement, and try the door there. The area was dank, the door in need of a coat of paint. The sky now was darker still, the colour of a sodden and dirty towel. I rang the bell. Still no one. Rang again. At last – I had heard no footsteps – the door opened a very little way: and round it came a male hand. I called out, but there was no response, 'I am from the Central Hanover Bank and Trust Company.' (A ridiculous announcement.) Again no response, but the hand slowly withdrew. Terrified, yet with the courage of desperation, I pushed that door open. It gave on to an empty stone room, furnished with a few pot plants and a bicycle. There was a door leading into the house at the far end: but surely the owner of the hand could not have reached it before I blundered my way in? No hiding-place, or so I thought.

I ran away in superstitious fear, ran almost all the way to the safety of bus and tube, my message undelivered. By that time, the rain was coming down vigorously, dancing along on the gutter, and the sky was lightening. That was a relief.

Did I then, or do I now, believe this was a supernatural manifestation? Certainly I do not. Someone had considered opening the door, had decided not to do so, and had either dashed for the inner entrance, or gone into some place of hiding that I could not see. It was a very real hand that had made its tentative way into my sight. All the same, I was shaken. I think many 'authentic' ghost stories have their origins in little events.

I also have another theory about people who see ghosts. I have met a few, some of whom I considered to be exhibitionists, and others whose good faith I could hardly doubt. Let us take the latter group. *Where did they see them?* In what architectural circumstances? Because I have been in a 'haunted house' or two, notably Monmouth's house in Chelsea, so contrived that one might expect to see anything: a figure disappearing around the turn of a passage or a stairway. Shadows, in these kind of tricky buildings, can easily seem like psychic appearances. I once had a flat in Beaufort Mansions, Chelsea, which wasn't haunted, but should have been: it had a twist at the end of a long passage totally obscuring what lay ahead. Our house in Clare was old: the foundations about the fifteenth century, the rest a pleasing conglomeration of the seventeenth and early nineteenth. Almost every big house in that little town had a legend of some sort – indeed, we were told that we had the Admiral's ghost, but he turned out to reside elsewhere. No legend attached to our ancient house at all. Why? *Because it was all so open.* There were no corners to peer around, no dark, half-hidden places to spring surprises. It was a sunlit, wide-open house. Would it be useful to have the relevant archi-

tecture looked at carefully when ghostly appearances are
investigated?

Incidentally, I do think these ghosts should be prepared to
appear to sceptics. It is thought that in the most haunted house
England can produce, Lord Blackett, for example, the late
J. D. Bernal, and my husband would have had a very blank
night, and that this would have been attributed to their scep-
ticism. Is this sporting?

Now let me be serious. I cannot claim to be a mystic – and
would not claim it – but one summer a year or so after Philip's
birth, I came home from London to Clare, in Suffolk, where
we were then living, after an appalling attack of migraine
(it was with me for over thirty years). That night I found a
lump, like a piece of cube sugar, in my left breast. And this
led to an extraordinary experience.

Next day I called my doctor, Alan Stewart, who was also my
friend in those rural days. He said he did not himself think it
ominous, but that I had better visit a specialist in Cambridge.

When Charles and I went to see one – he lived somewhere
off the Madingley Road – it was a clear, bright flowery day.
Not fair folk in fields, but cricketers. Blossoming trees bearing
their glorious weight everywhere. The specialist examined me.
No, he didn't think it was serious, but I had better go into
Addenbrooke's Hospital for an exploratory operation.

Charles and I walked, falsely hearty, back past the white
flannels, the swags of flowers, and the scents of summer. How
long I had to wait for a hospital bed I don't know: perhaps
not long, but it seemed so. And I was filled with dread. I
would walk round our lovely garden, leading down to the
river, and gaze at the flowering rockery, the little pools, as if
I might never see them again. (Though I was not afraid of
death particularly, but of mutilation.) I said nothing of this
to my mother, and certainly not to my elder children by my
first marriage, Andrew and Lindsay. I think I said little to
Charles, but the fear of cancer was strong in me.

Cancer, that damned crab. Why has it such a dreadful name? Sunshine, fear, the love of husband and children, dominated those days of waiting. Of course I should not die: but what if I did? The answer was somewhat undramatic: an inconvenience to others.

At that time, Philip had a nanny: Nanny Page, about whom I cannot write with too much love and gratitude. She *shared* him with me: at our first interview she stated that had I asked her to take total control she would not have wished to come. I had had no money for nannies for my elder children and I think they suffered for the loss of it. I had to bring them up as best I could and earn money by my writing at the same time. It was Nanny Page who took me into hospital.

A few days before that, however, while I was still waiting to go in, I had to make the journey back, alone, from London to Clare after a job with the B.B.C. Perhaps, because I was very tired, fear was heavier than usual upon me.

Then, on the little slow train between Marks Tey and Cambridge, it happened. We were just passing through the charming small town of Bures. It was, as it had been when I visited the specialist, a radiant late afternoon in spring. I was looking, lack-lustre, out of the train windows.

Then the glory opened.

I can only weakly describe it. The trees sprang to three times their normal height and burst out in blossom. Though it was the wrong time of the year 'the corn was orient and immortal wheat, which never should be reaped, nor ever sown. I thought it had stood from everlasting to everlasting.' All was a golden enormity, beyond anything I had ever seen or ever can conceive. Size and gold. A sky golden over all. Familiar and yet unfamiliar: something of almost insufferable beauty.

I suppose this vision, for that is what it was, lasted for two or three minutes. But when it had passed, I was free from fear. I went, free from fear (except for a cosmetic fear) into Addenbrookes, and was serene. When I woke up from the

operation I remember saying to a nurse, 'Am I *intact*?' Because
I did not care to touch myself and find out. She said, 'Quite
intact.'

The tumour was benign.

But will such an experience ever come to help me again, if
I have need of it? And was it, after all, a mystical experience?
I dare not say no, though as I said, I do not pretend to be a
mystic. Nevertheless, since it rid me from fear, how can I think
from where it came if not from God?

He may not be so generous to me again.

Yet I wonder why I have chosen to tell a silly story, and a
real one. Perhaps because I have an instinct that the latter had
some tremendous importance.

Anyway, I can't let the experience of the countryside beyond
Bures go by.

All this brings me, however, to the contemplation of death.

Death is a part of life: birth the opening, death the completion. I do not follow Dylan Thomas's rhetoric:

> Do not go gentle into that good night.

My only hope, and I think it is the hope of most people, is
that I may go very gently indeed. But there is always the dread
to beset us, of a lingering terminal illness, in great agony. Few
people are altogether free of this. There are, of course, the pain-
reducing drugs, but there comes a point when even they may
lose their power.

I have recently read a thoughtful and well-reasoned article
upon the intractable subject of euthanasia. It presented both
sides of the case sensibly but, of course, reached no conclusion.
Perhaps there can be none, for to legalise it seems impossible.
(Yet I suspect that there are often acts done out of loving-
kindness to put an end to unspeakable suffering, without a
word being said.) I wonder, if such suffering ever came to me,
whether I should ask my doctor to help me quickly out? I
think I should have a rather dishonourable hope that he would

do so without being asked. Dishonourable, on my part, because I should be laying a dread responsibility upon other shoulders. But I doubt if I am capable of ultimate stoicism. I can only think about these things (blessedly, infrequently) and come up with no answers. I must say that Cardinal Heenan's recent observation that if euthanasia became legalised it would therefore become compulsory is pretty bizarre. We have legalised homosexuality between consenting adults, and that hasn't become compulsory – yet. But I do not mean to be flippant, about this question, of all questions.

Perhaps, at the end, something like that transformation of all things seen from a train window, might come to me again? If only my faith were not so feeble, I might hope for it, or at least cling to the hope. *On mourra seul* as Pascal says: and which my husband has often quoted. With real faith, one does not. But I don't know whether I have enough of it.

I let my mother die alone, literally, because I thought she was 'crying wolf'. I shall write of that later, as briefly as I can, because it was one of the most terrible things that ever happened in my life, and because out of selfishness, I need the relief of the confessional. But not now.

5. Instructions on the History of Art

When I was in my penultimate year at school, a piece of great good fortune befell me. Miss Hedgeland, our art mistress, said that she would give, to a group of volunteers, a course in the history of art. I had always loved pictures – but in a fumbling, undirected way. Now, owing to her, and the work she unconsciously induced me to pursue on my own, I am by no means sure that I do not love painting above all the arts.

After a preliminary lecture, during which she showed us reproductions of paintings from all over the western world, she would take us to spend an hour weekly in the National Gallery. Here she first taught us not to dislike a painting (such as Duccio's *Transfiguration*) simply because we were disappointed by the absence of what, at the relevant time, *could not have been there*. Paintings such as this were for church decoration, and the backgrounds were of solid gold: nobody had yet thought of adding landscape. We were not to let our appreciation of Piero della Francesca's *Nativity* be dampened because the cow in it was such a peculiar shape: in Piero's time, animal anatomy had not been studied. Perspective? If we wanted to see the first fruits of that we could look at Uccello's ever-ravishing *Rout of San Romano*. And so, quite quickly, we began to concentrate upon what there was, and not expend energy and appreciation on searching for *what could not have been there*.

Gradually, we began to form our own favourites among the various schools of art. I was most profoundly moved by the Flemish Primitives, by Van Eyck, Memlinc, David, Bouts,

Hugo van der Goes, Geertgen Tot Sint Jans. Possibly my Belgophilia was again at work, for I had recently made myself familiar with the Groenings museum in Bruges. At any rate, my dominant tastes have remained the same until this day. And very lucky for me, as it turns out: what I most desire is unacquirable, even by the purse of the multimillionaire. So I have always been able to take comfort, as I have when viewing some item of dress and jewellery in a shop window, by saying, 'Well, you can't have it' – and have passed on, calmed and appeased.

Not unnaturally, when I think of the treasure I should most like to possess in all the world, it is Van Eyck's *The Mystic Lamb*, in the church of Saint Bavon, in Ghent. ('Well, you can't have it.') I pass on, freed from desire. Anyhow, where should I put it?

Miss Hedgeland taught us to pronounce most of the names wrong. She made something mysterious of Pollaiuolo, and as for pronouncing the Flemings, had very small idea. Few people have. I once asked a Flemish friend to write down the proper pronunciation of the names of half a dozen great painters. I have tried these out myself, but finding them quite misunderstood in England, have given up this somewhat snobbish habit. Who is Van de Hoos? Van Ake? Gairtgen tot Sint Yons? I have learned to stop it. But I still pronounce the name 'Brueghel' correctly. It is 'Brerghel' (with a marked guttural). It is not 'Broygel', as it would be if, in German spelling, it were 'Breughel'.

I learned who were the Italian painters in the various schools, and listed them carefully. I longed to travel extensively in France and Italy, but it was many years before I got as far as the Uffizi.

I took an examination in all this, for what was then known as 'Matric'. Never before have I sat down to a paper that really seemed to be child's play. It was one of my first few scholastic successes, English apart. In geometry I distinguished myself

by getting a plain O, which did not seem in the least like
Giotto's.

To Miss Hedgeland, then, I owe what was to be one of the
deepest pleasures of my life. On leaving school I read as deeply
into the subject as I could; I profoundly admired Max Friedländer. In his remarkable book, *Art and Connoisseurship*, there
is the reproduction of an extremely simple line-drawing by the
sixteenth-century German, Wolf Hüber, of *The Mondsee and
Schaffberg*. Why it so snagged my imagination, I do not
know: but it has figured many times in my dreams. It was
pure magic, to me – and who can account for magic? I have
never succeeded in obtaining a reproduction for myself.

Here I have, for a moment to pause: and to say that in this
whole field, I am the merest amateur, though I think I might
have made something of a living as an art speculator. When I
came into contact, on B.B.C. 'Critics', with experts, I shrank
with humility: though that didn't stop me from talking
vigorously about whatever we had been seeing that week. I
must say they treated me (most of them) with kindness and
indulgence.

In the fifties, Charles and I had enough money to acquire a
modest collection of our own.

My first serious purchase was a matter of pure chance. It had
become my habit to wander weekly through the galleries of
W.1., usually coming out 'by that same door that in I went'.
But one day, going into the Redfern Galleries in Cork Street,
I was struck with excitement. Here was an Australian painter,
Sidney Nolan, whose name I did not know at all, few in England did at that time. These were strange, authoritative paintings of unfamiliar subjects, bizarre figures in landscapes that
seemed to extend over a whole continent. They were the first
to be seen in London of the 'Ned Kelly' series. I called Charles
in to see them at once: and we bought, for a sum we didn't
have to think about – we would have to think about the purchase price of a Nolan now – 'Kelly 1954', perhaps the proto-

type Kelly, and the most widely reproduced. This shows Ned, in his armour made from ironmongery from the kitchen, astride his horse, his back turned to the spectators, his gun, which also looks homemade, under his arm. He is facing an almost empty landscape, perhaps a few far distant gum-trees. The sky is cobalt-blue, with two hump-backed clouds, and a few darker drifts of cloud that might be gun-smoke. The gum-trees? They might equally be a line of his advancing enemies, who shot it out with him at the Siege of Glenrowan, and later hanged him. There is a rectangular hole at the top of his square black helmet. This one must interpret for oneself. To me, it symbolises the fact that to many Australians in his own time, Kelly, though real enough, was merely a myth. It is a myth sitting there on horseback.

Since then, we were able to acquire, in those early days, a *Leda*, a magnificent painting of a dead soldier on the beaches of Gallipoli; and a mysterious, sea-borne painting of Ayer's Rock, which is a thousand miles from any sea. Two of his paintings he has lent us, for so long as he wishes us to keep them.

Australia was founding a genuine 'school' of painting, and astonishingly quickly too. Russell Drysdale appears to be the founder of the style, much more so than Dobell. Arthur Boyd is a fine painter, in his own peculiar idiom, with his emphasis on aboriginal life; but I believe the best of them all is Nolan, and, that though he may have his fluctuations of fortune, while, like Picasso, he may be experimenting to the point where he can not hope to bring everything off, he will be regarded as such. Some critic wrote recently that Nolan was out of the main stream of contemporary art. For God's sake, who wants to be in one? Did El Greco? And it seems to me that the mainstream today, in so far as it is discernible, is carrying along with it much that is shoddy, meaningless, or just uncertain. Sometimes it reminds me of a stream carrying along a miscellany of tin cans and derelict perambulators. If anyone told me that I was in the 'mainstream' of the contemporary novel, I should not regard it as a compliment. Marcel Proust was not in any stream but his own.

Among other things, including a Chinnery on loan, I have a good Greek island painting by Michael Ayrton, a drawing of myself by Mervyn Peake (1949), a Neizvestney sculpture drawing. I have no water-colours, except for a weedily romantic Varley.

But Varley brings me to a fisherman's story: the story about 'the one that got away'.

In 1945 and 1946, I was pretty poor, though not so poor as I had been. Whenever there was a show of English water-colours at Agnew's, I attended it. How absurdly cheap they were then! One day, I was sufficiently carried away to put my name down for Harpignie's *La Tour Saint Jacques*: which was going for forty-two pounds. After this daring stroke, I continued my way up Bond Street: and suddenly, Fildes-like visions came over me of Andrew and Lindsay starving, clinging to my skirts, outside the Casual Ward. I raced back and cancelled the sale. It is a sorrow to me, to this day. *Could* I have managed forty-two quid? Yes, just. And what would that lovely water-colour fetch today?

But then, I have never bought paintings as an investment.

I also lost a fine, erotic Etty, of a pearly and roseate nude with a fat bottom and decorous Victorian hairstyle, bathing in a studio background. All for sixty-eight pounds. I hadn't got sixty-eight pounds, or thought I hadn't. Relatively few people have a fondness for Etty: I have. He seems to me to have had a very rapturous time of it.

Just as a far greater painter, Renoir, had a rapturous time of it. For the first time in the Chester Barnes collection, in Philadelphia (which seems almost as difficult to penetrate as Fort Knox), I found myself a little satiated. Yet I suppose that, after Monet, he is my favourite Impressionist. Almost everyone takes joy in the Impressionists; Monet's *Terrasse de Ste Addresse*, now in the Metropolitan Museum, New York, can conjure up the pure joy of a warm, breezy day, when everyone is happy and life has no cares. Sisley is, to me, a particular delight. But I have no sadness that I do not, and cannot hope to, own one. Some of my American friends do, and I can see them when I like.

There is one way – this is purely idiosyncratic – in which painting has been more of a solace to me in times of distress or pure misery than either music or literature. In the National Gallery there is a large painting by Niccolo dell'Abbate, in which the miniscule figures of – I think – Abraham and Isaac, are shown in the foreground against a vast blue, mountainous, winding landscape. It is not a great painting, it is indeed, not one of my more eccentric favourites, as is the little Simon Marmion in the early French collection.

But in front of Niccolo, I used to sit, and gradually allow myself to be absorbed into it, stepping into the frame and travelling on, to where I did not know, through the mysterious distances. No one knew where I was. No one could get at me. I was safe. This was not, I emphasise, anything to do with mystical experience. It was an act of will and imagination.

It did not last long. After that I had to go out into the rumble and flutter of Trafalgar Square, and get my bus home.

6. Fever Hospital: 1922

In 1922 I contracted nasal diphtheria – a mild form, I believe, as it goes. I was then nearly ten years of age. I was sent to Stockwell Fever Hospital (no private patients here, and my mother could not have paid for me if there had been) where I spent some six Dickensian weeks. I say 'Dickensian' because it seems to me now that the circumstances of imprisonment there would have been well within the range of Dickens' imagination.

I did not feel particularly ill: my daily plague was a nasal irrigation, which I came to tolerate. I can't say that the food was horrible – but to me monotonous: because I had an allergy to fish, I lunched every day for those six weeks on mince and rice-pudding. (It is perhaps an oddity that I object to neither now.) But after that, I was hungry. For tea, a couple of pieces of bread scraped with margarine, and perhaps, as a treat, marmalade. But because I was not then *quite ten*, I was denied supper. I had to watch while the trays went round the ward to pretty well everyone except me. Also, I was cold: I complained repeatedly of this to my mother, begging her to induce them to give me another blanket, but my letters were heavily censored, whole lines blacked out, and this worried her to death.

My comforts were the magazines she sent me, the letters I constantly wrote to her, and occasional visits from an elderly Benedictine priest, who never attempted to convert me, or even pray with me, but simply to give me twenty minutes' fun.

Not all the children were unhappy. Some had come from such miserable homes that hospital was Paradise. There was a little boy – much younger than I – who was called by all

'Bloody Bert'; this because 'bloody' was his only known term of endearment. 'Bloody nurse!' he would cry, entwining his fragile arms, like sticks of celery, round the neck of a favourite.

Most of the nurses were kind. But I happened to fall foul of a bad one. Her name I shan't give: I shall call her Nurse Birch. She took a dislike for me which I now recognise as pathological. Because I happened to speak standard English – you can't come of a theatrical family without doing that – she thought me 'above myself'. Her habit was to read out to the whole ward my letters to my mother and – worse – my mother's to me. Having received the expected chorus of titters, she would remark: 'Pamela, you are too old for your age.' I remember her as singularly without colour. None in her lips, her eyes, her cheeks: I suppose such hair as appeared beneath her cap was a palish brown. She was tall, bony, slow-moving.

On night-duty, I dreaded her. She would usually fetch me a bed-pan and sit me up on it (I would never demand one till the last vital moment) but then leave me there, despite my pleas, for any time up to three hours. She was the only dyed-in-the-wool sadist I have ever personally encountered in my life.

Why did I not complain of her to the Benedictine Father? Because I did not dare. Somehow I was afraid the complaint would leak back to her, and be visited on me. (Schoolchildren often have much the same fears.) When I was at last released from hospital, I told my mother the whole story. She went with it to the Governor, and heard to her amazement that there had been many other complaints (disregarded) about Nurse Birch. But mine clinched it, and this dreadful woman was at last dismissed.

Apart from her persecutions, I settled down, for a cosseted child, fairly well into hospital life – after all, it would come to an end some time. There were the delights of *The Magnet, The Girl's Friend, The Gem*, and several other magazines of the same kind: there was the joy of my food – yes, mince, rice-pudding, bread and scrape – and of the nights when Nurse Birch was not on duty.

I believe a real attempt was made to provide a happy Christmas for the children, though I was released before that. But I remember Bloody Bert weeping because he was to be released too. He had so looked forward to it! He was going back to a home *more* wretched than any I could imagine.

There was one singular horror: that was the regular aperient; a breakfast-cup full of *warm* liquorice powder. This was wholly disgusting, and *cascara sagrada*, when permitted, was a treat. One day, due for the liquorice powder treatment, I overheard one nurse saying to another that the dispensary was almost out of it: so, in a burst of spirit, when my cup came reeking round, I deliberately spilled it. The ruse was successful. But imagine a ward-full of children daily and madly straining their bowels in the hope of escape from this particular torment.

I got better, of course. First I was allowed up in a chair, then was permitted to wander round the ward, and at last my mother came for me. She had brought with her a dress she had specially made for me, of peacock blue, and pretty voluminous: an unhappy choice, as it turned out, as I was as yellow as a lemon and my legs and arms were like sticks. We went home by tramcar, through the liberating streets: and then – she said – I ate more slices of bread and *real* butter than she had ever seen anyone eat in her life.

Conditions in fever hospitals have doubtless changed. I think now that it would be impossible for a child to complain nightly of cold without being given a second blanket. Liquorice powder appears to be a thing of the past. Nurse Birch, herself, has disappeared from history: I think she can have left no successors. But of course I don't know. She must have made her ghostly reappearance as a wardress in the concentration camps.

Apart from those several miseries I cannot believe that I was unhappy at all times. In fact, I certainly wasn't.

Still, my memories of this time are necessarily vague. Perhaps they have to be. But I do not remember, even once, crying myself to sleep. I had too much to look forward to – eventually.

7. Travels I

I had not been abroad till I was fifteen: in this, all my children were to be far luckier. Then, I went to Belgium with my mother and my Aunt Kalie, first to Knokke, and then to Bruges. I have written so often in my novels, both as total background or in part, of Bruges and the Belgian coast, that I shall say no more here: except that of all cities, Bruges arouses in me the greatest nostalgia. The attribution of 'Belgophilia', recently applied to me, is just.

I first crossed the Atlantic with Charles and with George Bosworth, then Personnel Manager to the English Electric Company, of which Charles was a director, in 1954, for a visit to the Canadian associates. It was a poor introduction to a North Atlantic crossing, for we had only just traditionally toasted the Captain (which it is well to do early in a trip, as one might not feel so enthusiastic later) on the old *Empress of Scotland*, then creaking and groaning into the last of her days – when we ran across the tail of one of those hurricanes with women's names. This is a nomenclature against which Women's Lib might well raise its voice. (Why not Hurricanes Edgar, Freddy, Gerald, Hector?)

Anyway, the night was rough-going. We went to our cabins after dinner, the tablecloth soaked with water by the stewards, so that the glasses might not slip about, to find the deadlights up in our stateroom. We were awake for the greater part of that night. Sleep was impossible. The furniture and luggage kept falling down. I remember making to Charles, with the idea of heartening us both, the idiotic remark – 'Worse things happen at sea.' I discovered that if I went to the lavatory, I could only get back to bed by taking a running jump, which, Charles assured us, was a funny sight. The ship creaked horribly, and the gales roared. We were not being helped by the fact that, at intervals, our Irish steward would come in, cross himself, and say, 'By the grace of God, we shall come through.'

Luckily, neither of us had (or has) the least tendency to be seasick. Whether Charles was scared, I don't know: but he read a book about the Lake poets serenely enough. I prayed for a bit, then read Nicholas Blake's *The Whisper in the Gloom*, which was remarkably successful in holding my attention. I think I had one minor triumph over Charles, for at five a.m. I had had enough of the other Blake's invisible worm, that flies in the night in the howling storm. I laid myself down, and slept deeply till nine o'clock when – I admit – Charles got up to breakfast (bravado, I always feel, as the ship was still listing at 30 degrees) but I did not. However, by ten-thirty he and I and George Bosworth – the last seemed to have had a thoroughly placid night – were up on deck. (At the end of that voyage, we were presented with little cards, showing that we had been in a 9-force gale, so that nobody could doubt our travellers' yarn.)

When the storm had calmed down, we sailed on a lake-like sea for hours, it seemed, past the island of Anticosti, where I was told there were bears and – could it be? – a ruined opera house, like the one in Manaos. Charles finished the Lake Poets.

We disembarked at Quebec, and I must say that for a whole day the stairs of Château Frontenac listed heavily under me, and I had to cling to the banisters. I had temporarily lost my balance.

Quebec is weirdly entrancing. I was only disappointed by the Heights of Abraham, which seemed to me pretty small heights: I could not believe that Wolfe could have had much trouble in scaling them. But if I use the word 'weird', it is because it was a city even then so nationalistically out on its own, a French city, fiercely defensive of its language and traditions. In the upper town, much English was spoken, though most of the bookshops were filled with French literature : down the great steps to the lower town, to the lovely eighteenth-century square of Notre-Dame des Victoires, all was French. It was not so much like being in France, as being in a segment of France, cut off, and transported across the ocean.

Charles and I were anxious to meet, and had made arrangements for doing so, a young Québecois writer called Roger Lemelin, whose novel, in English translation *The Plouffe Family*, in French *Les Plouffe*, had greatly impressed us, if it had not impressed anyone else in England. He telephoned us, and made an appointment for lunch-time. Here, I say somewhat ruefully, we fell into error. It seemed to us that a French-Canadian writer, with a naturally limited public, could not be making much money. We even thought, presumptuously, that he might welcome a square meal.

We could not have been more wrong. The telephone rang : he was in the lobby of the hotel. We went downstairs, to meet a tall, handsome, robust, and obviously well-fed young man. No, we were not taking him to lunch : he was taking us. We went outside. He had an enormous Cadillac which, to my dazzled eyes, seemed to take up the whole frontage of the hotel. Off we went, to a delectable French luncheon. Part of the way we walked, and it was like walking with the young Dickens : from every side, 'Bonjour, Roger !' 'Bonjour, M. Lemelin !'

What could it all mean ? Eventually we found out. He had written several novels, of which *Au Pied de la Pente Douce* seemed to me one of the best : but with only local success. *Les Plouffe* was different. This had been turned into a television series, so wildly popular (like our own *Forsyte Saga*) that churches not infrequently altered the times of their services, so that parishioners should not be deprived of their viewing. It was about a lower town family of racing cyclists, and it had made him rather more than a small fortune.

I was humbled when he arranged for me to view an episode.
'English or French?' he asked me. 'French,' I replied, airily.
I was hardly able to understand a single word of Québecois.

He had a brilliant gift. But what has happened to him now?
Is he untranslatable into English? Perhaps. I don't know. I
wish he would write and tell me, for we have by no means
forgotten him, and never shall.

We went from there to Montreal, then on to Toronto. That
city I have a particular affection for, as my son Philip was to
have many years later, when he attended a semester at Trinity
College there before touring Canada and the U.S.A. Central
Toronto is, as I suppose most people would agree, scarcely to be
described as pretty. But its people – half Scotch, as far as I
could tell – seem to have kept their identities: they are Scottish,
they are English (nowadays there are immigrants from all over
Europe), they are above all Canadian. In 1954, the influence of
the United States was surprisingly slight.

During the first forty-eight hours that we were there, the hur-
ricane which had been pursuing us across the Atlantic struck
the city. We were dining out with friends that night, and
being aware only that there was a high wind and – on emerg-
ing from the house – that several boughs had been blown
down – we thought nothing of it. Back in the steel-and-concrete
fortress of our hotel, we were stupefied to receive from my
mother a cable asking us if we were all right. We replied that
we were. Only next morning did the truth come to us; there
had been death and devastation throughout the area. People
had been clinging to the roofs of shacks, bodies were floating
in the river. It had been a horror.

Let us return to Toronto in calm days. In 1954, Yonge Street
on a Sunday night was the dreariest sight imaginable. Nothing
to see, nowhere to go, nothing to drink. The hotel lobbies were
often full of men who had overcome the third disadvantage –
presumably in the privacy of their bedrooms. The restrictive
liquor laws irked Philip in 1970, when, at seventeen, he was

unable to buy a glass of beer. (The same obtained in San
Francisco in 1960, where a boy taking his girl to the Top of
the Mark was unable, if both were under twenty-one, to entertain her to anything stronger than Coke.)

But as I say, I loved Toronto. The suburbs were leafy and
delightful, though in the heart of the town there was hardly
a decent piece of architecture to be seen. As the Duc de Guermantes remarked, 'If it was there to be seen, I saw it!' Perhaps,
like him, I missed something.

All things that happened to me in Toronto were pleasant
ones. Much later, in about 1963, we returned to stay with
John Conway, whom we had first known as Master of Leverett
House at Harvard. He had now become Master of Founder's
College, York University. He was a war hero, who had lost
an arm at Anzio, and one of the most compellingly attractive
characters I have met or expect to meet. At York University
I received, with Charles, an honorary degree. My citation was
of a kind that would have made a far more confident person
than I blush with a sense of unworthiness. I received it, I
hope, with dignity, but also with the dread fear that my
'square', or mortar-board, was going to fall off. It was far
too big. I wisely removed it before I made my speech of
acknowledgment.

But back to my first visit to New York. Charles and I went
there by train by way of Buffalo, arriving in a totally Polish
quarter, and eating station hamburgers of an unsurpassable
horror.

New York! Who has not hallucinated a first visit? Those
glorious sky-scrapers, by night all silver and gold, splitting
the indigo skin of the sky? The overriding exhilaration?
(Charles had made frequent visits, but this was my first. Now
I reckon my score, in 1973, is about thirty-seven.)

It was not at all like that. Pretty late at night, the train eased
into a murky, smelly station. From there we rose to a dark and
equally murky cab-rank. We were to stay at the hotel, No. 1

Fifth Avenue, just by Washington Square, which was to be our base for fifteen years or more. It was down-town and when we emerged into Fifth Avenue, it, too, was dark, apart from a few lighted shop-windows. Where was the glory and the dream? Nowhere, so far as I was concerned, in my bitter disappointment.

Next morning was not much better. The great avenues (Park Avenue excepted, which has some breathing space) were monstrous canyons of stone, cold on the shadowy side. Fifth and Madison caught the bitter winds, and the overall impression was of a magnificent engineering feat which had achieved only pomposity and discomfort. On Park, the Seagram building was a glorious exception.

I did not like New York then, even when it was a city in which (Central Park excepted) you had to seek for the dangers. Now, when it may be perilous to walk even the brilliantly-lighted streets at night, I like it less.

But when dusk fell, it was all it had ever claimed to be. The vast towers of gold and silver rose in all their majesty: the wonderful work of man who, perhaps, had slipped into the error of making all things too large for his stature.

Exhilarating? I did not find New York so. I found it too shut in. But intellectually stimulating – yes.

Soon, on that trip and those that quickly followed, we made many and precious friends. Charles Scribner, our publisher, and his editor Burroughs Mitchell, Lionel and Diana Trilling, whom I loved, but always found a little intimidating. (My lack of a higher education contributed to this.) Jacques Barzun, who had 'style' if ever a man had it, and his wife Marianna, whose figure is like something from the Parthenon Frieze. By these two, I was not alarmed at all. Brooke Astor, who gave me surcease from anxiety by wearing clothes I could never live up to, so had no need to try. She is a clever woman and most attractive, with a marked literary gift. We had fairy-tale excursions to her estate at Rhinebeck. John and Cassie Mason

Brown – all kindness – all 'style' – but who seemed innocent
of the latter quality. It just grew. Over the following years,
we were to acquire more and more friends, who are too
numerous to record here.

Later, as Charles became well-known in America, we were
to make friends in Harvard and Yale, to 'sit on' many
campuses, in a semi-teaching capacity, and in 1960, to visit the
University of California at Berkeley, with Philip and Lindsay,
too young to be left in England, for six months. But some of
that can wait.

Charles and I, with Philip and Lindsay (eight and sixteen
respectively), set off on the *Queen Elizabeth* for New York
in August 1960, and after a spell (in intense heat) then went
off to California by train. This was because we wished the
children to understand from the beginning that the U.S.A.
is a very large country indeed, and this they could not have
grasped by air travel. I can't say the train was very comfortable;
one tended to bang one's head on the iron ladders leading to
the upper berths: but the discomfort was worth it. The sight
of Salt Lake by sunset, like an ice-field illuminated by a rainbow, caused Philip to cry out. *What a lot of marvels I'm
seeing!* The Rockies seemed endless. Hour after hour we went
through their incandescent redness, until the excitement of
them began to pall.

Eventually we alighted at Berkeley. This was my first disappointment, for there was a thick mist and it was shivering
cold. We were met by a friend who drove us to the top of
Vine Lane, in which we had rented a house from a professor
on a Sabbatical. All the way across the continent, I had been
nursing a bottle of Scotch which had been given me as a farewell present on New York station. The moment I got out of
the car, I dropped it: and had the chagrin of watching it
stream away down the gutter.

Suddenly the weather cleared, as I soon learned that it

would do, about 11 a.m., and California was as bright and warm as I had always dreamed that it would be.

The house was charming, the interior all of wood, with a large living-room above which was a Romeo-and-Juliet balcony, off which were the bedrooms. Behind it was a strange mountainous garden, full of rockeries, fuschias, humming-birds and blue jays. Raccoons raided the dustbins by night, but I never caught sight of one. From the upper windows you could get a splendid view of the Golden Gate at sunset: I usually rushed upstairs not to miss this. The elderly, and as it turned out, wonderful, Irish housekeeper who had been found for us (here we were remarkably lucky to discover such a rare kind of help) came to greet us. We thought she would be deterred by the sight of such a large family: but not a bit of it. She had been working for one very old and sick woman, and the loneliness of it had preyed on her. She thought we would bring a little liveliness into her life – which I think we did. (Anyway, when we left in the dawn six months later, she cried to see us go, and we cried at parting from her.)

Philip's and Lindsay's schooling was all fixed up: so in a very short time Charles took up his appointment as Regent's Professor in the University, and we became acquainted, as far as one ever could, with the enormous campus.

Hurricanes of trouble have blown through it since, but then it was relatively quiet. I only had one warning, and that was from the Dean of Students. 'If I were you, I'd be careful whom Lindsay dates. There's a lot of drug-taking round here.' That was thirteen years ago. I must admit I never came across any evidence of it, though I don't think I should have known marijuana if I had smelled it. In fact, I'm sure I shouldn't. I wouldn't now.

Vine Lane was off Euclid Avenue, with a steep walk down to the campus, and a very stiff one back uphill. This I soon learned when I went to the shops at the foot, and tried to stagger back with the shopping. Our housekeeper soon found

out where to shop, which was nearby and more or less on the
level, so I soon abandoned my own Sisyphus-like attempts.

To return to the campus. We made our first visit on Registra-
tion Day, which looked like the gathering on the Day of
Judgment: white, black, brown, yellow. All races. How should
we ever get to know – properly – a single student?

We had an idea. On Tuesdays and Thursdays, from 4–6
p.m., we kept open house for any students, of whatever faculty,
who wished to talk to us. We tried at first to confine the
numbers to twenty-five at a time, but this never worked:
either there were about forty, or there were three – because a
big game was on. I learned later that the first batch were
disappointed in me: it appears that they thought I was going
to be very, very English, and dispense tea from a pot of
Georgian silver. In fact, I put a baize cover on top of the grand
piano: and what I did dispense were cans of Coke and beer,
with accompanying can-openers. I think that once the disappointed romance had faded, they liked it far better.

The discussions we had with our students were rewarding:
they ranged from the desperately serious to the purely frivolous.
But we did become aware that by some faculty members, we
were regarded as blacklegs: we were setting a pattern that
they had no desire (nor time) to follow. I can sympathise.
However, I am quite sure our pattern has not persisted.

Through all this, though, we did manage to see many individual students more than once, and it broke our immediate
impression of helplessness in the face of such prodigious
numbers. The complaint of many – and it was a true one –
is that they rarely came in touch with a senior faculty member
at all, until some years had passed. The numbers have so
swollen that it must be worse now.

Charles had an office down a long corridor, where his
colleagues in the English Department had theirs. He had to
keep his door open all the time – which he disliked – but it

was the convention. All was pretty peaceful. Violence had not then become a way of life.

One day a student did run berserk with a gun down that corridor, by-passed Charles's room, but shot a friend of ours, in the room opposite, through the jaw, not killing, but seriously injuring him. However, this was not an everyday event.

We made, of course, many friends. Neighbours who offered me that timeless and open-handed kindness that is typical of Americans. One lived just across the way, and we all went to her in time of need – or just because we loved to see her, her husband and her children. When we had to be absent she would keep a motherly eye on Philip and Lindsay.

Nobel Prize-winners grew thick as daisies on a lawn. It was nothing to see seven of them at lunch together.

In the mornings, and sometimes in the afternoons, Charles wrote in his office, at the same time available to anyone who wanted him, while I wrote at home, enjoying the glorious sunlight streaming through the window, and ate a solitary and invariable lunch of half an avocado and a slice of bread with peanut butter (salted and peppered, *not* with jelly). This seemed to me an admirably balanced diet.

Then came the cat. Outside my gate one morning, I found a ginger kitten, perhaps two and a half months old, rolling orgiastically in a bed of catnip. Of course I stroked him. Immediately he followed me into the house, jumped purring on to my lap, and made it perfectly clear that if he had a home (we never found out that he had) he was certainly not going back there again. Never have I known such a delightful animal. He was superbly athletic: he would leap several times his own length into the air after a paper mouse. He was affectionate to a degree; while I was saying goodnight to Lindsay, he would sit outside her door yowling till I came out again. Naturally he shared the bed with Charles and me: if you love cats, you do not deny them this simple comfort. We called him Skipton.

Our housekeeper, alas, didn't like cats at all, and moved him around out of her way – gently – with the toe of her shoe. But she endured him, as she endured all things, for our sake.

It was a sad day for us, due to return to England, when we had to part with him. A friend of Philip's had found a home for him. When Skipton finally went off on the school bus, I wept. To me, he is inseparably bound up with my memories of Berkeley. Where is he now? Dead? Or is he a huge, thirteen-year-old in Sausalito? And has he any vestigial, shadowy memories of his youth? Sentimental, I know. But allow me to be. There is little enough to be sentimental about in this rough world, good sirs and madams.

Andrew came out to us for a week or so in the Cambridge vacation. A young man whom Lindsay had met on the ship came to stay with us for a week, and somehow she managed to wheedle the headmaster into letting her cut afternoon games, so that she could spend more time with her friend. They went often to San Francisco, ate on Fisherman's Wharf, explored Chinatown. Once they bought Philip a really ghastly Hallowe'en mask, in which he nearly terrified Charles into a heart attack, by bending over him in the early morning and thrusting this hideous thing into his face. It was the product of a really nasty imagination.

There were other excitements, perhaps the greatest of which was the Kennedy–Nixon election. We were all passionately pro-Kennedy, and I had to stop Lindsay involving herself too deeply in electoral matters. I used to explain that this was not our country, and we had no right to intervene in its politics. But my heart was not in this stern moral prohibition. (I did allow her, on election night – I had weakened – to help man the telephone at the Kennedy H.Q. in Berkeley.) Philip's part in it all was unstoppable: every day, when he walked from the school bus home, he would tear Nixon stickers off cars and come triumphantly back with great dangling handfuls.

Our housekeeper was worried because, having moved up two

blocks to look after us, she was afraid she might have lost her vote in our electoral district. She asked me to make enquiries. 'It isn't because I'm a Catholic, and he's a Catholic,' she said earnestly. 'I just believe in Mr Kennedy.'

I telephoned the appropriate Kennedy H.Q., put her case and got a delightful, if improper, response.

'Who's she voting for?'

'Your man,' I said.

A pause. 'Then she's O.K.'

This was the first American election campaign that Charles and I had ever been able to witness. On election night, we did not stir for hours from the television set, and pretended we had not noticed that Philip had crept down from his bed. Here we were lucky in our ignorance as to how the voting would fall. By the early morning all seemed over for Kennedy bar the shouting. We went happy to bed and slept soundly. What we did not realise was that, during our slumbers, the Mid-Western votes were coming in. If we had been awake for them, we should have been plunged into an agony of apprehension. In the morning, we woke to find that Kennedy was indeed President: it was only later that we were to know through what dangers we had passed. I should say that both Charles and Philip, who are political animals, consider with hindsight that their emotional investment in this election was quite excessive.

Later that morning, I had to lecture to the girls at Mills College about some aspect of English literature, I forget what. Before me was the prettiest collection of girls *en masse* that I had ever seen, all yawning their heads off.

I began sternly. 'Yes,' I said, 'I know you have been up all night. So have I.' (This was not strictly true.) 'But I want you to stay awake and alert for forty-five minutes: after which, with the permission of your faculty, you may go to sleep again.'

I must say they were all very good. Mills College has now disappeared. It is a dreadful pity.

We were not supine during our months at Berkeley. We
visited and talked at every campus in the University at that
time, with the single exception of La Jolla.

While Andrew was with us, we made a trip to Los Angeles
which, once you are down from the heights of Bel Air, is one
of the most depressing towns I have ever set foot in. As
Gertrude Stein said of Oakland (not far from Berkeley itself),
'There's no There There.' There is not. No central point. It
is a great, shambling, shoddy conglomeration of buildings and
tangled motorways. What 'Hollywood' glamour it may once
have had, is all gone. I do not think even the snack-bar
waitresses hope to be 'discovered', and swept away to stardom.
Above all there is the smog: it gives the effect of the blue
heat-mist of a fine summer day. Actually, it is pollution that
makes the eyes water, and gets into mouth and nose, lingering
disgustingly upon the tongue. And when we went to Pasadena
we found that, incredibly, *worse*. But perhaps I am out of
date. In both places, the air may now be clean and pure. But
I admit that I doubt it.

They talk of the 'smog' in San Francisco. Actually, this is
for the most part heavy sea-mist, which clears pretty early.
On the heights of Berkeley, you are quite free from it, except
for the early morning hours.

One of the painful sights, for a visitor, was that place of
misery, the island of Alcatraz. It looked so charming, too, lit
up at night, out in the bay: but it was hard to enjoy a meal,
within view of it, with anything of an appetite. I am happy to
say that it is no longer a prison. But this, in a sense, is sweeping
the dust under the carpet. Did one really care what happened
to the prisoners, when that rock of hopelessness was no longer
on one's conscience? Did they go to San Quentin, which can't
have been much better – though it had then an enlightened
governor? Where did they go? Out of sight, out of mind?
Maybe. But when I was in California, it was neither.

We left for New York in January, by air. We rose before

dawn, when it was dark. But as we crossed the Golden Gate
bridge, the sun rose. First in a ring of scarlet, as on an electric
hotplate, then a shower of sparks. The sky paled to peacock
blue – above the scarlet came the gold: soon the whole sky
was ablaze. We had a singularly clear flight, and were able to
see, as if it were only a hundred feet below, the confluence of
the Missouri and the Mississippi.

New York was, of course, freezing.

It may be observed that we were now flying, rarely sailing,
more's the pity. A note on this.

I am afraid of flying. I will not say that I am terrified, or
I should have opted out, as some of my acquaintances have
done. But how Charles and I would have spent about twenty
years weaving our way from England across the majority of the
United States and great parts of Eastern Europe by other
means, I simply do not know.

I think Charles has, through sheer habit, come to terms with
the whole thing: as indeed, he comes to terms with most
things. He is stoical, philosophical, and to an extent knowledgeable about aeronautics – though this, he says, is really of
no advantage, in fact the reverse.

Any sensible person is aware that the moments of greatest
danger are in the take-off and landing. This I appreciate intellectually. But not emotionally. Our flight is called. We
board the plane. There is that awful step between earth
and the inevitability of air. Then I neatly fold my copy
of *The Times* so that I can begin on the crossword puzzle.
'For we have no help but thee,' is my sacrilegious greeting
to it.

After an interminable period, we taxi to take-off point. There
will be a long wait to the first cigarette, the first drink in the
air. Up we go and very quickly, too. I fill in three clues in the
crossword, often with a marked quickening of the intellect.
We are airborne! We are first allowed to smoke, then to release
(or just to relax – I am in favour of this, knowing what clear-air

turbulence can be like) our seat-belts. All is beauty below us. Ice comes clinking in the glasses.

At the end of it all, the landing. However dangerous I know this is, I simply do not care. The lights of New York or San Francisco below us, splendaceous maps of gold and silver. We are nearer the ground. I shall have less far to fall.

Silly, I know: but this is the way I feel.

My trouble occurs in mid-Atlantic. Never mind those absurd life-jackets. If I were plunged into the sea, even assuming that I could inflate the ludicrous things, blow whistles, flash lights, I should still die of cold before help could come. So I sit – at times – and wonder how this enormous tonnage of metal keeps in the air at all. I find my normal pace of reading abnormally slowed down: in a flight of seven hours, I will have read only a quarter of a novel, which, on the ground, I could have finished in two. My appetite for food is vestigial.

We flew several times with Captain Earthrowl, whose only ominous peculiarity was his name. (He never crashed anything in his life.) Knowing us quite well, he often used to come out from the flight-deck for a chat: never knowing that I was screaming inwardly, 'Go back! Go back! And fly this awful plane!'

Sometimes I myself was invited on to the flight-deck, where fear would mysteriously leave me, and something of the delight some find in flying would take over.

Indeed, on the short trip over swampland from Atlanta, Georgia, to Montgomery, Alabama, I was allowed to sit with the Captain – this was a tiny plane which had once belonged to General Eisenhower – and thoroughly enjoyed the precise and delicate skill of landing.

But on a jet in mid-Atlantic – I feel quite differently.

I have no tendency to air-sickness, even in the worst turbulence, and neither has Charles. I fear that if it is very bad, I may be far too scared to feel sick.

How bland are some of the passengers! The men who

regularly commute! David Frost, who can (and must) go to sleep. But the majority of air travellers are frightened, and the cabin staff know it. I admire the latter inordinately. They must beam all the time, and in the last resort, be prepared to die with stoicism. I particularly admire the apparently impervious Qantas stewards, who rouse one from gloom with 'Time for a drink?' or 'Time for tucker?'

I must admit that my very first transatlantic flight did not bring me much comfort. Charles and I had decided that, for the sake of the children, then young, we would fly separately. (We do this no more: they are adult, and they can cope.)

I was seated next to an agreeable old gentleman who had been a fighter pilot in the First World War, and who had emerged without a scratch. Soothing. But in the seat behind us were two men who obviously knew everything about aeronautical engineering. We were getting near to Newfoundland – how near I do not know – when one said to the other, in schoolboy French, 'Je crois que nous avons perdu une engine.'

Horrific enough, and my First World War pilot was blissfully unaware of what had been said.

Then: 'Je crois que nous avons perdu une autre.'

How true all this was, I can't tell: though I do know that we descended at Gander at a shattering, deafening rate, and were stuck in that abomination of desolation for the best part of three hours.

The passengers sat on stools at the bar, in the bleak airport lounge, gossiping, smoking and drinking. Having somewhat recovered from my fright, I asked an airport official what they found to do with themselves all day, whenever a plane was not coming in. Newfoundland, from the air, is a place of horror, consisting of ravines, and terrible strips of ice and snow. (What it is really like, I don't know.) He replied, 'Oh ... we play a bit of poker.'

I rejoined Charles some hours later in New York. Even he was looking somewhat put out.

The most horrible trip we ever had was from New Haven to
Atlanta, *via* Washington. The airline was a small one, the
weather was foul. At Washington, it became markedly worse.
In fact we were on a roller-coaster all the way. Several courageous old ladies stuck it out gallantly for a while, then resorted
to the sick-bags.

Atlanta, at last. We were met by representatives of Agnes
Scott College, where we were to lecture, and do a bit of
'sitting', and soon realised that only the airport was not Dry.
We dined there, stoked ourselves up more than our hosts approved, and then, longing for bed, made for our luggage. It
had been left behind, the lot of it, in Washington. The tem-
perature that night was 90° : we had no nightclothes, no
toothbrushes – nothing. When we got to Agnes Scott, they
did procure for us toothbrushes and paste, and for me hair-
grips. But, such is the efficiency of the U.S.A., all those bags
were returned to us by 7.30 next morning.

All the same, there are great aesthetic compensations in
flying, and I would not have missed them. I am enchanted,
when I think of what Shakespeare would have made of
flight.

8. Women

'I sit on a man's back, choking him, and making him carry me, and yet assure myself and others that I am very sorry for him and wish to ease his lot by all possible means – except by getting off his back.'

This epigraph from Tolstoy, with which I begin these series of reflections, may not seem particularly apposite at the moment – or to some it may seem all too apposite. But I hope to explain my meaning in due course. A hint: Tolstoy was not really thinking of domestic help. I am, among other things.

I am naturally in sympathy with many of the aims of the Women's Liberation Movement. Equal pay for equal work, equality of opportunity, in so far as it is possible (sometimes it isn't), and the relief of women not devoted to domesticity from the intolerable boredom of the daily round. Some take great pride in the smooth-running perfection of the home: home and children are fulfilment enough, and good luck to them. If this is so, only a bigoted meddler would want to interfere. Some like it partially: a great many women and, incidentally, some men, really enjoy cooking. But *every* day? *Every* meal? And I confess that I do not know how anyone in her senses can enjoy making beds.

There are aspects of Women's Lib that I dislike, and I don't only mean inanities, such as brassière-burning. (Some figures can stand it, but most cannot. Also, let us remember that the brassière was a liberating influence in itself: it enabled us to run for buses without having to grab at our chests.) What I do detest, are those persons on the fringes on the movement – I hope they are mere fringes – who want to stir up sexual hate, to make bitter enmity between woman and man. Hatred is always detestable: we have enough of it in our world already, without adding to it by pure silliness. I like the company of men: the idea of a society without them, a perpetual hen-party, would to me be unspeakable. (I do not want to charge like a rhinoceros into men's clubs. Do leave them in the peace they deserve.) But let me tell this outrageous story, and fuel the fires of Women's Lib. by doing so. A year or two ago, a wedding reception was held in a men's club of great repute. Alas, when it came to getting in, it was found that the only way into the room of celebration, was through the library which no woman's foot was permitted to tread. What do you think the men did? They rigged up a ladder to a convenient window, and *made the women guests crawl in that way*. I am sorry this ludicrous event wasn't televised. Anyway, it is one wedding that I should not have attended, and I am stunned by astonishment that so many of my sex were content to do so.

Sexual tensions do exist: they are psychologically inevitable: and any attempt to increase them is irresponsible.

To begin with – though it is here a side issue – why does it seem so impossible that women priests should be ordained in the Church of England? The Congregationalists have had their successful ministers, such as Dr Maude Royden. I believe the true, if concealed, opposition to this is a deep psychological one, and hard to break down. In the great monotheisms, God is presented to us as a *man*, made in man's image, and the priest is regarded as His surrogate. Silly? Perhaps. I am not interested in the opinions of agnostics in this particular matter. I, personally, should like to see (experimentally) women admitted to the priesthood. But they won't be, not in the foreseeable future. Something deeper than common sense, something deeper than all reason, is militating against them.

In marriage, there are, and always will be, such depths: deeper than the bed of the deepest sea. I do not believe any normal woman can give one rap of respect for a man who is not prepared to care about her, and, within possible limits, protect her from harm. I am not now talking about financial protection. (Do I expect to 'look up to' a man? In the physical sense I have no option, since few men are smaller than I.) In the more serious sense, I need a man I can admire: and if there is anything at all admirable about me, he may if he pleases, return the compliment. Marriage is, after all, a small part bed to a deal of conversation. I expect discussion of all vital matters, above all, those dealing with the children. I expect it, and I get it.

I should not expect my husband, after an exhaustingly hard day's work, to help me unduly (though I am sure he would, if driven by necessity) with household chores. *I might not wish to humiliate him.* Do you know why I say it might, in our present social *mores*, be humiliating? It might even be regarded as a jail sentence.

Listen to this. Only a few weeks ago, a magistrate sentenced some young sinner, whom he did not wish to send to prison, *to a hundred hours or more of housework*. So the cat is out of the bag! Housework, for most women, *is* penal. The magistrate regarded it as punishment. And of course, certainly, it is equally penal to those whom we can induce to work for us.

By the way, I have often noticed how little Soviet husbands will help their wives, though they will certainly both have been out to work (equal pay for equal work is the law there). Some of them will scarcely help to stack a couple of plates, while she plods from table to kitchen on her doubtless sore feet. This mostly applies to couples in middle age: and believe me, the wives complain about it. Among younger married people it is often different: the work gets shared: it is quite *chic* for the man to do his part. But that is in another country.

Let me, for a moment, consider the position of the working-class wife in our own. She will very likely go out to work: not to find 'expression', not to 'liberate' herself, but because she has to have the extra money. Can we 'liberate' these people?

Of course we cannot. Not if we wish to 'liberate' ourselves. Let us not talk 'bourgeois' nonsense, even if we ourselves are inescapably bourgeois.

Naturally, the woman who goes out as a daily cleaner needs the money she is paid for her work, by those able to afford someone to do the 'rough'. But can she possibly *enjoy* it? Of course not. No one could. It is dead-end labour. And it leaves the rest of us free to do the work we do enjoy, or at least, have some interest in.

For years I was pretty unliberated. I had my writing to do; I did so because I wanted to, but also because it supplemented a wretched pension, for my mother, from the Crown Agents, and an inadequate army allowance for myself. I had my two young children to rear, I had my fair share of the domestic work. The rest of it was done by my mother, and a cheerful woman from nearby called Maggie, who did most of the cleaning. But with all this help, I invariably went to bed dead tired.

With my remarriage in 1950, my circumstances inevitably changed. So did my way of living. Charles and I were both writers, and he was other things besides. We wanted to do our writing, as far as was possible, in the mornings and early afternoons, when we were fresh. My mother was ageing, and badly needed some rest herself. So we embarked upon a series of cook-housekeepers and daily women. In Clare, we were cared for by the gardener's wife and her daughter-in-law. When, in 1957, we returned to London, to a large flat in what is now the dilapidated Cromwell Road (we were there for eleven years) it was to take over the former tenant's housekeeper and her ready-made baby. She was with us for a long time. We, during that period, were travelling extensively in the U.S.A., so there had always to be someone at home. Our last housekeeper, Conchita, is still with us: but she is over retirement age, and must soon return to Catalonia. She has been hardworking and over-conscientious, for twelve years; I have tried to help her as best I could, but half the time she would not let me. She had, for a long while, five of us to look after: Charles and me, Andrew and Lindsay, and Philip, when she first came, was only ten. Conchita worked hard. In later years, she has worked too hard, and though I have found relief for her as best I might, she is getting tired. So I am 'the man on her back'.*

If I am to be liberated, how can I be so, as a married woman, a professional woman with three children, *without enslaving another woman*?

More guilt, and I see no solution. Has anyone a practical answer?

I think it not inappropriate to say a word here about the deliberate illegitimising of children. It has become fashionable in some quarters to downgrade marriage. It has been made so by various notabilities of stage, screen and television, who have glowingly announced that they have, or are about to have, a baby, and have no intention of marrying the father, even though they may have been living with him for years. Now, one should not have a child for any therapeutic, or 'liberating' reason. That child is of primary importance. This attitude is irresponsible.

I once met a young woman – unmarried, and in something of a state – who said that only having a baby could help her psychologically. Help *her*? Procreation is for the child's benefit, and should only be brought about by a care for its future and for the love of it as an individual. I believe that a child needs two parents, and that the father should play his part from the beginning. By this I do not mean that he should be dragged through the ugliness and blood of the labour ward, as if to punish him for his part in the event. I would not have had my husband near me, to hear me gasping and grunting, and see me in ridiculous postures, at any price. The actual giving of birth is my business, only mine.

To return to the problem of illegitimacy. It is no longer, we

* 1954. She has by now gone back to Spain and I have had the remarkable good fortune of finding Doris.

are told, a 'stigma'. No? Here we are reverting to our usual bourgeois thinking. To millions of 'unenlightened' people it will remain a stigma, causing pain, or at least embarrassment, to the child from the innocent questions of its friends (children's questions are, by the way, very rarely innocent), and a host of complications, some of which these hopeful unmarried mothers, delightedly withholding a real family background from their babies, cannot possibly foresee *as yet*. It is too early. I would bet that there is still many a household in England, from which the trendy daughter, following the fashionable *moeurs* and proud of her coming illegitimate child, will promptly be slung out. These girls might be in a minority, but I feel pretty sure they exist.

In the newspaper, only this morning, I read of a young girl discovered dead in her own blood over a wash basin, in a bed-sitter, with her dead baby in a carrier-bag by her side. She had been afraid to tell her parents. This was obviously a pure accident. Most illegitimate births are accidental. But are some thought to be, in the new 'freedom' of the well-to-do, acceptable?

To marry is, of course, to take on a responsibility. To make a good marriage, needs a lot of patience and good faith, respect on both sides, common interests, and an enormous amount of understanding. Also, it needs love, which is something more, much more than sex alone, and more lasting.

I am sometimes suspicious – perhaps cynically – of some of those girls who will not marry the father of their child, even though they profess a loving relationship. *Could it possibly be that the man doesn't want to marry them?* In many cases, the desire for 'freedom', however misguided, is genuine. But have either the man or the woman really looked ahead? I think if the woman did so, too, she would find that she had merely liberated the man – and with no advantage either to herself or to her child. She can be left flat and penniless – unless she is a 'celebrity' – and often, in the long run, she is.

My daughter, Lindsay, who naturally knows more about her generation than I do, thinks I am all too sanguine about the benefits of sex-education and the Pill. She is probably dead right, and I listen to her with respect. Her claim is that many young girls, say of sixteen or seventeen, have no idea, even after all the publicity, where they may obtain preventatives, but go blindly on in the conviction that nothing will ever happen to them. But it does.

She also suggests that few of them know anything about the current ideas of doing away with marriage altogether. Perhaps they don't, although if so, they can't read the popular papers. All I say is that, despite our new 'freedom', tragedies continue. And I have small sympathy with those who would boost these optimistic ideas on their way.

The chief trend-setters of our society are film stars, T.V. celebrities and footballers. Let them be careful what trends they set, for to their example thousands and thousands cannot bear to say no. They must bear a load of responsibility.

To quote the late Stevie Smith:

> All these illegitimate babies ...
> Oh, girls, girls,
> Silly little cheap things,
> Why do you not put some value on yourselves,
> Learn to say, no?
> Did nobody teach you?
> Nobody teaches anybody to say No nowadays,
> People should teach people to say No.

She was a wise, stern woman, Stevie.

9. A Sharp Decline in Income

I have no clear idea from what income we had to decline. My grandfather (C. E. Howson) had died before I was born, but my memories were of comfort: of deep larders full of preserves, raised pies, hams, bottled fruits, and whatever else one finds in what might grandly be described as 'still-rooms'. I wouldn't know now.

On my mother's side, we had been a theatrical family for generations. My grandfather, Australian-born of English parents, had begun by taking out band-parts for fourpence a sheet: he had played the violin in a theatre orchestra; danced as Harlequin in pantomime: and by some transition I do not know about, had become Sir Henry Irving's treasurer, which job he held for twenty-five years. (I might say, in passing, that he seems to have been a good linguist. Some years after his death my mother and Aunt Kalie discovered in the summer-house at the end of the garden, half a lifetime of diaries, written in violet ink in his lovely script, *in Italian*. And on the grounds that nobody would be able to read them – perhaps on other grounds too – they incinerated the lot. I am intrigued to think what may have been lost by this ridiculous action.)

So far as I can recall, my grandfather's sister, Emma Howson, was the original Josephine in *H.M.S. Pinafore*. I cannot check the truth of this. A relative of a still older generation introduced the Carl Rosa Opera into Australia. And a lady (probably Mrs Albert Howson) who called herself Madame Albertazzi was a singer of no mean repute. One of my great-great-uncles was in the touring company of *Our American Cousin*, after Lincoln's assassination.

But it was to Sir Henry Irving and Dame Ellen Terry that I owed any lustre of my background. Irving liked to deck his stage with good-looking people, whether talented or not: so my stately grandmother (born in the Old Kent Road and rigorously educated in speech and deportment by my grand-father) walked on as the Duchess of Norfolk in *Henry VIII*, carrying the infant Elizabeth. My Aunt Kalie was with the company for some time, and went on one of the later American tours: her most ambitious role, however, was as the Ghost of Marie Antoinette in *Robespierre*. Non-speaking.

Here, I think I must break off to tell a story. It was one of Irving's spectacular crowd scenes, in this play, and Aunt Kalie was yelling with the others. After Irving's great speech to, I believe, the Goddess of Reason, the crowd was to cry, 'To the Champs de Mars!' One night, unfortunately, Aunt Kalie mistook her cue, and raised that solitary cry *before* Irving had spoken. Whereupon the curtain came down. My aunt, in desperate distress, rushed off into a corner to hide: she did not know what was to happen to her. But Irving found her out. Standing noble and beetle-browed above her trembling body, he contemplated her. Then he remarked, 'Original, Miss Howson, but don't do it again.'

My youngest Aunt Emma, already stout as a child, but extremely beautiful, was called upon by Irving to act as a cup-bearer: but she fidgeted and he had to get rid of her.

My mother Amy, however, having a small but pretty singing voice, went to join the D'Oyly Carte Company: she never rose higher than understudy to Yum-Yum (who did not fall ill) but it is from her that I gained an extensive knowledge of the Gilbert and Sullivan operas.

I have often thought that we had no recognisable class at all. We were thought of as 'Bohemians'. I am afraid my family was afflicted with a degree of snobbery: the thought of 'marry-ing into trade' afflicted them as it might have afflicted a noble Victorian. But none of us ever did.

Our house, despite its ugly façade, had a bizarre attraction within. My grandfather had a charming taste in wallpapers:

the drawing-room, deep blue and gold-flecked, was adorned in
the middle by one of the innumerable perks that came from
Irving – a chandelier from his production of *Henry VIII*. I
cannot say the same of his taste for furniture: he brought
some horrible rocking-chairs back from San Francisco, and
some really dreadful pieces of yellow maple, including a desk
that was also a souvenir cabinet, filled with such objects as
emus' and ostriches' eggs.

The hallways were hung with Irvingiana: Beckett loomed
just inside the door, Ellen Terry as Lady Macbeth, hung beside
it. Satin programmes, from Royal performances at the Lyceum,
abounded: I now regret that I have given so many away, kept
so few, of those left to me by my Aunt Kalie. Though I could
never have seen Irving or Terry, I was told so much about
them, that I began *to believe I had*: they remain a cult with
me. I especially love Ellen Terry, because she was so ginger-
golden, and because she had been so kind with gifts of toffees
to my mother and my Aunt Kalie who, as children, had been
at school at Eecloo, in Belgium.

But I was most permanently impressed by the books in my
grandfather's library, mostly Irving's rejects. There was, above
all, the Irving edition of Shakespeare, enthrallingly illustrated
by Gordon Browne: it was from this that I learned my
Shakespeare at a very early age, just spelling out the captions
and then seeing where they fitted into the text. I had read the
whole canon by the age of eight, though with what degree of
comprehension I shouldn't like to say. Then there was *The Life
of Sir Stamford Raffles* (dull), *The Arabian Nights* (ex-
purgated), the complete works of Washington Irving, a few
volumes of Dickens, and a medley of other books.

One book we did not have, was one grandfather had destroyed in a rage. He had always detested Irving's secretary,
Bram Stoker. One day he came home with a greyish volume
in his hands, and said to his children, 'Stoker has written a
beastly book. It's all about people who suck other people's

blood and lunatics who eat flies.' He put it straight on the fire. It was, of course, the first edition of *Dracula*.

After his death, and during early childhood, prosperity still seemed in the air. My Aunt Kalie, theatrical ambitions forgotten, had taken a job at the Ministry of Transport. My Aunt Emma married, though it did not turn out so well for her. Our chief sadness was for my grandmother, diabetic and now going blind. She was to be totally blind for the last ten years of her life. She loved to cook, and was magnificent at it: it was a tragic day when she was told that she must stop, since a nail and a dead mouse had been found in successive rice puddings. She took her consolation later, such as it was, in teaching cooking to me, and questioning me closely as I followed her instructions. I regret that all her teaching has been mostly forgotten, and that my cooking today is no more than mediocre.

It was some time before my father's death that we began to feel the pinch. No more were we able to keep open house, as my grandmother had done, on Sunday nights, the table covered with roast chickens, pies, jellies and wonderful trifles. Our 'musical evenings', which we much prized, became fewer and fewer. (They were somewhat better than average, because we were able to draw on many professionals.) My mother and I left our flat at the top of the house to make way for lodgers, and shared the semi-basement sitting-room as a bedroom. All manner of lodgers passed through our hands: one was speedily removed, being suspected of sleeping sickness: one, a rubicund Welshman, got into fights on the stairways with my Uncle Charlie: one, who posed as a doctor living with his sister, sat quietly upstairs manufacturing pornographic literature, until the police caught up with him.

All this seemed to me great fun, and I was surprised to hear my Aunt Kalie mourn that my grandmother, could she see, would be deeply distressed by the relative poverty indicated by the state of the larder.

But when my father died, things had to alter more radically.

I was then at Clapham County Secondary School, for which my mother paid fees of £5 a term. She had to plead with an acquaintance among the governors that this should be remitted, which it was. She took in typing, to bring a little money into the house, for R.K.'s debts lingered on, and death did not appear to cancel them. She had some interesting clients, among them Mr Hsiung, author of *Lady Precious Stream*, and the son – or grandson – of Buffalo Bill. To see the last coming down our area steps on Battersea Rise, with Stetson hat and long white flowing locks, was something of an experience.

And I – few clothes, and meagre pocket money. But I adapted to all this without pain. I had my own plot in our long back garden, with poplars and a cherry tree, and had cultivated it as I pleased, never at a loss for bedding-out plants and packets of seed. Now, at times, my mother would find me a hard-to-spare twopence, and I would go out in a delight hitherto unfelt to buy a root of pansies, or of pink-tipped daisies: to put in this one plant gave me more pleasure than putting in all the plants previously at my disposal. Poverty was rather fun, though it was nicer whenever it stopped hurting, like the old story of the lunatic banging his head against the wall because it was such a joy when he ceased to do so.

On my way home from school, I would call in once a week at Grandmother Johnson's house; usually, with great laboriousness, she would extract from the reticule beneath her skirt, a sixpence. I did sense that she could ill-afford it, and indeed, when she continued the practice after my adolescence, was very embarrassed.

Of course, all this put an end to any hope of higher education for me. My headmistress, the splendid Miss Ethel A. Jones, who remained my friend till her death at the age of 84, wanted me to go to Oxford to read English: how she hoped to overcome my mathematical difficulties first (I am numerically blind) I do not know. But her wishes didn't matter. Grants were very slender then, and that I could have supported myself, let alone my mother, was inconceivable. I spent one year in the sixth form, left at sixteen-and-a-half, and at seventeen – this must have been a severe strain on what were my mother's now very frail resources – took a six-month course at the Triangle Secretarial College in South Molton Street, which was rather smart.

Then I had to go out to work. I found a job as The Junior in the West End branch of the Central Hanover Bank of New York in Lower Regent Street. Very little banking was done here: it was really designed for looking after the needs of travelling Americans. The offices were sumptuous and brand-new: but I was paid the not-so-sumptuous sum of £2 a week, which, after four years rose to £3.

The joys of Friday, of pay-day! By Thursday, I was so hard up that I could barely afford a cup of tea and a bun for lunch, for part of my salary went to my mother, who gave me back 10s a week for fares, food, and the ten cigarettes which I could not even then do without. But on Friday I deserted the ABC and went to Slater's, where I would have an omelette and chips, and a blackcurrant sponge pudding. I should wish to say that I have never enjoyed, in my life, any meals as much as I did those.

My mother's typing earnings went largely to my grandmother to pay for our keep. With the little she was able to save, she bought material to make me new dresses.

I should hate anyone to think that I am romanticising poverty: if I am romanticising it at all, it was my own *semi-poverty*. True poverty, sleeping rough under bridges, on freezing nights, protected by newspapers, hardly entered my head. For I had a warm bed, a supper usually brought from the delicatessen over the way, a loving family, and nothing to hate but my daily journeys from Battersea Rise to the office. In autumn and winter, wrap up as I would, I was invariably cold. I would look out from the top of the bus upon the windows of the Piccadilly clubs, upon peach-fed men stuffing what

I believed to be kidneys and reading *The Times*: and I hated them all. Curious this, as I never liked kidneys myself.

Now, the thought of real poverty, above all that of very old people, lonely and friendless, struggling to keep warm with, at best, a one-bar electric fire, distresses me beyond measure. For what can I do, except subscribe to charity? I admire the young people (a maligned generation, except for the nihilistic minority who cannot be maligned too much) who do try to take practical action about these things, and who see far beyond them to the horrors existing in the Third World. I feel far older than my years, and perhaps more helpless than I need be.

My only excuse for writing this chapter is that we had a 'come-down': a wretched thing for my elders, but a stimulus to me. What became of Irving's chandeliers? The Japanese kakemonos, brought back by my grandfather from one of his American trips, on the walls? But Ellen's picture hangs in my study still. Contemplating it, I can only think that her Lady Macbeth was, as Shaw put it, 'such a dear'.

Three years after my father died, my handsome young uncle, with his dark curling hair and bluebell eyes, died also, from a duodenal ulcer too long neglected. Then, when I was eighteen, my grandmother. I remember the times when I ought to have read to her, but didn't. I played the piano, I sang her favourite songs, but I hadn't the patience for very long bouts of reading. Something else of guilt. Many years later, when Charles, my second husband, temporarily lost his sight – or most of it – I would read to him for hours, and love every moment of it. But in youth is cruelty.

10. *Edith Sitwell*

She was said to sign her letters sometimes with 'Edith Sitwell, D.Litt., D.Litt., D.Litt.', representing her three honorary degrees. (I am by no means certain that there is any truth in this, but it would be characteristic.) She delighted in the honours that came her way in a manner almost childish – as if she had been, say, a Girl Guide awarded a medal for rescuing some infant from a watery grave. Her pleasure in academic recognition came, I am sure, from the fact that she had had no education to speak of. Not that she needed it. She did very nicely without. She may have made herself into a Queen: but at heart she was humble. She was not really arrogant. When she seemed to be – and arrogance was a favourite dressing-up part – it was all façade. (I intend no pun.) She liked to behave like a great lady, which of course, by birth, she was: but spiritually she was more like a gentleman. So, come to that, was Queen Elizabeth I.

I should like to tell the story of how we happened to meet her (in 1959: alas, we had far too few years of her joyful company). I had written my novel, *The Unspeakable Skipton*, and I was rather pleased with it. This is rare with me: some of the novels of my later years, including *The Honours Board* and *The Humbler Creation*, were saved from incineration by the efforts, in the first case of my younger son, and in the second, by my husband. This is not mock-modesty. I always feel, on the completion of almost any novel, that it is no good at all. But *Skipton* was quite different. I dropped it in, with the greatest confidence, upon the then Managing Director of my publishing house: and waited for, in due course, cries of delight. Nothing. Only a mysterious silence. Then an awful silence. I felt bound to break it. What, I asked, was wrong?

The answer came. *Did I realise that I had libelled one of their most distinguished authors?*

Let me make this point quite clear. When accused of this sort of thing, one is almost invariably guilty. But on this occasion I was not. I was as innocent as a Blakeian cherub riding the blast, and totally bewildered. I asked, who on earth did they mean?

The answer came. Dame Edith Sitwell.

Now I had, in my novel, a female poet, given entirely to the subject of maternity (she had seven children, and wanted more) whose literary output was slender. Her name was Dorothy Merlin. It seemed to me that she was as unlike Dame Edith as anyone could possibly be: in any case I had never had any contact with the latter whatsoever. Letters were exchanged. I urged my publisher to take legal advice: he did, *and the cards fell against me.* I fought against this. I agreed to make certain trivial alterations: Dorothy was tall and fair, so I made her small and dark. I even made her Australian. Still it would not do. After six weeks' deadlock, Charles said he could stand no more.

He wrote to Dame Edith, saying first that he was sorry neither he nor I had had a chance to meet her: but that his wife was in great trouble, and he could see nothing for it but to go to the fountain-head. He explained the position precisely, offered to send her the manuscript and to let her see for herself whether it had any offence in it.

The response was swift. It came at breakfast next morning, on the telephone. Edith herself, roaring with laughter. The gist of it was that I was to go ahead and publish. She took my word for it that I had meant no offence to her. She would like to see the typescript for the pleasure of it, *but no more than that.* There was no need to show it to her at all. She added, 'I am writing a book about Catherine de Medici. Since your wife is not a Roman Catholic, and does not massacre Protestants, surely I am libelling her? Do come and see me.'

A gentleman, as I have said.

I need hardly say that I did, immediately, send her a type-script, which only made her laugh more. This was the beginning of a friendship cherished both by Charles and me.

We met her for the first time, at luncheon, at the Sesame Club, where she was supposed to hold court. I say 'supposed', because I think this a psychological misconception. She just sat in her corner, looking spectacular, and courts formed around her. I have seen people, whom I shall not name, bow so low before her that their buttocks shot up at an angle of forty-five degrees.

She was not a 'room-talker', a type I detest. Like to talk, she did: but she was also a good listener. She could be a savage foe (though this was really another dressing-up part, consisting largely of schoolboy japes) but I, personally, have never known her to be the first to attack. And attacked she was, cruelly and vulgarly, during the thirties, by persons without a moiety of her talent. If a friend of hers came under attack, she would fight for him quite as vigorously as for herself. To one's misfortunes, she was very kind: but to say she suffered fools gladly would be a misstatement. She didn't.

The miseries of her youth are well known, and I shall not dwell upon them. But she is the only person I have ever known who made a work of art out of herself, and with complete success.

She was an exceedingly plain child, and Sir George Sitwell's enforcement of a steel contraption to straighten her nose, did not improve matters. But it was characteristic of Edith that she would not let even nature defeat her. She must have planned, with great deliberation, that it should not. She contrived for herself a unique style of dressing – sometimes reminiscent of Elizabeth I, sometimes of the Pope, more often of the paintings of Van Eyck – which she wore so splendidly as to acquire something that could be called (and often was called) beauty. She usually chose majestic, hieratic hats, not at all like the late

Queen Mary's, and robes of the richest embossed materials.
Round her neck were exotic ornaments of heavy gold. On her
exquisite hands were loadings of aquamarines. One wondered
how she could even lift them from her lap.

I only once saw her without a hat, and this when she dined
at our flat. Her hair was fair and sparse. But she was magnificently robed in a gown presented to her by the Metropolitan
Museum of Art (New York) for her poetry recital there. She
told me at once that she had worn it to give me and my guests
pleasure. She did, we were all delighted. But, so robed, she
did not overawe us. It was not part of her plan. Her plan was
simply to please.

I came to know her famous brothers, Osbert, now dead,
then suffering with the utmost gameness from Parkinson's
Disease, and the handsome Sacheverell (the present baronet)
whose prose works, *The Quick and the Dead*, *Splendours and
Miseries*, are absurdly underrated. As a trio, they were – at
least, in their earlier years – so united, so bizarre – a sort of
six-legged race – that they not unnaturally became targets for
parody. (One must parody someone.) Sir Noel Coward was the
first, and most effective offender. (Young men usually are:
remember the days of *TW3*, and *Beyond the Fringe*.) But I
am glad to say they made it up before Edith died. Because, had
things been different, they would have enjoyed each other's
company so much.

Edith's last days were not particularly sad ones. She was
confined to her room, where she occupied her chair as if it
were a throne, and then to her bed. This had a green velvet
coverlet, and her lovely hands were always displayed above it.
She was cared for by her devoted secretary, Elizabeth Salter,
and by the equally devoted Nurse Farquharson. There was a
Siamese cat called Shadow.

Her parties continued, but no longer at the Sesame Club. We
were invited for drinks to her flat – not 'summoned', as I have
heard someone say: a parade of that sort was not in her nature.

She was enormous fun, even when old age had made some of her 'practical joke' stories repetitive. They were so good that one didn't mind hearing them again; even as no one has ever minded hearing again the most famous songs of a great music-hall star.

When she died, how we missed her! She had that capacity to linger in the memory fully-blown. For we are pitifully short these days of people who have 'style', that mysterious and immediately recognisable attribute. Edith had it. So has Harold Macmillan (*in excelsis*), Sir John Betjeman. But we are fast becoming a grey lot.

Of Edith Sitwell's poetry I shall only speak briefly. She was in love from the first with metrical intricacies, and the golden Hesperides of words.

Some clown has announced this week, in some periodical, that poetry should only be reviewed by poets. For whom, then, is it written? Should plays only be reviewed by play-wrights? or novels by novelists?

This demand means that poetry should only be reviewed by technicians. The rise of the hair along the spine, as Housman put it, has no place in this new aspect of criticism. It is a mere engineer's conception.

Edith, until her later years, did not approximate to the status of more than a minor poet. Few hairs rose along the spine. Yet she was gay, delightful, and absolutely original.

I think her main early weakness was her passion for Swin-burne. A magnificent manipulator of words, he had no sense at all: I do not know anything sillier than his record of Sinister Queens.

'I am the Queen Aholibah', etc.

Poets need to have something to say: see Shakespeare, Dante, Milton, Donne, Herbert, Pope, Dryden and so forth. Edith found it during the war, when her religious feeling and her social conscience grew side by side. 'Gold Coast Customs' and 'Still Falls the Rain' are very considerable poems.

Who should blame her that in her younger days, she chose to employ her very great gift in giving fun? She had had little fun herself.

11. *Being in Love*

It is not an entire advantage to be fluent in reading, as I was, and my children after me, at the age of four, nor to understand what is so laboriously spelled out in front of you. 'N-O-T B-E-F-O-R-E T-H-E C-H-I-L-D.' Of course, this pricked up one's ears. And sometimes one's ears could be sources of grief.

I was amusing myself with a playmate of about my own age – say, four and a half – one afternoon. I think we were dressing up: doubtless she was the princess and I the handmaid. She was extraordinarily pretty: indeed, she grew up to be the prettiest woman I have ever seen in my life. She was killed in a bombing raid during the Second World War.

Watching us indulgently was her mother, and a friend of her mother's, Mrs T. Suddenly I heard the latter say, as part of a conversation, but with her eyes on me, 'She seems a clever little girl. What a pity she's so U-G-L-Y.'

When my mother came to call for me, I could hardly wait to get outside the door.

Me: 'Mamma, am I ugly?'

My Mother (indignant): 'Certainly not! Whatever put that idea into your head?'

Me: 'Mrs T. said so. She spelled it.'

My Mother (always just): 'No, darling. You're quaint.'

Quaint! A horrible word. It dogged me for years, when I could not believe that any of my young passions could possibly be reciprocated.

I was, in fact, a plain child. Photographs of the time show me as a Chinese doll, with an odd slant of eye (this runs in the family: my grandfather liked, mysteriously and ridiculously, to attribute it to a Mandarin – it *would* be a Mandarin – of whom we were all the descendants), a snub nose, and a bob of thick dark hair, with a low and unbecoming fringe, this topped by a big ribbon bow fashionable at the time.

After the incident of Mrs T., the subject of my looks tended to worry me. Later, strolling with my beautiful friend on the Common, hoping to pick up boys from the Grammar School, I would automatically take second place when these hopes were realised. It was while staying with the romantic novelist Jeffery Farnol and his wife Blanche, that comfort came. I was fifteen and I remember it well: it was the first really lavish household I had ever visited, and an exciting one. Jeffery, in the spirit of his novels, would cry out, when carving the Sunday joint, 'By Jesu, a goodly baron of beef!' I was happy there, and their daughter Jill took me to tea-dances and presented me, diffidently, with two of the most beautiful dresses I have ever possessed – or, I suspect, ever shall. At that time my mother and I were very hard up.

But one afternoon I heard a brief conversation between my mother and Blanche Farnol.

My mother: 'Yes, I think she shows promise.' (I was then writing long poems about the Golden Fleece, Hylas and the water nymphs, and others of similar classical inspiration, all deeply influenced by Tennyson.) 'But I'm afraid she isn't going to be a beauty.'

Blanche (comfortably): 'Just give her a year. She'll improve.' At sixteen, in fact, there was some improvement, and my fears of a lifetime of non-reciprocation faded.

I should like to return, however, to an experience I had at the age of eight. I was returning on the bus from a trip to Richmond Park, with my mother, my Aunt Kalie, and a man friend of hers whom I shall call Henry. Henry must at that time have been in his early thirties: and women, except platonically, were of no interest to him. This, naturally, I was not to know. I was sitting next to him in a front seat on the top of the bus. It was a blue and brilliant afternoon (wasn't it always like that, when we were children?). I was suddenly taken with a passion for him so violent that I shall never forget it. It seemed to me that I had never met anyone who seemed so handsome (he was, in a bleak way), so adorable. So much what I wanted for myself, for ever and ever.

The duration of this *amour* was, I suppose, about an hour and a half, if that. But what I want to emphasise is that it in no way differed *in kind* from any love I experienced later. It seems to me that our youthful loves and our mature ones differ very little, in essence, except in their duration. Proust knew this: his devoted love for Gilberte, frustrated, soon died, and he was able, without the slightest feeling of remorse, to give her precious gift of an agate marble to Albertine.

My mother was, in some respects, a wise woman. So that I should not sneak off to meet boys round street corners, as she (fearing grandfather) had done, she kept, from the day I was fifteen, open house for the boys and girls I cared to invite. These were the dancing days: we rolled back the carpet in our pleasant semi-basement sitting-room and danced for hours. We then drank tea and ate my mother's special and much appreciated treat, called for for many years after that – of bread pudding, full of currants and spice, hot from the oven. Afterwards we graduated to something called Reo, a red wine that seemed racy then, but which I cannot now admire.

Babs, Teddy, Jack, 'Take Plato' (see *An Impossible Marriage*), Reg, Peter, later Ian (this was not his name, but I liked it better than his real one) and later still F., but F. was older than we were, and in a sense a disruptive influence, for by then he and I had become engaged. I think of them all with affection and gratitude.

Of course, that basement became redolent of romantic attachments, but in those days, for boys and girls of our middle-class upbringing, these were only expressed in flirtation and in surreptitious kisses in the hallway. I am speaking of a time when we were between fifteen and nineteen. No one went to bed with anyone else, nor would have thought of such a thing.

(If anyone did so, he or she kept it dark.) No one suggested to us that otherwise we would be frustrated, would wither on the vine. My mother, who had had my horoscope cast and who had been informed that I should need 'a strict moral training', would certainly have seen to it that I did not fall into error. But then, nobody asked me.

None of us was any the worse for all this. It was a carefree time, the only one I have ever really known. The end of the twenties: the beginning of the thirties. To my second husband, Charles, they did not seem like that at all. Seven years older than myself, they were days to him of hard work and anxiety: he was politically conscious, while we were not.

We were, on the whole, a literary set, though only a few of us cared for serious music, and only I had a smattering of knowledge about painting. Every week there was some new discovery. Someone had found out Dostoevsky, someone Liam O'Flaherty, someone Nietzsche, I think this was 'Take Plato'. And one day, Teddy burst in, full of excitement, to tell us of a novel called *Look Homeward, Angel* by Thomas Wolfe. This was a profound influence upon us all – for it is a book for youth – and many years later I was to write a critical study of Wolfe's work.

I am not going into a recital here of my love affairs, green-stick or otherwise, except to say that my engagement to F. had been broken off. Before him there had been Ian, whom I met many years later as a middle-aged man, handsome, a combination of fun and *gravitas*, with a charming wife and family. A grandfather. He died before his time, and I remembered Bruges, where we first met at a band concert on the Grand' Place, all gas flares and carillons.

Of my two marriages, I wish to say little here. I married Neil, an attractive, Frenchified, twenty-four-year-old Australian (his education had been mostly in France) in 1936. We were married for fourteen years, and the marriage was broken up, I think, largely by the war and the irrational hostility of my mother, with whom we lived. It was some years after the war that we were divorced, but the strain had been increasing. But I remember the pre-war trips we were constantly making to France – mostly to Paris, but sometimes in rucksack hikes around the Seine Valley – Les Andelys, Caudebec-en-Caux. We were both extremely pressed for money, for my writing brought me in little, and I do not know how we managed it. But we did. For him, I have little but gratitude. He has remarried and has a daughter.

In 1950, I myself remarried. This was to C. P. Snow whom I had known, from an exchange of letters on the subject of literature, and from casual meetings, for many years. He has been all I could wish. More might be said, but it isn't going to be.

12. A Higher Education

I once said of Aldous Huxley, that he was loved by the young in the twenties and thirties, because he had the gift of making them feel that, if only they really tried, they could become as clever as he.

I was fascinated by his novels, and repelled: repelled by his own loathing of ugliness wherever it was to be found – in a human countenance, in a dog falling from an aeroplane and splattering with blood two naked lovers on a flat roof. Implausible, I have always thought, but unforgettable just the same. He had a certain in-built life-hatred and life-contempt: when I met him in his old age this seemed to have moderated. He was very gentle. Age had even brought him a handsomeness that he had lacked in youth. Nearly blind, happy with his wife, he found in California a way of life that appeared to satisfy him. He became a mystic and, I must add, the most gullible man I have ever met. He really did appear to believe that dolphins were cleverer than he was.

It was not, however, the novels, or his later mystic-philosophical works, that had such a deep and life-lasting influence upon me. This was a book published in 1933, called *Texts and Pretexts*, which was an anthology with critical commentaries. It opened miraculous doors to me, and for a group of my friends with literary interests, who were as excited as I was. (When I spoke of it to him in the sixties, he said he intended to write a sequel: he died before this became possible.)

He was my 'Higher Education', and the only one I ever had. At least, it was the only real help I ever had: the donkey-work, which a university would have helped me through, such as a long struggle with French literature, had to be done in solitude, and with no further instruction. Here I am not asking for sympathy, holding out the tin can, as it were: I believe that, to a creative writer, a university education would have been nothing but a hindrance. A course in Eng. Lit. has rotted many a promising writer. It is only as a critic that I should have welcomed it.

At my excellent school – a very good grammar school – we were on the whole admirably taught, and made to work where we were not absolutely unteachable, as in all the mathematical subjects I was. When it came to trigonometry, the mistress threw me over in despair: and actually gave me permission to sit at the back of the classroom and write poetry. (After Charles and I married he, disbelieving in my incapacity, said that *he* would teach me trigonometry. The lessons, with me really trying hard to understand, came to an abrupt halt, when I insisted that a sine was something that just didn't seem to exist, an invisibility you were supposed to move around anywhere between an angle. He became in total sympathy with my maths teacher.)

English, and particularly French literature, were thoroughly taught, and I immensely enjoyed both: but I never realised how narrow the syllabus was in both cases. English: Shakespeare, Keats, Coleridge, some Milton, Wordsworth, some Blake, Byron's lyrics, Tennyson, Palgrave's *Golden Treasury*, Browning (a little) and 'Modern' poetry concluded with the 1914 war. French: Racine and Corneille, Lamartine, Victor Hugo, various minor poets. Much to be grateful for, of course.

But when I started to read *Texts and Pretexts*, I felt like the industrious girl in the story of *Mother Holle*, who was rewarded by a shower of gold.

Crashaw, Vaughan! I had never heard of them. George Herbert, my most beloved poet – I am making no value judgments, of course – hardly at all. The more esoteric Blake. Manley Hopkins, the great intoxicant. Sir Philip Sidney. Sir Thomas Wyatt.

And French! Baudelaire, Rimbaud, Verlaine, Valéry, Mallarmé, Gérard de Nerval!

In Latin, which my friends and I could all read adequately, though mine is badly rusted now, there were anonymous delights such as this:

> Spatiari dulce est
> per loca nemorosa;
> dulcimo est carpere
> lilia cum rosa;
> dulcissimum est ludere
> cum virgine formosa!

Among Huxley's many chapter headings were 'Visitations', 'Country Ecstasies', 'Self Torture', 'Loneliness', 'Desire', 'Earthly Paradise', 'Conceits', 'Magic', 'Serenity', 'Death'.

The chosen poetry under each was embedded in a commentary full of wit, insight, sharpness and sometimes, where appropriate, high humour and comedy. We knew that if we could never hope to vie with him in learning, he was with us in enthusiasm, that he had got as much kick out of the writing as we out of the reading. But the most important thing was this: he led us on. He pointed out to us, by mere suggestion, without the slightest touch of the pedant, where to read further – and this partly by leaving a great number of poems tantalisingly incomplete.

I am afraid that, at first, this newly-acquired and delightful learning, led us to bluff somewhat. With Huxley behind us, we could always show off – and we did. But later we needed to bluff less, since we had continued, many of us, on the courses he had set for us.

My copy of *Texts and Pretexts*, once bound in jade and lettered in gold, is now a brownish green on the spine – which is loose – and a mere memory of jade on the front and back. When I lent it to my sons, I was always terrified that I would never get it back, for the book must now be extremely rare, if not virtually unobtainable. I hope, in the names of education, delight, exhilaration and discovery, that it will one day be reprinted.

I have written a good deal about these poetic excitements, since I have found the poetry of the past can rarely have verbal appreciative expression after one's early twenties. One can mention a new book of poetry: one can talk of a new play and a new novel: also of classic novels. But poetry? It makes one feel a fool. Even when I meet a young poet whose work I admire, I cannot tell him so: I am awkward and tongue-tied. After all, what could I say but, 'I liked your poems'? Impossible to quote, or to attempt any sort of verbal analysis.

Just conceive of an ordinary literary party, among the talk of royalties, agents and general injustices, where someone broke out in praise of, say, Crashaw, and insisted on quoting from him. There would be a deathly silence. Yet some of those silent would not be incapable of continuing the conversation. They would just be too frozen to do so.

At small gatherings with literary friends, I have found it possible to discuss Dickens, Trollope, Proust. Even Philip Larkin, Richard Eberhart, Charles Causley, Ted Hughes. But Crashaw, Vaughan, Wyatt? Not a bit of it. I have not frozen in my own enthusiasms, but have frozen within them. And I think my readers will thus have frozen inwardly, unless they are teaching academics: in which case they may release their skills in the classroom. Somehow, these enthusiasms have become socially – well – unbecoming.

This is why I remember some of Victor Neuburg's garden evenings with affection. If we talked of Blake, we damned well did talk of him: we were at least uninhibited, even if we were raw. Contemporaneity was not all, though of course it entered it.

I think it is only on my rare meetings with Edmund Wilson that I was able to talk about Proust, Dickens, Kipling, in a spontaneous way – mostly in answer to his sharp questions. He was a great critic, and I was in awe of him, but somehow or other he made things easy. If it had been poetry – that unspeakable subject, when the poetry is over a hundred years old – I think I could have done the same.

But it is of no use repining: and my friends need not have the slightest fear that I shall suddenly break out in delirious praise of Wyatt, or anybody else. My excitements are not silenced: my tongue is. Even to my son, Philip, if I strike something in poetry that seems to me magical and may strike him in the same way, I will not read it aloud: I will simply pass him the book.

I gave *A la Recherche du temps perdu*, volume by volume, to Andrew, many years ago, when we were sitting on the sands of a small Belgian resort. I was rewarded, on occasion, by bursts of laughter, when Proust's comic scenes had struck home. It was very satisfying.

> Mais, O, ces voix d'enfants
> Qui chantent dans la coupole!

Little by little, the great arch of our heavens shrinks, the blue fades, and the dome of the cupola is smaller than we thought.

For all of us? I doubt if that was true of Huxley at any time. He was not a 'Gottgetrunkener mensch', but he was drunk with literature: and in our youth he made us so, too.

Now, as the years go on, we are becoming retiring and mock-modest; at least, among our contemporaries. It is sometimes possible to exchange enthusiasms with the young, *but only if they raise the subject*. That is one of the reasons why they please, and stimulate us, so much.

13. When Daffodils Begin to Peer

Shakespeare. All the international millions who are devoted to the plays, know him of course: as something more than an elusive shadow, just out of sight. Sometimes he seems very much in sight: and he is not Francis Bacon, or the Earl of Oxford, or some strange consortium – the last conception an impossible one for anybody of the slightest literary insight.

I first visited Stratford in the spring of 1940. It was beautiful spring weather: I am sure that the meadow flowers were more abundant then than they are now (fewer insecticides). Ladies' Smocks were indeed silver-white. The walk to Shottery was not so abominably built up as it is today: one could imagine the young Shakespeare making that trip, perhaps not altogether to his advantage. The doxy was just over the dale.

I was particularly happy: I had begun to suspect that I was to have a child, which proved to be a correct suspicion. What did I see at the theatre? I don't remember very well. But I think I saw Margaret Leighton in *As You Like It*: I know I heard three little boys sing: 'It was a lover and his lass', as though it were the first song ever sung in the world.

Of course, I had gone regularly to the plays long before that – (though not at Stratford) whenever I could. From the ages of eleven to about fourteen, I and a few like-minded school-friends saved up for our Saturday treat. This was invariably the same. We would climb to the top of the Monument, where we would eat our sandwiches, and look out on the panorama of London. Then we would go to the Old Vic – Lillian Bayliss' theatre – to sit on a hard gallery seat – price 6*d* – (or, I should say, two and a half 'new pence') – and watch Shakespeare. No scenery: just curtains, a few banners, a throne, some leafy boughs for pastoral scenes, fanfares and tuckets. Baliol Hollo-way, our hero, a dashing Falconbridge in *King John*. We were drunk with it all.

> Thou wear a lion's hide? Doff it for shame,
> And hang a calf's skin on those recreant limbs!

What is there about Shakespeare that can intoxicate many children, and carry that intoxication (though it will grow an increasingly critical content, where production is concerned) into age? God knows. But, of course, there is something.

The war interrupted my playgoing. But from 1950 onwards, Charles and I visited Stratford once every year for a week – in so far as it were possible.

I maintain that the town in itself is altogether delightful: in shape, it is as it was in Shakespeare's day, and the Stratford Trust has done wonders to preserve it. Of course there are some blots: some people will insist that it is 'commercialised'. It isn't, or only in some minor respects. But who, knowing anything of Shakespeare, that man of the theatre, businessman, builder of New Place, *armiger*, aspiring bourgeois, can con-ceivably believe it would have pleased him if it had run at a loss?

The most wonderful season at Stratford was, for us, when, under the general direction of Glen Byam Shaw, the whole tetralogy of the history plays was performed: *Richard II*, *Henry IV*, Parts i and ii (these two plays remind me of one magnificent novel), *Henry V*. The overall theory seemed to me based on the writings of E. M. Tillyard. What a cast! Harry Andrews, as Henry IV himself, bulging-eyed Hugh Griffiths as Glendower, and the delightful but obviously chilling young Richard Burton, first as Prince, then as King.

Burton now seems lost to the theatre; it is a tragic loss. I cannot but think that despite his fame in the cinema, and the plutocratic glitter with which he has surrounded himself, he has let us down: and by 'us', I mean the English stage.

I shall never forget his first entrance in *Henry IV*, Part 1. It was entirely consistent with the rejection of Falstaff, which was to come. Here he was, cold-eyed, pale-eyed, smiling rarely – and then only because Falstaff forced him to – among his companions in the Boar's Head, sowing his wild oats because time was running short, and he knew he had to accept a royal destiny in which they could have no place. The scene in which he and Falstaff were fooling, pretending to be king in turn, was singularly glacial; and a clue to everything that was to come.

Falstaff (playing the prince) was indulging in delightful false pathos: 'Banish plump Jack, and banish all the world.'

A dreadful pause. Then, in a voice of ice, the real Prince's reply: 'I do. *I will*.'

He had that rare star-quality which can be expressed by absolute stillness. Lydia Sherwood, Gertrude in Burton's *Hamlet*, was speaking to me of the first Court scene. 'You remember how he stands there with nothing to say, until "a little more than kith and less than kind"? Well, he just stood. He was doing nothing naughty, not even the faintest fidget. *But the rest of us could have turned handsprings before an audience would have paid us the slightest attention.*'

His *Henry V* was a little disappointing: perhaps he was not quite ready for the sudden switch to heroic acting. But in his scene with the soldiers by night, he was as magical as ever.

I remember sitting next to him – he didn't know me, and wouldn't have cared if he had, he was lost to the world – on a bright spring morning, on the terrace of 'the Dirty Duck' as it is called (the Black Swan, an actors' pub by the river). He was studying *Henry V* then. There he sat, not very tall, his hair still worn in his Prince Hal fringe, quite immobile, except when he had to turn a page.

Paul Scofield, that splendid actor, and most thoughtful and

modest of his kind, told me on an Atlantic crossing, that he
and Laurence Olivier, and almost everyone else, were invest-
ing every hope in Burton's future. Well, Richard Burton has
had his future : he and his second wife became predominantly
successful, and 'glamour-figures' of the highest order. But I
am afraid the glory has departed.

Between whiles during the Tetralogy – the weather was fine
– I walked by the river, watching the famous 'backward eddy',
and the weir where the swan's feather stays motionless on the
peak of the fall. This last was pointed out to me by Mr Timms,
the head porter of the Shakespeare Hotel, who is a remarkable
amateur Shakespearian and – I find – a very sound critic. He
had been pondering the lines, from *Anthony and Cleopatra*
'the swan's down feather that stands upon the swell at full of
tide, and neither way inclines', and had gone to the weir to
find out if they were accurate. I think Mr Timms has never
missed a performance : he was in love with Shakespeare from
his early youth, when the old theatre had been burned down,
and all that was to be seen was a performance of *Macbeth*
(live) in a local cinema. I rarely go to a play without asking
his opinion beforehand. His answer is often sly. 'Well, Madam,
since I expect you are a bit of a purist ...' I suspect that I am.
Sometimes I walked to Shottery, but in ten years that walk
had been ruined. No daffodils. No ladies' smock. No violets
blue. And only a modicum of daisies. New houses, concrete
schools, allotments, fences. But I had seen it in better days.

I must admit to a visceral dislike of Peter Brook's *A Midsummer Night's Dream* – a world success, and dispraised by
only one or two English critics. I was that year attending the
international Shakespeare conference, and saw this with
scholars from all over the world.

Now Peter Brook is brilliantly inventive : but on this occasion he invented too much. *A Midsummer Night's Dream* is a
play shot through with moonlight and moon-imagery. A
truism? All right. Why not, then, believe it? The play opened

on a scene of blinding whiteness – which was to blind the spectator throughout. A kind of gymnasium, where it might have been appropriate to hang war criminals. The first part went well enough – obviously we were to have an evening of perfect verse-speaking, and so we did.

Then – the wood near Athens. Oberon and Puck, in clown's costumes, high on trapezes, like accomplished conjurers playing between them a sort of cup-and-ball game. My attention was wholly distracted from the text by apprehension lest they should drop the damned things. Still worse, when the lovers began to climb vertiginous ladders attached to the wings. Who would be the first to fall? Worse still, when poor Hermia, hanging by her arms to a trapeze a good way above the stage, had to make a longish speech. Could she hold out? Was she suffering? Well, she was young. Let me comfort myself by pretending that she was not suffering so much as I thought.

Bottom and the workmen came off better. But when Bottom was carried off by the 'fairies', shaggy men in something resembling boiler suits, to Titania's bower, someone thrust an arm through his legs to suggest an enormous phallus. Influence of Jan Kott, probably. But so hopelessly out of key with the poetry.

I asked Marko Minkov, Professor of English at the University of Sofia and one of the world's foremost Shakespearean scholars (he was soon to be honoured by Birmingham University), what he thought of it all. He was sitting next to me. He replied, 'If I keep my eyes tight shut, all the time, it is beautiful.'

I cannot recall all the marvellous performances I have seen at Stratford. There was Olivier's unmatchable Malvolio, a canting, nasal-speaking Puritan who could yet arouse pity: so that on his release from the 'dark house', his exit line – 'I'll be revenged upon the whole pack of you' – struck a second's dead silence into the babbling gossips of Illyria. When

I saw *Twelfth Night* recently, this line was greeted by the audience with hearty laughter. Surely that was wrong? An Elizabethan audience would have laughed, but then, I think that in four hundred years we have learned to recognise something of Shakespeare's extraordinary ambiguities. Shylock, for example: don't we find some pity for the isolation of the Jew? Hadn't he eyes like other men? If pricked, did he not bleed? If poisoned, didn't he die? I think that in our laughing and our refraining from laughter, we may be wiser, and closer to him, than his contemporaries.

Paul Scofield's famous Lear was powerful and original: I just had one fleeting doubt. He looked so fit that he might have spent six weeks out on the heath without any damage to his health. But I reserve my supreme admiration for his towering Timon. *Timon of Athens* is scarcely a cosy play. Despite Wilson Knight, I think it is poorly composed, and suffers from being on only two notes. Yet the moment it was done, I could have instantly sat through the whole thing again, just for the moral splendour Scofield brought to it. This so impressed me and carried me away that I lost my head somewhat and actually shouted my applause, which emboldened several others to shout too. I must say I thought that, for a fleeting second, Scofield looked a little surprised.

To a non-Shakespearian scholar, to toy with new and recent Shakespearian scholarship is always fun, provided you don't mind being snubbed occasionally when you are wrong. I remember my son Philip, then aged about thirteen, and intimate with all the plays, going round at a party during one of the biennial Shakespeare conferences, and politely asking authorities from many nations if they knew in which play Matthew Gough appeared and what was remarkable about him. No one did.

The answer is, *Henry VI* Part II. What is remarkable is, that he has a quicker entrance and departure from this life than anyone in the canon, and nothing whatsoever to say. The stage directions in the Irving edition (I admit it is not now commonly read) and the O.U.P. edition, 1964:

'Alarums. Entry, on one side, CADE and his company; on the other, Citizens, and the king's forces, headed by MATTHEW GOUGH (or "Goffe"). They fight: the Citizens are routed, and MATTHEW GOUGH is slain.'

It was, of course, impudence on Philip's part, at his age, to tease scholars like this: but it was not quite motiveless. He believed that poor Matthew must have had more of a part once, but that something had been lost. Or perhaps the editors had been in an inventive mood? But this I can hardly believe. I should welcome enlightenment. The oddity appears to be this: in neither The Folio of 1623 nor The Quarto of 1594, does Matthew Gough 'enter'. He is only slain. What happened?

The positive discoveries of Leslie Hotson, who seems to have had all the luck in the world (and, of course, the industry) were exciting when they were revealed – Shakespeare's lodgings in Silver Street, the Mountjoy marriage settlement. But I think much of *The First Night of Twelthe Night* has its implausibilities. Could Shakespeare, even on a Feast Day devoted to licence, possibly have made fun of the Comptroller of Queen Elizabeth's household, Sir William Knollys, actually in the Queen's presence? I can't swallow this.

But, among other interesting things, he has this extremely interesting one. When the Fool in *Lear* closes the first act with the couplet,

> She that's a maid now and laughs at my departure
> Shall not be a maid long, unless things be cut shorter.

This is absolutely meaningless, unless we accept from Hotson that Shakespeare must have written 'deporter', the word for a fool's bauble, which could be made to represent an outsize phallus. (It would be interesting to know whether 'deporter' makes its appearance in any other Tudor-Jacobean writings.)

Dr A. L. Rowse is a good friend of mine: a most stylish writer, with an inordinate appetite for voyages of discovery. He is so self-confident that he does induce other scholars to rise in their wrath. At the time of writing he is much under attack because, although he has undoubtedly unearthed a Dark Lady, he is dead sure that she was Shakespeare's. I do not think there is sufficient evidence – unless he has something up his sleeve. His sleeves are capacious.

But I do have a strong feeling that he is right about the dedicatee of the sonnets: that he was the purveyor, not the subject of, the poem. (W. H. Auden agreed with this.) That they are dedicated by the printer, Thomas Thorpe, to – according to Rowse – Sir William Harvey (who would, again according to Rowse, have been called 'Master' Harvey). Sir William Harvey was the second husband of the Countess of Southampton, and would have been a likely person to have the original manuscripts in his hands. This seems to me far more plausible than the attempt to reverse Southampton's initials, to suggest that they meant quite a different golden lad, or to go into dithyrambic Wildean imaginings.

I am not pretending the false humility of a Joey Bagstock – of which there are far too many in the population, and among writers in particular – by insisting on my ignorance. I have a right to my fun, and sometimes to be convinced by something. After all, scholars do not presumably write only for themselves, a sort of closed, tape-worm-like society. They write, in part, to put their ideas to people who care about Shakespeare, and who do their best to learn as much about him as they can. At least I hope so.

When I am in Stratford, especially in the gardens of the New Place, I feel Shakespeare all around me. (Note: with a certain strained regret, I am not going to reply to any letters from Baconians. I have had too many of them already.)

Did he sit under that mulberry tree? It is old enough, poor thing. It was once suggested to me by somebody – I forget whom – that if he had indeed inhabited New Place, his study would have looked out on to a blank wall. And very sensible, too. Who, when he is absorbed in writing, demands a view? In my youth, I knew a young man who had rooms overlooking the river at Rotherhithe. He couldn't stand – being a writer – too much of that: he was constantly diverted by the shipping. This is why I sympathise with Proust, who chose to be encapsulated in a sound-proof room.

I deplore the fact that the chancel of Stratford Parish Church is now only accessible by paying a fee, and a relatively high one. This puts it out of bounds to most schoolchildren. We are barred sternly off from the Clopton tombs and now, in fact, can scarcely see them at all. Fees needed for the upkeep of the church? I do not believe the world will allow it to fall down.

On Shakespeare's birthday, 23 April, I like to walk in procession bearing my flowers, from the theatre up Bridge Street, where the flags of the nation are unfurled, to the church, passing by (or through, if privileged) the birthplace on the way. (It must, anyhow, have been one of two or three houses.) Visitors who come from all parts of the world, join in this exquisite ceremony. Flowers are heaped high above the grave, and below the Stratford bust.

Of this, what nonsense has been talked! Janssen was obviously an able craftsman, but uninspired: nevertheless, this was roughly what Shakespeare must have looked like. Substitute, for those eyes of stone, bright-darting eyes, hazel or blue. Not like Shelley? Of course not. Why should he have been? He must have had a pretty mesomorphic component, in Sheldon's terms, to have done all he did. There can have been no suggestion about him, of what someone, speaking of Shelley in an unkind mood, called a 'faerie slug'. He was too busy writing, acting, travelling, becoming a partner in his companies, making his pile, moving between London and his grand house. He did not die at a particularly young age, by

Elizabethan standards – especially considering the rigours of
his life.

I find it hard to write about him without understatement.
It is especially hard, because he has been among the great joys
of my life. But there is much more than this. He has the uncanny knack of hitting us where we live.

There is scarcely a state of mind which disturbs us for which
Shakespeare has not something to say. His human understanding is so vast that it may be dismaying – or a comfort.

He knows where the nerve is, in its innermost centre. He
knows where the heart misses a beat; and he fills the pause.
And he knows how to make us forget, for a while, our ageing.
There was a one-time pop-singer, Jim Dale, playing Autolycus
at Stratford a year or so ago. He is an extremely talented actor,
and has a sense of joy. He made me, for a while, oblivious of
my years.

> The lark that tirra-lirra chants,
> Sing hey, sing hey, the thrush and the jay,
> Are summer songs for me and my aunts
> As we lie tumbling in the hay.

No generation gap here. Shakespeare's high spirits, a re-
awakened awareness of mine.

Out from the theatre into the car-park, then down to the
black river, where a few of the ghostly swans were still gathering, even so late at night, though most of them had returned
to their residence on the island under the bridge, in a dormitory
of feather-scattered grass.

14. Crime and Punishment

I have always been interested in crime. I don't think this is morbidity: it is more an itch to find out why some people behave as they do, and to discover the point at which the thought of a deed becomes the doing of it. It seems to me that between this is a thread finer than a hair, but of enormous tensile strength. Somehow before, say, murder, can be committed, that barrier must be broken.

I attended several days of the Moors Trial in Chester, perhaps the most appalling in British criminal history, in 1967, at the request of the *Sunday Telegraph*, to write about my general impressions. The impact of this led me to write *On Iniquity*, a series of reflections on, but mostly arising from, the trial: an attempt to see where it slotted into society. For it seemed to me that out of some root and bud sprang this poisonous flower.

The Moors case was, if it may be so defined, a case of *folie-à-deux*, where two people are stricken with a kind of hysteria, mutually egging each other on, to do things that perhaps neither would have done alone. I was cynical enough at that time to suggest that the murderers might become cult-figures as the Manson 'family' have done in the U.S.A., and as Hitler has, to an extent done here. (I was revolted, in a magazine catering for teenagers, to see an advertisement for trench coats called 'Stormtroopers'.) The Moors murderers, I am glad to say, have not yet. And perhaps they never will.

But the worst part of the Permissive Society (which has many benevolent aspects also) formed the earth in which that flower grew. Obscene literature, the pervading idea that anyone is free to do anything – all this played its part.

Crimes of violence are greatly on the increase, some of them, such as 'mugging', having duly floated across the Atlantic. Violence on the football terraces (mass hysteria) seems endemic. Our underground stations are by no means wholly safe: New York's have been dangerous for a long time. The courts seem powerless to deal adequately with the offenders, when they are caught; and judges have given voice to this. Heavier sentencing might help: the Notting Hill Gate race riots were brought to an abrupt stop when Mr Justice Salmon gave the ringleaders four years apiece.

I was elated when the hangman was put out of a job. It seemed to me a cleansing of our society: and I still think it was. But I now think that a life sentence, for the most savage of our murderers (there are, of course, gradations of murder which most of us will recognise) should mean *life*. That might be a real deterrent: most people have got it into their heads that everyone gets out after nine years, which is not true. (Incidentally, it is an anomaly of the law, and always has been, that property is valued more highly than life. See the sentences passed on the 'Great' train robbers. This calls for law reform at its very roots.)

Don't think I have not the slightest idea of how appalling many of our prisons are. During the war I often visited the Borstal Institute at Feltham (a decrepit building, apparently run with humanity, and the food was decent). After the war, I gave a lecture at Pentonville. The place was a horror, Piranesi's *Carceri* seeming gay beside it. The greyness, the sound of the rattling keys, ugliness and malodorous age everywhere. The attendance for my not-very-interesting talk, 'On Being a Broadcaster', brought a full house; it was not compulsory to attend, but what else was there to do? I was younger then, and was greeted with wolf-whistles. After that there was quiet, but below this was a note of hysteria. Question-time brought dozens to their feet: I was hard put to it to cope with them. Some sensible questions, some grotesquely resentful ones.

'You say they gave you a gin-and-orange. *Who paid for it?*'

'The Corporation,' I said, adding feebly, 'but there wasn't much gin.' (This was slander.)

Later, I was stupefied to see, in the front row of prisoners, a friend of mine from the days of the Wardens' Post. He was beaming cheerfully: he gave me a surreptitious little wave.

As I was leaving I saw, going down the sad grey halls, a harmless necessary tabby cat. I hope the prisoners were allowed to pet it.

So it appears that, if the punishment fits the crime (Gilbert's appallingly sadistic lyric in *The Mikado* shakes me with repulsion as it would not have shaken a member of a nineteenth-century audience) we shall lay still heavier loads on the prison service. 'Open' prisons? More, I hope, but that makes the burden still heavier. I cannot believe that all prisoners will respond to reformation. This is just sentimentality. But I would urge that they have every opportunity to do interesting and productive work (payment to their victims, if you like) and have the opportunity, if they wish, for study. But remember, during a prison sentence, a man is metaphorically castrated. I believe the Swedes have a method of dealing with this, but I do not know enough about it to expand the matter here.

Someone asked me the other day, whether I thought restoring the birch for crimes of violence might put a stop to it? (We have recently seen the introduction in Libya of Colonel Gaddafi's penal code, which permits the mutilation of hands and feet, *humanely performed in a hospital under anaesthetic*, as though that did not make it seem nine times as horrible. Wyndham Lewis, in *The Human Age*, thought of something very like this – a kind of penal surgery. There is nothing new under the sun.)

I had to think rather more hard than I should have done ten years ago. Then I replied, 'Very probably it would. *But we cannot do it.*'

Society must not regress in these ways. Regression would soil us all.

I have come to the tragic conclusion that violence, if met by judicial violence, might come to a sharp halt. But even if it did, *still it would not do for us.* We must cope as we may, and do it as humanely as possible. (See my remarks on that most admirable of prison reformers, Captain Alexander Maconochie, of Norfolk Island, in *On Iniquity*.)

Now I come to a more general matter: the effect of 'the Permissive Society', particularly in the cinema, and also though somewhat more rarely, on the television screen. It is here that the dread yell tends to arise – 'Censorship!' Yet we have censorship in all, literally all, countries now. (People object to censorship only when applied to things of which they don't disapprove.) One form of our censorship, not the only one but in some ways the most stringent, is contained in the Race Relations Act. That was applauded by all liberal opinion. Would we repeal it? It is by-passed by many people, but there is no doubt that it must have spared a good deal of suffering.

One of the effects of the Permissive Society has been to make sex ugly, and 'love', almost a dirty word. No, it doesn't make sex beautiful in its freedom: it cheapens it. And as sexual activity is the most pleasurable activity known to most men and women it should not be cheapened. We might, as children, have liked liquorice allsorts. Is that a reason to make a staple diet of them? We might do better with the allsorts, as they could ruin the lining of the stomach, but would not be the cause of ever-spreading venereal disease.

Pre-marital sex, after a certain age (not for children of fourteen) is permissible wherever the idea of love is, and may indeed, prevent certain difficulties from arising after marriage. No marriage? Out of date? Nonsense. Marriage is a mutually responsible affair. And we shall have to wait for a while before we see what the problems of illegitimate children bring about. For they need two parents, and the father's role is of great importance.

Abortion? Necessary, of course, when some silly young creature is likely to give birth to a child with whom she is too immature to cope. Or when some overburdened mother, having several children already, is in danger of bearing the straw, as it were, which breaks the camel's back.

Necessary, yes. I admit that the general idea fills me with repulsion. Life is there, for me, as soon as life is diagnosed. We must kill it, sometimes, the future circumstances being impossible. But do we know what we are killing? What that minuscule life might have become? Sometimes there are serious genetic reasons for destroying it, and these I accept: sometimes serious social ones.

Birth control? Of course. It is essential on a wide scale, even if some doctors find it repellent to provide the pill or the diaphragm (too difficult the latter, though) to the miserably immature. And, if accepted by the rest of the world, the pill would, of course, be an immense blessing, and a check to mass hunger and poverty.

Pornography? The flood of it makes us look, at worst, childish and dirty-minded, at best, silly. I feel strongly about pornography, if it is cruel – which it frequently is – and if it degrades women, which it almost inevitably does.

For Lord Longford, I have respect, and admire his courage during a campaign of vicious ridicule; I can go along with him some of the way, but he is a Catholic, and I am not – which makes a difference. He said to me, one day, 'I am visiting Myra [Hindley, one of the Moors murderers] this evening. May I give her your good wishes?' What could I say but 'yes'? Could I give her my ill ones?

Mrs Whitehouse I also respect for her courage, though her views are all too often far too narrow for me: she subtracts from the real issues. The 'Permissive Society' has in some

things, and not always bad ones, established itself already:
no Mrs Partington can sweep it away with a broom. But Mrs
Whitehouse occasionally has the right ideas, and, in any case,
it is no joke to set oneself up as an Aunt Sally for the Trendies
– especially the middle-aged ones. (Trendy? the word is beginning to have an old-lace and lavender aura already.) All
Lord Longford and Mrs Whitehouse really have in common
is a social conscience, and some of us are all too free from that.
Can pure bravery ever be completely disregarded?

When I wrote *On Iniquity* I was not infrequently praised
for moral courage. In fact it was thoughtfully received, although one anonymous correspondent accused me of being as
bad as Brady and Hindley. That seemed to me rather odd.
But where on earth should lie the courage, in an avowedly
'liberal' society, in saying what one thinks? It makes nonsense
of the whole conception. This 'liberal' society, not infrequently,
howls down what it, itself, doesn't like. They call this being
'liberal', 'permissive'? To do so is rubbish, if they cannot
listen to some unpopular views. (In the thirties, we generally
gave a quiet hearing to Sir Oswald Mosley – till the fights
broke out. There was a capital old lady whom I once saw, in
Chelsea Town Hall, defending herself and her views from the
Fascists by the use of a chair – the seat against her stomach –
its four legs forming something like a *chevaux de frise*.)

I remain on the Left. But I know what happens when its
fringes turn to anarchy. Anarchy never has produced a good
society: what it has produced are the Hitlers. If things get bad
enough, it may produce such phenomena again. For there can
be no doubt that the complete destruction of a democratic
society will not produce a *tabula rasa* upon which blessed
wonders can be built: no more than I have ever met an an-
archist who had the slightest idea how it could be done.

Baudelaire, whom no one could possibly accuse of being a
stuffed shirt, wrote, as an ideal, in 'L'Invitation au Voyage'.

> Là, tout n'est qu'ordre et beauté,
> Luxe, calme et volupté.

Notice which he put first: before beauty, luxuriance, calm, voluptuousness, he put ORDER. Without which, of course, the other four ideals could not exist.

Meanwhile, on stage, cinema and sometimes on T.V., we are glorifying the Destroyers. In effect, the criminals. Those who 'put the boot in'. Never mind whether or not they come to a bad end: the 'heroes' they are, in ultimate effect. Dr Frederick Wertham wrote to this effect; 'When I see a couple of teenagers heading in my direction after dark, I hope to God that they have not seen *Bonnie and Clyde.*'

Of course, only a minority of people act out what they have seen (or read). But I believe a great number become desensitised by being exposed to scenes of, or ideas of, violence. I have seen the young become increasingly unshockable by the screened or staged display of cruelty. What would it be like if they met with the real thing? Such as Hitler's public humiliation of the Jews? Crowds excitedly gathered round old Jewish victims in Vienna. They were laughing.

Are we preparing ourselves for a good laugh?

15. Sitting on Campuses

It is always called 'sitting'; though of course, one does more than just sit, like a smiling Buddha, on a stretch of sunlit lawn. Indeed, we worked so hard on some campuses – lectures, seminars, teaching, that we had finally to ask for a 'free period' – say two hours in the afternoon – during which time, if the weather was right, we could sit beneath the trees, or if it wasn't, sleep.

Of the smaller campuses, I will write later. But first, Harvard, which we visited often, and where in December 1960, we flew from Berkeley for Charles to give the Godkin Lectures on Science and Government. These concerned, for the most part, the row over the bombing policy during the war, as fought out by Professor Tizard and Lord Cherwell. They were presented in three parts – Charles has his own brand of cunning – very much as a detective story. The first two lectures ended, in fact, in cliff-hangers. After the first, one professor was heard to whisper to another – 'And *did* the butler do it?'

Our experiences at Harvard were invariably happy. So far as I can remember, we did a minimum of teaching there. But it was a lovely sight, at sunset, to look at the campanile, and over the blue, green, red, white and gold cupolas of the colleges. The falling leaves on Harvard Yard. So many friends. Old Professor Arthur Nock, now a long time dead, in his incredible book-cluttered room. Harry Levin and Elena, who became close friends. The Master of Leverett House, John Conway before he moved back to Canada; with him, life was – to use my husband's pet word – apolaustic, to say the least of it. The young Henry Kissinger at luncheon – obviously *someone*: but who knew what he was to become?

At Yale, at Timothy Dwight College, we stayed with Pro-

fessor Tom Bergin and his wife. All was fun. My only objection
to New Haven, is that it is hard to find one's way around:
everything looks, primly, decorously, so much the same. I
was always getting lost.

I don't know what Charles and I did there. Probably he
lectured. I talked with groups of students. But one thing I
do remember is this.

It all started late at night, at a party. I was talking to a lady,
who, knowing my theatrical interests, asked if I would like to
see the theatre collection. I eagerly assented. Next day my
appointed bear-leader called for me, and we set out on the day's
travail, which began, I think, with a Proustian talk by me to
the French department. He and I then went out into the street,
and – his English being fluent but imperfect – said we must
now go, if I wished, to see the theatre collection. (As I
thought.) But I did feel he was fidgeting. So I asked him of
what it consisted. He fidgeted worse. At last he replied, 'Of
reserved books.' Still dense, I persisted. 'What do you mean,
reserved books?'

Then it all came out. He had been telephoned at seven in the
morning to be told I was anxious to see what he took to be the
Zeta Collection. Now, this is what, not to beat about the bush
and confuse my readers, is Yale's collection of classical dirty
books. (Prohibited books, if I may put it more stuffily.)

I stopped dead in the middle of the street. No, I said, there
had been a misunderstanding. It was the *theatre* collection I
wished to see. It was not my habit to dash into a university
town and at once demand to see obscene literature, however
worthy of its kind.

What, then, did I want to do?

I wanted to get my hair done. By this time he was a bright
scarlet. However, we made an instant appointment on my
behalf. I had only been under the dryer for ten minutes, when
he came and found me. 'Of course, I won't say anything of
all this.'

'No, do,' I said, 'it's a good story.'

I might add, in all sincerity, that I should have *loved* to see the Zeta Collection. But for a first visit, this seemed to me too much. I do wonder what it's like?

Charles and I were later to make strong connexions with Yale, he as Fellow of Morse College, I as a Fellow of Timothy Dwight. We shall return there, eventually – all things being well. (As I grow older, I find my superstitions growing. Never superstitious in youth, I now touch wood, throw spilled salt over my left shoulder, and cross my fingers when passing under ladders. It does not chime with my religious ideas and I know it. But the old gods are distressingly potent. I do not choose to take risks.)

I cannot speak of other campuses in any datal order. My diaries of the fifties and sixties are lodged in a bank, and I'm damned if I am going to unearth them, break the seals, leaf them through, and then pack them up again. I am too tired, and my methods too disorderly.

Haverford College, in Pennsylvania, near Philadelphia, was a pure delight. (It was here that we first begged for two hours off in the afternoons.) Haverford is a Quaker College, with a tradition of cricket and a ground where they still play it. The beautiful Meriden cricket ground nearby is obsolete, so far as cricket is concerned.

Haverford was charming; flowery, bowery, as Manley Hopkins might have put it, but *dry*. This meant, that a drink was officially outlawed, and it led to a degree of comedy.

Our first day, when we had been working very hard, ended in a visit to the Principal – and all there was, after a joyous sound of tinkling ice, was water. On the second day, we entreated our student host to procure for us a bottle of Scotch, which we would drink squalidly out of our tooth-glasses when the going was hard. Next day it did, indeed, seem hard. We were due at a dinner party at another faculty house, so we attempted to stoke ourselves up for a dry evening. Dry? It was

like any party in New York. We made our way home across
the cricket field, and I fear we were compelled to walk with
even more delicacy than Agag. We never really got into phase
with all this.

This was the early fall so far as I remember: warm days,
gold weather, our two hours under the trees, and students of
exceptional quality – or exceptional graciousness: when we
spoke to them formally, they were extremely attentive. Not a
yawn showed. Yet I fancy that, on these occasions many a yawn
must be suppressed. Yet where lies true courtesy, but in the
suppression of a yawn?

St Paul's, New Hampshire, was what the Americans would
call a private school: we certainly shouldn't, though their term
is more exact than ours. We, ridiculously, call such schools
Public. It is the nearest American equivalent to Eton. Here,
I suppose, are educated some of the richest boys in the world.
There *are* scholarship boys, and it is a beautiful delusion that
no one knows who they are. (What happens when the talk
begins of where they are all to spend their vacations?) Eton,
at least, does segregate its scholars unless they wish to be
Oppidans, and to pay maximum fees.

Charles and I were invited for, I think ten days, financed
by an elderly lady who never appeared and never has appeared,
not once, and whom we were never able to thank. We were
given a pretty house of our own with ample service – though
we took our meals with the boys. Charles had one formal
speech to make. For the rest, we were to be 'available' (this
has always seemed to me a very pleasant thing to be) for any
boys who liked to drop in and talk to us.

The terrain, hilly, dropping down to the 'ponds' – which we
should call sizeable lakes (Thoreau's Walden Pond is an
example of this) where the boys did their rowing, was very fine.
I cannot say that the nearest town, Concord, was. But some
American small towns, no matter what glamour is cast upon
them by neighbouring institutions, can be amazingly drab:

others, in New England, one thinks of with pleasure still.

We were a trifle unlucky in our fist student contact, who turned out to be a rigorous John Bircher. However, that early impression was very shortly erased by the boys whom we met later. They were extremely courteous and – to my mind – extremely long-suffering. Our meals with them would have been ordeals, if the boys had not been so nice: for the food was revolting. On Friday, they had, God help us, a day of 'self-denial'. Nothing could have made the diet worse than it normally was. It was pointed out to us, though, and rather pathetically, by one of the boys, that they did eat it off very good china. That was quite true.

All the same, food does not matter much to either of us. We enjoy it when it is first-rate, merely use it as fuel at other times.

We met a great assortment of boys. The most dazzling, perhaps, was one of noble Hungarian descent, who actually owned a house of his own in the Ile de France. We were amused by the school grape-vine. We had a small party, one evening, with some of the masters. Next day, the word went round that it had been an orgy. How this rumour spread, we wouldn't know: but it certainly had no basis.

I have often wondered about what rich boys (by this I mean rich parents) pay for. I think it is primarily for two things: small classes, and good manners. It may conceivably include kindness of boys to one another, but obviously there are such glaring exceptions that I could not make a point of it.

Small classes? I shall say later in this book that I wish passionately that they could be the prerogative of all children. Well, in our present circumstances, they can't be. I believe that schoolteachers should be among the most highly paid of all social workers.

Good manners? This has an inevitable 'class' ring for some: yet all it means is the consideration of one child towards another. Sometimes, it is inculcated by the home background.

Sometimes, it isn't. But it should be rubbed in from the primary school onwards. (I can hear again, the agonised outcry of teachers; 'You should see the job we have *simply to keep them quiet*.') They are right, and I have seen this. But an education to live in society, at peace, is far more than knowing the academic drill. That is why I am so dubious when educationalists come up with enormous solutions for enormous anomalies.

St Paul's, New Hampshire (please pronounce it 'Saint' – not 'St'). A school, I think, not nearly up to the academic standards of Eton or Winchester, having less required of it: the American university course starts at a lower level than ours. But their graduate courses! They are rigorous in the extreme, and if Englishmen take part in them, they are kept running. I have often marvelled at the difference between American undergraduate and postgraduate education, and have wondered how many young men and women make the leap.

Other campuses have seen us, all over the Continental U.S. Ithaca, in upper New York State: one of the most beautiful, built, like Rome, upon seven hills. (It probably isn't seven.) Cornell, in the depths of winter: the appalling night-ride on the old Lehigh Valley railroad, now defunct, and a good thing too, crashing and bumping all night, as if the train had wheels, all right, but no rail-bed. Cornell, hung with icicles, every waterfall a shower of diamonds. Our friends Rosemary and Arthur Mizener (the biographer of Scott Fitzgerald). We went with Rosemary to read the unpublished letters from James Joyce to Nora, and made the interesting discovery that 'objective' was not really the word for Joyce. His letters to his wife, often written on paper with a little design of roses or forget-me-nots, represented a long masturbatory dream. It was when he was away from her that the fantasy would flow so easily: in some cases he actually broke off abruptly, because he had obviously come to a climax.

As we left the vaults of the library to return across a snowfield, Rosemary was looking shaken. 'I don't think I shall ever forget those letters,' she said. I told her comfortably that she soon would: it is astonishing how the brain acts as a shock-absorber.

Kansas. It seemed to me that everything was indeed 'up to date in Kansas City'; I liked it very, very much. One day in Lawrence, when we were staying in our small house, lent us by the university, Charles was out at a football match, and I was reading in the living-room, or rather, looking at a book of photographs by Andy Warhol, the monotony of which was utterly bemusing me. They were all the same, and if there were any variant between one and the other, I did not perceive it. I was so absorbed in wondering how a presumably intelligent man could be so ineffably boring, that I failed to notice that an earthquake was going on. Certainly the ceiling light swung wildly around, but that, I felt vaguely, might be what it was used to doing. Is this a point to Warhol? That he could hypnotise, even to indifference to an earthquake, by a display of mere emptiness?

There was considerable excitement about the earthquake afterwards, but to this I was unable in any way to contribute.

Texas. Houstan, Dallas, and a drive to Austin through roads lined with wild flowers, blue bonnets, Indian paint-brushes. These do not grow by accident: they are encouraged by municipal policy. At Austin, a scientific conference arranged by Jagdish Mehra, glittering with famous men, Abdus Salam, and the great Paul Dirac.

A note on Dallas. Of course I wanted to inspect the scene of the J. F. Kennedy assassination, and here I got a jolt. I had always suspected that this was not done by Oswald alone, because, from pictures I had seen, the book repository was a large and high building, and that, even with telescopic sights, his chance of a direct hit would be small. But when I saw the building, I realised that it was not particularly high, that the road was surprisingly narrow, and that the actual feat of killing

would not have been too remarkable. I am now prepared to
accept the verdict against Oswald as assassin.

But one thing still sticks in my throat. We all saw on television, not once but many times, the killing of Oswald. As
Ruby stepped forward, the police appeared to force Oswald in
front of them into the line of fire. Was it perhaps better that
no more should have been said about the whole thing? Had
this demented man been *used* in any way, by others? This we
shall never know. But that Oswald himself could have, and
did, fire that shot, I am pretty certain.

A final campus – I shall come to California later, but I
regret my many omissions. They are not deliberate. They are
simply the result of a shaky memory. In the autumn of 1961,
we went to Wesleyan University, Middle Town, Connecticut,
as Fellows of the Centre for Advanced Studies: and here our
job largely was *to sit*. We were presented with a house – daunt-
ingly large – to live in, and beautifully appointed offices in
which to work. At what? *At our own books.* We did give
certain lectures – I gave a couple on Proust, and I suppose we
talked to students. But we did what we were paid for, which
was, write. I finished a very difficult novel called *An Error of
Judgment*, and went on, for light relief, to an American
comedy called *Night and Silence, Who is Here?* Among our
colleagues at the Centre were Hannah Ahrendt, Douglas Cater,
and our beloved friend, the American writer Paul Horgan:
who should be beatified one day, for his sweetness, generosity,
and absolute kindness, if ever a man should be. But he has not
yet performed any miracles, except where we were concerned.

Night and Silence, when it did appear, certainly caused a
stir. Everyone took me to be satirising Wesleyan – whereas the
book was an amalgam of many campuses, with Wesleyan, in
some respects – notably our first weekend there – in the lead.
But there is not in it a single campus character *à clef*. There
are two, certainly *à clef*, well beyond campus bounds, but they
both know this and I think have been much amused.

We arrived in the late afternoon, tired, since we had spent a busy morning elsewhere, and were longing for a drink. But we were first taken on a tour of the campus, saw the graceful Faculty Club, where we were to eat (when it was open), and called on the President, with whom we drank ice-water. At last we came to our house: not quite Charles Addams, but nearly: and far too big. We decided at once, when we were left alone, that we would occupy only the first floor. We now – being hungry – made our way to the kitchen. And here in the fridge we found a bottle of milk, a carton of orange juice – stiff-frozen – two eggs, the scrag-end of a knuckle of ham, some bread: and that was all.

The Faculty Club was shut. We walked down to Middletown: the shops were shut there. So we made the best of what presented itself. Incidentally, we had no car, so could not drive to the nearest restaurant – several miles off.

I must make it clear that this was an obvious failure of administration. The Americans, and the Russians, are the most hospitable people in the world so far as I know it. We had a good breakfast at the Faculty Club next morning, and adjusted to our situation. We were eventually saved by Paul Horgan, who was anxious to know when we had last had a square meal, and who promptly drove us to one. (That was his miracle.) My novel's connexion with Wesleyan goes no further than this first comic weekend. (It was true that I had to ask for some kind of domestic help two or three times a week since otherwise I could not have done the work I was being paid for.) It is greatly to the credit of the Americans' sporting-spirit – never lacking – that *Night and Silence, Who is Here?* had the best critical reception, in some places rapturous, that I have ever had on that continent, though the book did not sell particularly well. I keep these yellowing cuttings with love – even at a time when I keep very few things written about me. Somehow, nowadays, I find it hard to care.

Now, in praise of Wesleyan. It was a college for men, but not now: it is, in fact, rich. It has a very pleasant campus, near to an ugly little town. When we were there, town and campus were safe to walk in at night: now, Paul Horgan says (he later became Director of the Centre), they are not. This seems to me miserable, but it is the way our world is going, and how we are to stop the Gadarene rush, I don't know. It is, educationally, of the highest excellence. It has a distinguished faculty. And it has this Centre, which provides, for many a hard-driven scholar, peace in which to work. This peace it gave us, and we were grateful. Occasionally, we went to New Haven, to enjoy the fleshpots of friends near by: the Howard Sachses, the Gordon Haights. (He is the George Eliot scholar.) Mrs Sachs had a Seurat cigar-box painting, which tended to hold my eyes to the exclusion of all else. We also had the hospitality of Beecher Hogan, the great expert on English eighteenth-century theatrical history, and his wife 'C.C.' who is a musician. From these trips we returned feeling that our golden attire had turned to rags, and our glass slippers shuttered about our feet.

But the generosity of Wesleyan, in paying us for *getting on with our own work*, is something I can never forget. It was a noble conception, and I think no Fellow of the Centre was ungrateful. I should like to visit it again, under the guidance of Paul Horgan – 'Oom Paul', as we call him, though with no special reference to Kruger. However good it was, I think he must have made things better. He makes everything better. (Alas, he has retired now from the office of Director.) So perhaps I shall never again be *persona grata*.

16. Amy

Amy was my mother, the second of three daughters. Her elder sister Clélia (by eighteen months) was handsome in an Italianate style. Her youngest, Emma, was downright beautiful, though destined to become irremediably fat.

Amy was pretty, in an extremely delicate way. Rather small eyes, very small tipped-up nose, tiny mouth: a white skin, and that very rare kind of black hair with a blueish gloss on it. She was, in the modern sense, something of a 'pin-up'. Photographs of her, as a super in *Dick Whittington, Bluebeard, Mikado, Patience, Princess Ida*, found their way as far as Kimberley. She kept her black hair, and her strange appearance of youth, until her middle sixties, when osteo-arthritis and depressiveness took over.

Following the death of my father, we became very close. She had a great sense of fun, a huge repertoire of music-hall songs (all of which I, at some time, passed on to my children), and a brilliant talent for mimicry, which talent she could never produce on demand. No. But on thinking of someone, she would immediately look like him or her: we would guess of whom she would speak before she even opened her mouth.

In her heavy widow's weeds, she looked very nice indeed. None of the family, myself included (and willing) doubted that she would soon marry again. But she never did. She was absorbed in me. I, of course, in later adolescence (I was too busy before in trying to look after her) occasionally wanted to cut the cable. But when I suggested that I should like a flat somewhere of my own, her answer was tragic: 'So I have completely failed!'

She lived with me and my first husband during our entire married life. When I suggested to my second husband, Charles,

that she should now make a home with my Aunt Kalie, his
answer was one I shall never forget: 'How can we build
happiness upon the unhappiness of other people?' It was
splendidly unselfish, but I am not sure that it turned out to
be wise.

However, that was many years ago.

As I have said, there was great fun in her. If she played the
duenna, my friends and myself hardly realised it. She danced
to the gramophone as we danced, she was a good dancer; she
had a flow of anecdotes: and she supplied our peculiar refreshments. It was only when she felt me old enough to go unes-
corted by her to dances with a young man, that she would
become nervous. Then she would stand at the window watching for me. She had watched before, because my spectacularly
good-looking friend, Teddy, had been brought up in Malaya
and she had a strange fear that he would slay me with a *kris*,
and leave me in some awesome hiding-place on Wimbledon
Common. A sillier fear could not be imagined: Teddy was the
soul of gentleness.

In 1934 we moved from 53 Battersea Rise (it had become a
David Greig's shop when I saw it last) to Chelsea, our Mecca,
and the Mecca of Dylan Thomas, who had by then absorbed
my attention. The place was on the first floor of No. 1 Tedworth Square: it had a sitting-room, two bedrooms, and a
kitchen with a bath discreetly hidden under the kitchen table:
the lavatory was one floor down. We had not been moved in
for long, before Amy discovered a bed-bug. What horror!
(My own opinion is that a squashed bed-bug smells of gar-
denias.) So we had to be fumigated. To my mother, this was
degradation beyond belief: to me, merely funny.

The trouble was, however, the rapidity in which we made
our move from Battersea Rise. Aunt Kalie was going off on her
own. I was busy writing my first novel, *This Bed Thy Centre*,
on packing-cases with the removers removing about me. God
knows what we lost: none of us had time (and I no inclination)

to find out. What did disappear among other things was a first edition of the Sherlock Holmes stories, not rebound from the *Strand Magazine* (of which I had acquired a full set) but published as a whole for the first time.

As I say, God knows what else we lost: I was too occupied with my writing to concern myself.

I had always been writing: and for years earning a pittance to supplement my income from the bank. Some of it was trash and I knew it. I then fell in with Victor Neuburg's circle: he had been a friend, if you can call it that, of Alastair Crowley, and appeared to have of him, even now, an unwholesome fear. (It might be valuable to refer to Arthur Calder-Marshall's *The Magic of my Youth*.) Victor had contrived to get a poetry column in the *Sunday Referee*, somewhat gruesomely called 'The Poet's Corner'. With his beautiful friend Runia (or Sheila McLeod) he managed, himself on a pittance, to keep open house for his 'poets' at various swiftly-changing addresses in St John's Wood. He was an eccentric with a vast literary knowledge, especially of Blake, whose *Marriage of Heaven and Hell* he would expound to us in a ragged, rambling garden, while the green twilight fell. Summer nights. Sunsets. Did it ever rain?

Amy was at first much alarmed by all this, since she had heard scandals about Vicky from a barrister friend. But when she met him, she was completely won over. Apart from his tendency to facetious blasphemy (which worried nobody but me) he was respectful of his young friends, and treated them impeccably. To the garden came David Gascoyne, David Haden Guest (who was to die in Spain), A. L. Morton, Geoffrey Pollitt (a poet who took his own life), and eventually Dylan Thomas, who was to make a fairly rapid withdrawal. Dylan was so much aware that he was better by a thousand times than the rest of us. The story of Dylan, as much as I care to say, I shall save for another chapter.

I was the first to win the *Sunday Referee*'s annual poetry

prize, which was the subsidisation of a book of poems. They were chosen from the prize poems published each week: mine was called 'Chelsea Reach': it was not devoid of rhythmic interest, but totally devoid of sense. It had probably pleased Vicky's Swinburnian leanings.

How excited I was! I made the most careful choice of my own work; I corrected the proofs. It was only when I finished surveying the finished production, that it dawned on me that I was no poet. Of that I was sure. And the majority of critics agreed with me. (Many years after this, during the war, I was offered the remainder, if I wanted them: I accepted, and burned the lot. That is the reason why *Symphony for Full Orchestra* – an impossibly pretentious title – is so rare, and fetches such a relatively large sum today.)

The next poet to win the prize was Dylan. I cannot refer to him as 'Thomas' anymore than I can refer to Yevtushenko, a braver man than many think, and my friend, other than as 'Zhenya'.

Everyone at the bank was delighted with *Symphony for Full Orchestra*: not so I. For I knew what I thought, and worse, what Dylan thought. As I say, the second year's prize went to him. The *Sunday Referee* and Parton Press publication was the famous *18 Poems*, no portrait, no absurd introduction – just the poems. Amy found it hard to believe that I held myself a poetic failure, but to an extent she was realistic: she believed I could turn what gifts I might have to something else.

Short stories, of which I wrote a good many and sold a good many too, failed to satisfy me. I had more to say than would pack within so small a compass. So I went resolutely on with my novel.

Here I had a stroke of luck, though it didn't seem so at the time. In the autumn of 1934, my mother and I went to stay with Dylan, and with his parents, at 5 Cwmdonkin Drive, Swansea. Amy and I shortly moved out to an hotel at the Mumbles, where we saw Dylan every day. Before long, I began to feel ill. (Was this because I knew things were going wrong between Dylan and myself?) Anyway, I consulted a doctor, who found out a heart murmur. But nothing serious. Could I take a month or so's absence from my office job?

I could, and I did. Within a month that book was finished (the title, *This Bed Thy Centre*, was an unwise suggestion of Dylan's: it had originally been called *Nursery Rhyme*) and within another month, was accepted for publication by Chapman & Hall. No trouble at all.

So I said to Amy, 'If this book brings me in any money, and I can live on my writing, may I leave the bank? I promise you that if it doesn't, I will look for another job.'

She considered. Then she said, 'All right. But in the meantime, I can only allow you half a crown a week for pocket money.'

This offer was accepted, but of course it meant hardship. At last the book came out, and by today's standards would be considered a signal success; the nearest thing to it that I can think of is *Lucky Jim*, in the very early fifties.

I had not known that it would bring me so much misery. The book was not at all autobiographical: but I believed it was a pretty faithful portrait of the ambience in which I had lived. And I believed that it told the truth, so far as any girl of twenty-one, carefully nurtured, knows what the truth is. The reception of *This Bed Thy Centre*, was widespread and startling. It was considered 'outspoken' – which means dirty. The late Richard Church, who later became my friend and my supporter until his death, used the word 'lewd'. (I have since republished this novel, which is very mild by today's standards: and no one, naturally, raised a voice.) But there it was. I was sick with fear lest it should become a subject for prosecution, and I mean, literally sick, as well. My father's family, for a while, virtually disowned me. Persons at the Ministry of Transport asked my Aunt Kalie how she could have allowed her niece to do such a thing. The local (Battersea Rise) library

refused to stock the thing. A friend of my mother's, also a
minor novelist, wrote to me more in sorrow than in anger,
pointing out that books could sell without 'sex and cancer'. I
received many obscene postcards. Throughout all this, Amy
was stalwart: I had her entire support.

But, apart from Vicky's circle, I had few literary friends:
and certainly no academic ones. Dylan wrote me, however, a
somewhat embittered postcard: 'God, aren't you successful!'
He could not have foreseen his own future. (Charles later told
me that, a young don at Cambridge, he had much admired the
book, and had been on the point of writing to me about it. If
only he had done so! It would have meant so much.)

I was saved from further suffering by Cyril Connolly, who
had written in praise of the book, and who asked me to call
upon him. I was both awed and terrified, but he gave me much
comfort. That the book was in any way 'shocking' *had not
occurred to him at all*. A second meeting with him took place
in the Six Bells in the King's Road, Chelsea: his friend John
Banting was with him, and I forget who else. I was so enthralled by the conversation, that I did not notice five pints of
beer stacking up in front of me. When I did, it seemed to me
obligatory to drink them.

How I got home I do not know – I can remember nothing
of the walk there – but when I arrived I smiled blissfully at
Amy, and passed right out. Oddly enough, I had no ill effects
from this.

I owe Cyril Connolly much.

A year or so after that, came the beginning of a series of
anonymous postcards, which were to plague me, two at a
time, at intervals of between five and eight years, and continued
for the best part of twenty. They were horrible. The writer
knew both Amy and myself, knew about my history, about
my goings-out and comings-in. There was a terrible closeness
about them, as if an invisible presence were at my very elbow.
I took them rather ridiculously. If anyone could say such things

about me, surely I must be wicked? I should not be so much of an ass nowadays. Nevertheless, I have never met anyone receiving an anonymous letter, who had not been disturbed by it. (Charles' friend and mine, Harry Hoff, who writes as William Cooper, later scoffed at me: until he received one of the beastly things himself.)

I believe that such letters give pure delight only in the writing: pleasure may cease when they fall through the slit in the pillar-box. I do not believe the writer is still living, for I have not heard from her (it was obviously a woman) for a long time. All I can say, if she can still hear me, is that yes, she did give great pain. In what she set out to do, she succeeded. Is that a comfort to her? I don't give a damn now whether it is or isn't.

Letters, now infrequent, from lunatics (mostly paranoid) have now no effect at all.

When I married Neil, we lived with Amy for a while, in close quarters, in Tedworth Square. Then, our prospects having become rather more bright, all three of us moved in 1937 to a flat in Beaufort Mansions. This, after Tedworth Square, was grandeur. Now we had five rooms, kitchen and bathroom, accommodation many Russians would envy. Neil had a job, Amy her small pension, and I the increasing – though not glittering – earnings from my writing. I had published two more novels, decently received, though no more than that. Amy had given up her typing and was acting as cook-house-keeper.

Marriage: politics: Spain: A.R.P.: war: children. Through all these things she was faithful, though I do not believe that we gave her loneliness a thought when we disappeared in the night on 'yellow messages'. Was she afraid? I never thought to ask.

In 1946 Neil was discharged from the Army and returned from India to the son he had only seen briefly in infancy, and the two-year-old daughter he had never seen at all. At first all was well. And then, I am afraid, Amy began gradually to play her part in what was not. She did the shopping, and part of the cooking, I looked after the children and had to do my writing, necessary to our joint incomes, late at night. I shall never work at night again. I was always tired, and I think some of my earlier books show this strain. But she had had me (and the children) too long to herself: and I think she became jealous. Tensions developed over three years, and the end was inevitable. But it was very sad.

In 1950, I remarried: C. P. Snow, who had been a friend of the family since 1941. That we are both writers was never a source of rivalry or jealousy: it has been a binding factor: after all, there is always something to talk about. We moved first into a large house in Hyde Park Crescent, taking with us the children, Amy and my Aunt Kalie. Amy's spirits revived: her old sense of fun came back to her, and she enjoyed having the work taken off her shoulders. Then, when I found with joy that I was pregnant, it was Charles' idea that the coming child should be born in the country. He was perhaps more enthusiastic than I was, but when the ideal house seemed to present itself, I caught his excitement. This was a half-timbered, yellow house in the wide main street of Clare in Suffolk, with a fine garden running down to an arm of the Stour (where Andrew fished, and had a canvas coracle) and, across the way, a cottage, with a vegetable garden behind it, which housed the gardener and his wife. We had seen it before, by chance, when visiting friends in Glemsford, and had been enchanted by it: suddenly it came on to the market.

It had been built largely in 1644, but the foundations were much older. From the huge stone entrance hall there rose, contiguously, then branching out into the east and west wings, two fine staircases; one built by the proud say-maker who had come to prosperity while in possession of the house, the other and wider, was of the time of William and Mary. We arrived in the heat of high summer, and only later learned that the draughts rushing down these interesting architectural features, were to make the hall uninhabitable for the greater part of the year. Now, really, Amy didn't like it at all, and I had a reason for disliking it myself, for Charles went up to London from Tuesday to Friday each week, and I was lonely. No sound by night. Not even the mooing of a cow. For this was sugar-beet country. Perhaps the occasional soft plop of beets falling off a lorry. But there was, both for Amy and me, the compensation of the coming child. We moved to Clare in June. In August, the baby began to manifest itself, a full month early, at about four in the morning. Charles called Dr Stewart, who said I must go at once to the Mill Road maternity branch of Addenbrookes, in Cambridge, and sent for an ambulance.

Meanwhile, the dawn broke: a magnificent dawn, the sky raging vermilion and gold. Charles and I looked out of the garden window, while we waited, and both imagined we saw on the lawn blackbirds larger than life: celestial blackbirds, harbingers of our coming son – for Charles had always said it was to be a son.

When I was installed in Mill Road, there came something of an anticlimax: for nothing happened at all, and no one seemed to expect anything for some time. Twenty-four hours passed. Charles came in to see me: he was due to dine in Christ's that night, but was apprehensive, and afraid to go. I told him he must; nothing would happen yet. I said this with the utmost sincerity. But just as I was listening to his footsteps retreating along the passage, I suddenly knew that the birth was imminent. This gladdened me: he would spend the evening free from anxiety, and by morning it would be all over.

In fact, it was over by a minute or so past midnight on 26th August. Curiously enough, it was rather a more painful birth than I had previously experienced: Philip only weighed 4lb 6 oz. but seemed to have an abnormally large head. (I am pleased to say that he has grown to it since.) So Charles, who had finished his dinner and his port, and had retired from the

Combination Room to bed, was telephoned with the joyful news that he had a nice little son. The word 'little' might have warned him, but it didn't. When he came next morning to see me and the baby, he was first shown one of only three pounds; presumably this was kindly meant, so that he should find his own son much larger, but it gave him a shock, all the same.

Philip was not allowed to leave hospital till he weighed five pounds. This was a slow process – a quarter of an ounce, at most, at a time, was added to his tiny bulk. I hung around Mill Road as long as possible till my bed was required, then moved over to the University Arms to be near him, and from where I could visit him every day. But after a week, I was taken by such appalling post-natal depression that I had to return to Clare. Every day, early, I telephoned to Mill Road: yes, a quarter of an ounce. Once, half an ounce! At last I was allowed to bring him home, and obtained the services of Nanny Page, who was to stay with me for a fortnight, and remained for eight years.

When Philip was about two years old my Aunt Kalie, who was staying with us, had a serious accident. She fell, fracturing her femur, over one of our treadworn seventeenth-century steps. After an operation, she appeared to make a rapid recovery: but her condition deteriorated, and she needed expert nursing. So she went into a small nursing home, in Callis Street, no more than a quarter of a mile away, where one or the other of us could visit her nearly every day, myself on my bicycle, my mother (whose arthritis was bad by now) driven in our very old car by the gardener, who despised it, because every time he shut the door a window was liable to fall out.

Andrew was now at Uppingham, Lindsay at a local school. I had become one of the B.B.C. 'Critics' (a delightful job), and would, periodically, go to London three days a week, for spells of six weeks at a time. I was able to stay with Charles then, in a guest room at Dolphin Square. I was invited to these 'Critics' sessions about three times a year. I was also on the committee of the Book Society, which met monthly and invariably gave me migraine headaches.

All this my mother hated. It robbed her of me. She was often in pain, and she felt dreadfully the loneliness caused by my absences. She was, like my Aunt Kalie, hypochondriacal. She became afraid of a heart attack, but a cardiogram showed nothing wrong. Her high spirits had gone, and she was in a constant state of depression. Once she had been proud – over-proud – of my career. Now, when my voice came over the radio, she would often pretend to be asleep.

She would brighten a little when she heard me singing to Philip—

> When father papered the parlour
> You couldn't see pa for paste—

or the Nightmare Song, from *Iolanthe*, in which I had become adept. But such moods would not last. One of the things she did was to ask me frequently whether there was an afterlife. On this I felt insecure: she needed comfort, and I could not give it her. I had not the decency to lie for her sake. I did not know, I said. This is one of my greatest regrets.

One day she came into my bedroom looking ill. She had violent pains in her left shoulder. This was at first diagnosed as a sort of muscular rheumatism, and she was given morphia. She passed a restless day and a very troubled night: I sat up with her. She kept on saying it was breakfast-time, and trying to get out of bed: and later began those ominous plucking movements at the sheets. I was alone in the house with Lindsay and the baby. Charles was in London, Nanny Page visiting her home in Bedfordshire. I shall never forget that night.

Next day, however, Amy's condition seemed greatly improved, and went on being so, though she was still in bed. A week or so later, I had a meeting of the Book Society Committee coming up. I asked her if she would mind going, just for one night, to the nursing-home where Aunt Kalie was. I was very anxious to attend this particular meeting early, as there was a book for which I very much wanted a Choice. I promised Amy that I would be back by the earliest evening train on the same day.

She made little demur. Indeed, as she got with difficulty into the car, she said, 'The Transit of Venus.'

François Mauriac says somewhere, that a person bore imminent death like the brand on a sheep's back: and that nobody recognised it. Certainly I did not – or did I, and would not look?

I left her in the nursing-home, sitting with Aunt Kalie and drinking cocoa.

On the following morning, when I was due to catch the London train, the telephone rang. My mother was very ill. Could I come to Callis Street?

I knew, of course, that she was dead.

After seeing her, I had to break the news to my aunt. With her customary kindness, she thought first of the living. Almost the first words she spoke to me were these: *'You must not let yourself feel guilty.'* This! To *me*. (Though Aunt Kalie had meant well.) I had left my mother to die alone.

Her death had been sudden. She had spent a good night, had slept well. In the morning the nurse had asked her what she would like to eat. Grapefruit, perhaps? Amy agreed. Grapefruit would be nice. When the nurse only a little later brought up the breakfast tray, Amy was dead.

I passed through a period of intense grief and guilt. I can write nothing about that. Amy. I had greatly loved her.

Possessive, I suppose, she always was, though in my earlier years I was not aware of it. She gave me so many good times, and my friends liked and were amused by her. She had pinched and scraped, and all in good humour. I am quite sure that if osteo-arthritis had not attacked her, things in those later days might have been quite different. But she was getting old, she was frequently lonely, and she was in almost constant pain.

But what fun she had been! How much I owed her! The songs she had sung in her small, pretty voice! The anecdotes, always enthralling, about her schooldays, her memories of Ellen Terry, her theatrical experiences! I now try to think of her only like that.

17. Politics and War

I have written so extensively about the Left Wing in the thirties, in my novel, *The Survival of the Fittest*, that I can only approach my political life at that time from a very personal angle.

Believe it or not, to the young the years leading up to the war and the earlier years of the war itself, may have been days of acute anxiety and activity, but they were often *fun*. Great fun. The problems for the Left were simple: you didn't like Hitler, nor Mussolini, nor Franco. The extreme complication of political life today for the young, fills me with apprehension. The young whom I know best are making a very good try at tackling it. Their main method being, *to find out precisely what the facts are*. I am afraid we did not always – or more properly could not – do that. For our children, there may not be so much fun in it.

I married in 1936. I was a member of the Chelsea Labour Party, member of the Left Book Club and frequently at polemic odds with the Right Wing Trade Union element; we ran, from the shabby party headquarters in The World's End, a cyclostyled weekly, written mainly by myself, called *The Chelsea Democrat*. It was rather successful: it was even rumoured that Sir Samuel Hoare's butler subscribed to it, but this may belie him. The magazine did not fold up through lack of funds – subscriptions just covered costs, but because of editorial exhaustion: I had too many other things to do.

The trauma of the defeat of the Spanish Republican forces in the Civil War was something beyond which the earlier trauma of Munich almost paled.

I remember standing in Belgrave Square, when the Republican flag was hauled down, and Franco's went up. There was a vast crowd. The inevitable band was playing (I believe it played for Mosley's men as well as for our side) the *Hymno del Riego*. I could not stop crying: and there were many, men and women alike, in the same condition.

We were grieving mostly because of a defeat for our cause; but also because we believed that in the coming war – yes, we believed in it, all right – Gibraltar was lost to the Fascists, and thereby the Mediterranean. In this we were wrong. I cannot achieve any love for General Franco (in fact, I have never been to Spain and will not, while he is living) but I am lost in admiration for his shrewdness. For it was not his intention to 'come in', but to keep well out. Our political judgment had led us, as it had led many others, astray.

What deeply distressed me was George Orwell's *Homage to Catalonia*. I realise his stature as a writer (though *1984* is on the hysterical side) and that *Animal Farm* will one day seem a fairy tale for children as remote from politics as the nursery rhyme, *Hector Protector*. But, when the Republic was in the gravest danger, he was a divisive factor within it. And that, very few of us of the non-Trotskyist Left were able to bear. In such times of crisis, it seems to me, ranks have to be closed, however beastly some in those ranks may be. But, to be fair, nothing could have saved the Spanish Loyalists by that period. Perhaps it isn't God who is on the side of the big battalions, after all, but Someone Else.

But then there was the time of struggle against Chamberlain and the 'Men of Munich', as they were later to be called, when Chamberlain had succeeded in getting there. This struggle was carried on by large forces in the Trade Unions, all left-wing parties, and had many allies on the Right: not the least of them Churchill, Eden and Lord Cranborne (later Lord Salisbury). 'Demos', as we called them then, and still do, were serious: there was no playing of guitars.

I remember walking home from a Labour Party meeting the night the Munich Agreement had been announced, with

Sibyl Wingate, sister of the famous Orde Wingate of Burma.
She was a bleak young woman. She said simply (and correctly),
'*Now war is certain.*'

I have never subscribed to the theory that Neville Chamberlain was either misguided or silly. He wanted, ultimately, a
four-power pact between Hitler, Mussolini, Daladier, and ourselves. He was an able man, but self-deluded. I believe now,
that with all our (left-wing) efforts, to promote a defensive
pact with Russia, Hitler might only have been stopped when
he made his bid to re-occupy the Rhineland.

How scornful we all were when the Government sent Mr
William Strang, now Lord Strang, a 'foreign office clerk' (we
weren't knowledgeable about the Foreign Office hierarchy and
I think we conceived of him as a Bob Cratchett, sitting at a
dusty high desk on a Dickensian stool) to the U.S.S.R! (Later,
in more sophisticated days, I met Lord Strang and found him
an accomplished Proustian.) But all was slow, slow, and the
newsboys cried disaster in the streets. 'Only a sallow dawn
and newsboys crying war' as Louis MacNiece put it.

Munich night I shall not forget. Members of Parliament
(with honourable exceptions) and a good many of our own side
also – in fact, a majority of the population – behaved like
political lunatics. A friend of mine, trying to convince the
rejoicing populace in a Lyons' Corner House, that they were
done for, so far as peace was concerned, was hurled roughly
and joyously into the street.

Neil and I joined the Air Raid Wardens. I, I admit, being
small, looked ridiculous in my brown boiler-suit and steel
helmet. Our post warden was John Freeman, later Ambassador
to the United States. We had a Warden's Post at the World's
End, which was later moved to the basement of 94 Cheyne
Walk, within easy distance of that plausible military objective,
the Battersea Power Station.

In both these places, I encountered the Classless Society: it
was genuinely classless: I have never met with it since. We

waited for yellow messages (preliminary warnings) and drank cup after cup of revolting stewed tea, which left an orange film on the tongue. At intervals, I worked at my novel, *Too Dear for my Possessing*. With us were Ron, ex-printer, ex-everything, one of the cleverest self-educated men I have ever met; 'One Arm Harvey', an ex-sailor, Bob Brent, H., an ex-chef from the Savoy, who presented me with an omelette-pan which I still cherish, and four extremely pretty women.

That was the period of the 'phoney war'. Nothing happened: nothing was to happen for a long time. At Cheyne Walk, 'yellow messages' became more frequent; and Neil and I were often called out to go down there in the middle of the night. He had the enviable trick of going straight to sleep again on a bench, with his head resting on the rubber rim of his helmet. I never met anyone so utterly without fear: and so it was with him when he was in the jungles of Burma.

Then, early in the spring of 1940, an event much longed-for, I became pregnant. Realising that no one would want a pregnant warden, and that Neil's call-up could not be long delayed, I resigned. When I handed in my uniform I felt like Dreyfus, except that I managed to retain the three stripes I had earned for proficiency, a verbal examination on the peculiarities of poison gas. (It always struck me that phosgene, said to smell of hay, would have had a poor chance among the various odours of Chelsea Embankment, though Charles sensibly assured me that a poor chance – of being instantly detected – would be precisely the enemy's idea.)

We moved to a bungalow near the river between Staines and Laleham. That bungalow was unremarkable, but it stood in a delightful garden (with red hawthorns, a medlar tree and a small apple orchard) which I found less delightful when I tried to cultivate it myself. I suppose it covered about one-third of an acre.

The spring and summer of 1940 were golden.

'Mai qui fut sans nuage et juin poignardé,' as Aragon wrote.

France had fallen, the Germans were at the Channel ports, and there seemed to be no reason why we should not lose the war. *But no one seemed to believe that we would,* even when we were quite alone and likely to remain so. I do not know why Hitler couldn't have been content simply to starve us out, and only then turn his attention to the U.S.S.R.

Neil was called up for a period of training on the Norfolk coast. My mother and I were managing to live on her small pension, my writing, and my army allowance. I did all the shopping on my bicycle.

In September, the bombing of London began. A few bombs came our way, but they were very few: we heard the sirens, heard the bombers overhead, and the noise of the anti-aircraft guns. I cannot stand sudden noise; I sat placidly and incompetently sewing a layette with Quies in my ears, balls of pink wax that softened on insertion. I do not remember being unnerved, except that I once put the sleeves into a smock the wrong way round.

On most nights, we slept in a horrible cemented garden shelter, three steps down, the walls running with damp, a bench, or bunk, on each side, and beneath that, water to a depth of three inches. My mother and I made ourselves comfortable as best we could, and the Siamese cat (I have always had Siamese cats) came to join us. We would read for a while by candlelight, and later try to sleep. When the all-clear sounded, we would go back into the house, make tea and smoke (I date my really heavy smoking from then) and at last go to sleep.

My son Andrew was born in the early hours of New Year's Day, 1941. His was an easy birth. There was no question now of going to the shelter: we stayed in our beds. The night preceding his birth was free from raids: not so the following night. I was attended by Dr John Sanctuary, whose grandfather Archdeacon Sanctuary, had been, oddly enough, a personage in that part of Dorset where my father's family had lived for generations. He was a fine doctor, and a friend.

I had a nurse for a fortnight, whose name I now forget: but I do recall her fear of men. One night she said to me, 'To think of all you have had to go through!' I demurred, pointing out to her that the bearing of my son had not been particularly onerous. She replied, 'I didn't mean that. I meant, *what you must have been through just to get him!*'

The bombing went on. One night we watched, from our garden, the City burning. It was a beautiful and terrible sight, the sky a vivid rose-colour behind our apple-trees. In the summer, there was a mysterious pause. Everyone speculated as to what it might mean. Then, in June, Hitler invaded Russia. It may seem the height of callousness to my Russian friends, but our first thought was: *now we are no longer alone.*

The addition of the U.S.S.R. to the Allies put the B.B.C. in a quandary. They were accustomed, before the 9 o'clock news, to playing the anthems of all friendly nations, defeated or otherwise. But could they possibly play the *Internationale*? Heaven forbid. So someone had the idea of playing something called 'Kutuzov's March', which was unknown to anyone, the Russians, I have been told, included. The idea was destined to failure: after a very short while, the B.B.C. gave in, and the *Internationale* was played with the other anthems. Later of course, the U.S.S.R., fighting a nationalist and patriotic war, invented an anthem of its own: it is in the main a very good tune, though with rather too lengthy a middle section.

To say much more about my war, after all the books that have been written about other people's, would be superfluous. Neil went to India and subsequently to Burma. My D-Day daughter Lindsay was born in May 1944, a few days before the V.1 bombings began. These, I admit, made me afraid: my nerve almost broke at one time. My mother's, never. By then we had a Morrison shelter, a steel table-like structure designed to take anything but a direct hit. The trouble was that my mother, myself, Andrew, Lindsay and the cat could not all sleep in it together: so Lindsay and I retired to my study beneath the large mahogany sideboard where I myself had been sheltered during the Zeppelin raids of the First World War. It had certainly taken the weight of most of the ceiling during the 'Little Blitz' of February that year. The v.11 bombs I did not mind so much, since you could not hear them coming. If you did hear them crash, you had not been hit; if you did not, either they had not been coming at all, or you were dead.

So I began to go up to London more frequently, to look for houses. In 1945 the Chelsea Council offered us (as old residents) the lease of 6 Cheyne Row, at the rent of £3 a week. We moved there at the beginning of the following year. That house, when I saw it last, had lost its elegant window, and looked squalid. It may look better by now.

The war. It seems to me the only war in British history – or perhaps any other history – which was worth fighting. I have never doubted that at all. (It is, beyond dispute, a gothic thought that the war in South-East England began and ended with a thunderstorm). Goering, with his customary *élan*, committed suicide. The remaining German leaders (Hitler and Goebbels dead, Bormann probably) were hanged in a gymnasium by what seems to have been a peculiar bungling (and inexperienced) American sergeant. A settlement was reached, better than Versailles in 1919, but with all the seeds of dissension left to burgeon. But I was still looking forward to a better world and, in our country, a welfare state, which to an extent we did achieve. The thought of a protracted illness in Britain does not carry with it the dread of financial ruin which it does for so many in America. We can still have children free of charge: and we can die free of charge, too.

In 1946, Churchill made his celebrated Fulton Speech in Missouri, and I was filled with horror. Was it all to begin again? Were we casting about for a new enemy already? It proved to be the beginning of the Cold War which God help us, we haven't totally been rid of to this day. I think I hardly realised that Churchill had only brought into the open what had been building up for some time past.

The unthinking, or unimaginative young, who blame my generation for leaving them a world of mess, anger me. We fought a savage war and we won it: which was a good thing for them. Afterwards, we fought for a far greater social security: reforms were sweeping, though of course some people were still untouched by them, and I am now afraid that some of those reforms (I refer particularly to the Health Service) are slowly becoming eroded. Some of us lost a sizeable part of our youth in almost incessant political activity. So where did we go wrong? It is for the intelligent young, whom I like and respect, to put us right. The unemployment figures remain bad, though not on the scale of those of the thirties. The housing shortage continues. Old people, often lonely, cold and neglected, have to struggle along on completely inadequate pensions. The appalling poverty of the Third World is always before our eyes. Organisations such as Oxfam, Shelter and Help the Aged, do what they can, and it is just a little more than a drop in the ocean. There is plenty to worry about.

Then there is the war in Vietnam, on which successive British governments have tended to keep a cowardly silence. Did America learn no lessons from the reaction both of British and Germans to heavy bombing? It was almost useless, militarily, and it simply served to stiffen resistance. But if President Nixon's bombing policy does contribute to any kind of peace settlement (I am writing on the 17 January 1973) I shall still say that it was indefensible.

My many American friends will not misunderstand me. Most of them feel precisely as I do. Are we, in this, 'all guilty'? Do we share a 'collective' guilt, and if so, what does that mean? Am I personally guilty in any way for the dropping of nuclear bombs on Hiroshima and Nagasaki, for the recent saturation bombing of Hanoi? No, I'm not. It would be absurd if I did 'share' in it. I have much to be guilty about, but not about these things.

Yes, we have left the young some fearful problems. But it was not written into our Wills – in two senses.

18. Kipling's 'Natural Theology'

I ate my fill of a whale that died
And stranded after a month at sea ...
There is a pain in my inside:
Why have the Gods afflicted me?

I began to smoke cigarettes sporadically, I regret to say, at the age of fourteen: both my father and my mother were very heavy smokers. My grandfather – curious this, from a Victorian papa – liked his girls, in their late teens, to have a cigarette with him. By sixteen, I was well confirmed in the habit, and now I cannot stop any more than can a drug-addict. If I do try to stop, the nicotine level in my blood falls, and I suffer withdrawal symptoms. Frightened nowadays, I go regularly every eight months for a lung X-ray. So far, nothing has shown up on the plates. But in the last year I have developed chronic bronchitis. I could not possibly be stealthy, even if I had a reason to be, because my cough heralds me from the top of the house to the bottom. (Of course, I do not really want to stop: I relish each cigarette from the first in the morning to the last at night.)

Remember, when I started to smoke, no guilt was attached to the habit. There was no fear of lung cancer, because we knew nothing about it. Furthermore, it was even cheap; sixpence for ten, a shilling for twenty.

I hoped my children would not develop the habit, knowing how important this was. Andrew doesn't smoke at all, and Philip very rarely – perhaps three cigarettes per annum, and then only in circumstances of extreme stress. But Lindsay! I promised her money on her 21st birthday, if she hadn't smoked by then. She since tells me that the sum was too small. But I don't believe a sum twenty times larger would have stopped her. She is making a gallant try now to curb the habit.

I have led a singularly sedentary life. Of course, I have spent hours at my desk, or writing on my knee. But I have never had the slightest inclination for exercise. At school, I was remarkably bad at games, though at that time I had, I suppose, a reasonably athletic physique. When it came to picking teams for netball shooting (a detestable game), I was always picked last, and by someone with obvious reluctance to pick me at all, for my team would inevitably lose. I would be shooting on with increasing despair while all the rest had succeeded. I hated gymnastics, and invariably collapsed on to the middle of the vaulting-horse, though by some strange freak, I could climb ropes better than anyone else. Tennis I tolerated, but no more than that. Was I really so inept, or did I *want to be*? When I won two green 'gym-stripes' – for 'pluck' because I had volunteered to undergo some particularly frightening performance on the wall-bars for a second time – actually, I was too much of a coward not to put my hand up and so face contumely – hardly anyone (including my mother) could keep a straight face.

I have never liked walking except in Venice, where, spurred on by the anticipation of some marvel likely to be around the next corner, I would happily walk for miles. At home, I try to shop within a very small area. I sit most of the day in my orange-coloured chair; working, reading, or doing crossword puzzles. At sixty, quite naturally, my figure is not what it was: it has not deteriorated too rapidly during the past five years, but it still deters me from shopping for clothes. When I do go shopping for them, Lindsay accompanies me so that I don't return – which is almost inevitable when I go alone – empty-handed and profoundly out of love with myself.

During the past two years, my health has been a little

dubious. Two minor operations, a subacute intestinal obstruction (no fun this, no fun at all), and a minor stroke. I recovered rapidly from the last, except that I could hardly use my right hand for holograph. This was dreadful, since I had to tap out my last novel, *The Holiday Friend*, straight on to the typewriter. Few American writers would think this a deprivation: but I did. I am a very good typist, and I type *much faster than I can think*. So page after facile page found itself in the wastepaper basket. This is the first book since that I have managed to write by hand, and that hand has become crabbed and not too easy to read.

For these last rather dramatic misfortunes, I think I am not to blame. I had eaten none of that stranded whale. But for general debility, I am. I have brought it upon myself, and it is not the Gods who have afflicted me.

> Si no fagas tus deudas,
> Dios se las cobrará,

as the Spanish proverb has it. Or, in the version, not literal, but more familiar in English, 'Take what you want, and pay for it, says God.'

My doctor of many years, David Sofaer, has watched over me like a hawk: and does not rebuke me. Perhaps he should. I am all too often bringing to him minor neuroses, though sometimes I bring him troubles which are not the result of whale-eating.

Longevity has usually a genetic basis. If your parents die at seventy-eight, or perhaps eighty-eight, your chances are good. We have no such examples in my family, except, perhaps, from Grandmother Johnson. Charles has a better chance. His father died – willingly – at eighty-four, when he was no longer able to play the organ in church. His mother at a good age. Am I being morbid? Possibly I am. It is the mood of an hour. But I do realise, that had I looked after myself better, there would be no reason for morbidity. What a fool I shall seem if I reach eighty myself, a sort of Empress Dowager, with a silver-topped cane – I like to imagine this – lashing out at those who do not please me!

Yet, as George Herbert says—

> I once more smell the dew and rain
> And relish versing. O my only light!
> > It cannot be
> > That I am he
> On whom Thy tempests fell all night.

A poem that has meant more to me, personally, and has been of greater encouragement, than any poem ever written.

On the other hand—

> We had a kettle: we let it leak:
> Our not repairing it made it worse.
> We haven't had any tea for a week ...
> The bottom is out of the Universe!

19. *Dylan*

It was in 1933. He had won a prize for a poem in Victor Neuberg's column. It began,

> I sit at open windows in my shirt sleeves.

I knew it was derivative and I knew from what. Nevertheless, it seemed to me more distinguished than anything I had seen in the *Sunday Referee*. I wrote congratulating him. I received a stately little reply, complimenting me pleasantly on my own work. He could not have meant it (and he didn't) but it was nice of him. That led to a long literary correspondence, letters to and fro sometimes one a week, sometimes twice or more. The letters grew very long and confidential. He told me all about himself (but lied about his age : it was long afterwards that I learned he was two years younger than I), his aspirations, his enthusiasms. He sent me poems, sometimes typed, sometimes fragments incorporated in the letters themselves. I sent him mine. Here he could not bring himself, out of literary honesty, to deceive me very far : his criticism was sound, astringent and not infrequently hilarious. I, on the other hand, could not come to terms with his, when they were of impossible obscurity. I think, in most cases, I was right : and that 'Fern Hill', in its basic simplicity, was later on to prove my case. But I succumbed to his word-magic, even while I sometimes made fun of it. His 'poppied pickthank' became a joke between us : why not 'pippied pop-thank'? I asked. I believe he found several other variants.

I knew beyond the slightest doubt, even then, that he was to become a very important poet, even a great one. Where he will eventually find his place, it is far too early to tell : but he is established permanently among the poets of the twentieth century.

He wrote me word-pictures of his father and mother. He was to tell me many stories about them, sometimes quite apocryphal: but while he thought his mother feather-brained, he was fond of her: and he worshipped Jack Thomas, his father. I was later to know both of them well.

It was obvious that we should have to meet. In February 1934, if my memory serves me – which it very often doesn't – I invited him to stay with us for a few days in the house on Battersea Rise. By this time we were, of course, fully prepared to fall in love.

He arrived at the door, palpably nervous. After a brief exchange of courtesies, his first words to me were 'Have you seen the Gauguins?' There was a Gauguin exhibition in London at the time. He afterwards told me that he had been rehearsing this query, which seemed an appropriate form of opening an exchange between artist and artist, all the way in the train from Swansea.

He was smallish: and looked smaller than he was because his clothes were too big. A huge sweater exaggerated a boyish frame. His trousers were baggy. (Though a maudlin Welsh friend who saw them hanging on a clothes-line, was once heard to drool – 'such *little* trousers!') He wore a pork-pie hat, revealing, as he took it off, the most beautiful curling hair, parted in the middle, the colour in those days – when he washed it – of dark gold. But in the curiously-shaped face, wide and strong at the top, tapering to weakness at the mouth and chin, there were those marvellous eyes, dark brown, luminous, almost hypnotic.

Then, there was the magnificent organ voice. At that time, it had lost all the Welsh lilt: Dylan, like his father, spoke standard English. He was to recover the lilt later on, when it came in useful.

My mother was as enraptured with him as I was, and spoiled

him as though he had been a child. He didn't in the least
appear to mind this; even, he welcomed it. He would offer no
resistance when, going off to meet friends, she suggested that
he might wash his neck.

Dylan and I talked late into the three or four nights that he
stayed with us. About art. About music. About the novel. About
poetry.

He knew all about the last. Otherwise, he was inclined to
stupendous bluffing. He did not, I think, know much about
the classic novels, except in the most surface fashion. Of painting, very little. Of music, very little too: though he chided me
for admiring Wagner. But he could hold forth, in that resound-
ing voice, upon all these things, and he did. After all, he was
only nineteen.

Between these sessions of one-upmanship, we played the
gramophone: Dylan particularly liked an old 78 record of a
then popular, but now forgotten, favourite: a jolting tune,
with the rhythm of a train, called 'The Beat of my Heart'. I
cannot pretend that whenever I hear it I think of him: because
I never do hear it.

We drank a little beer, which Dylan fetched from the off-
licence. I must emphasise that at this time, and for some time
afterwards, whatever he himself said, he was not a habitual
drinker. It was true that he arrived at our house with a quarter-
bottle of brandy in his pocket, but that could not be expected
to go far. Drinking was, for him, one of the great romantic
necessities of the poet's image: he fantasticated his drinking.
Later, tragically, the fantasy became the reality. The other
two necessities were, to become tubercular, and – extremely
oddly – to get fat.

The few days drew to an end, with tension between us, but
nothing said. The letters went on: Dylan wrote to me that he
loved me. In the spring he came back to stay with us. I don't
know how long the stay was scheduled to last this time, but in
fact it lasted about six weeks. We were deliriously happy. We

talked of marriage, certainly we would marry some day, when Dylan had a job. He talked of becoming a bicycle salesman, doing his rounds in yellow rubber hood, cape and boots. 'When bicycles hang by the wall,' he would sing blithely.

We would make trips across the river to Chelsea – to both of us having an aura of high romance – and sit in the garden of the Six Bells, near the little fountain that dripped its tears, while we watched the shadows of the players on the bowling-green grow longer as the sun fell. (A part of the Six Bells, including the fountain, was destroyed in the war. On my sixtieth birthday the Manager – prodded, I think, by an imaginative friend of mine – sent me a piece of that fountain as a present, in memory of Dylan and myself. It is in my own small garden now.) We had great walks over Clapham Common, over those vast fields above which the stars were clear and the lovers lay in the dark – it was hard not to tread on them – to a favourite pub. It was about that period, or before it, that Dylan wrote 'Altarwise by Owllight'. An American critic bemused me by saying that it revealed Dylan's deep knowledge of astronomy. All Dylan knew about the subject was that he could recognise the Plough. 'Look!' he would say, pointing ecstatically upwards, 'I do know that. That's Charles's wain, "over the new chimney!"'

During the six weeks, he was making friends widely, and becoming rather well known. He was also getting introductions to persons of influence. I shall never forget the day on which he first met T. S. Eliot. He didn't come back, and he didn't come back: it was late when he did. He was sober, but glowering, and for a long while would not speak. When he did, it was to say with awful bitterness – 'He treated me – he treated me – as if I were "from pit-boy to poet"!' This unfortunate beginning, however, had a happy ending. Eliot became one of his most sturdy backers.

But the canker was beginning to appear in the bud. Dylan did introduce me to one or two of his older Welsh friends: but

to no one else. He believed in keeping his friends in compart-
ments, and the friends of his boyhood didn't like it. If we
came out together into the King's Road, and he spotted a poet
whose acquaintance he had recently made, he would leave me,
cross the road for a conversation and join me later. It was a
wounding habit.

Life continued to be, for the most part, idyllic. Then, later
on that year, my mother and I were invited to stay with Dylan's
parents in Swansea. (Someone has just pointed out to me that
my mother's continual presence seems to them pretty peculiar.
It did not seem so at the time. But now I cannot think of the
late Jack Buchanan's plaintive song 'And her mother came
too', without laughing.) I realise now that he did not wish this
to happen. At Paddington, he got us carefully on to the wrong
train, where we remained until my mother realised this, and
we raced to catch the Swansea one. I think he knew it was the
wrong train in the first place, and was prepared to go to Torbay
or anywhere else, so long as it wasn't home.

Florrie and Jack I became instantly attached to, and this
affection lasted for many years, long after I had parted from
Dylan. She may have been a light-weight, but she had a delightful sense of the ridiculous. Jack I respected and admired,
though I was not to see the odder side of him till later.

The holiday began favourably. After spending a few days
with the Thomases, overlooking the 'capsized hill', my mother
and I moved to an hotel at the Mumbles, where Florrie and
Dylan met us every day. Dylan would be intensely affectionate,
then moody. These moods worried me. I had not seen them
before. I was struggling to finish *This Bed Thy Centre*, and I
was not feeling well. A doctor ordered rest: and I took time
off from the bank. Meanwhile, Dylan's letters continued as
before.

I am unable to be sure of the chronology of the events which
followed, for ten years after Dylan's death I released my diaries
of our friendship and his letters to me to the University of New

York at Buffalo. But they went something like this. Dylan was often in London, and things seemed well between us. Then he and two friends acquired a one-room flat in Finborough Road, between Chelsea and Fulham. They begged whatever furniture I could spare and I did my best. Divans. The odd chair. A dozen yellow dusters. They would not let me see the result till they were thoroughly moved in.

Then I did go to see them. They had reached a peak of artistic romanticism. It was the setting of an up-dated *La Bohème*. The divans had been upended, so that their legs looked like tiny truncated posts of tester beds. The dusters, for decorative purposes, adorned the walls. They greeted me uproariously; and at once I knew that I was not wanted. I was no longer of their kind. That I had written a successful book made it, for Dylan, worse: like Scott Fitzgerald, I don't think he wanted another writer in the family.

I went away stunned with misery. But even that was not the end. Dylan began coming round again, telephoning, and at last insisting that we must marry. We would go to Chelsea Register office next day and put up the notice.

I had an appalling night. I might love him, but I knew it would be no good. I was not right for him. I did not care to wear the arty clothes he liked – I never have – and I feared and detested the Fitzroy Tavern, the denizens of which all seemed much cleverer than I could ever be. In short, I had no self-confidence.

Happily as it turned out, Dylan felt likewise. Morning brought no sign of him. One day went by, and another.

Slowly, he began to reappear, but it was only too plain (if it hadn't been before) that we had come to an end.

Late in 1935 I met Neil. Our plans for marrying were fixed for the end of the following year. We met Dylan quite often – sometimes in the Six Bells – and sometimes he would come to spend the evening with us. (From a period of intense misery, I had recovered remarkably quickly.) A short time after Neil and I were married, Dylan came into the Bells, full of excitement. He had met the most glorious girl, the most beautiful girl in the world. Her name was Caitlin Macnamara. (At that time, he pronounced it 'Cathlin'.) He showed us a photograph of what was indeed a beautiful girl, who appeared (this may be a false memory) to be standing on her head. He was alight with happiness. He married her soon after that.

I never met Dylan's wife, but I believe she was right for him. When I read her book, *Left-over Life to Kill,* I was sure of it.

I saw Dylan again shortly after the war began, when he signed a photograph I had induced him to have taken in 1934 : he inscribed it, 'August 12, 1940. Dylan–shooting begins.' However, the army would have none of him.

Did I see him again? Once, when the war was over. I was walking along the King's Road, when I saw a fat man who seemed vaguely familiar. I had gone past him a good way when I realised who it was. Dylan – fat. Well, he had always wanted to be. I didn't turn back. I don't think he would have wished it.

The later Dylan whom others, like John Malcolm Brinnin, knew so well, was not known to me. There was a whole war between us.

In one thing I cannot believe; and that is in the figure of Dylan as a sort of congenital womaniser. He was not like that, basically. He admired Harpo Marx, thought himself not physically dissimilar – which was true – and liked to mimic him. I think he took the Harpo Marx side to America, and let it overcome him till he was as powerless against it as he was against alcohol.

He was thoughtless and unreliable : but he did have the wish to please. I think he would have found it hard to deny the longings of any ardent young girl, but I doubt whether his heart was ever much in it. He was very kind-hearted except when he felt a real and violent opposition to his own wishes.

In 1937, Neil and I visited Florrie at her sister's house, Blaen

Cwm, Llangain, Carmarthenshire. There were Aunt Polly, Aunt Dosie, Uncle Dai, her husband (a minister), and poor Uncle Tom, who could hear threatening voices coming to him over the wireless even when it was turned off. It was idyllic: the purest and sweetest and floweriest countryside. Through the cottage garden ran a little, stream edged with rushes and primroses. Dylan spent much of his boyhood here. The most wonderful thing Florrie showed me, was a wayside bank so thick with violets and primroses that no green was visible. This has all gone, I suppose. Insecticides, again. The oddest thing she showed me was a village in which the inhabitants had only two surnames between them. This, she airily assured me (she was far from being a prude), was the result of generations of incest. Brother and sister, inheriting a farm between them would wish to keep the property intact; and that was that. Whether it was true I do not know; nor do I know whether it was true that the majority of these villagers were imbecile. Incest is no guarantor of imbecility and may be far from it: but there could have been something wrong with the original genes. Anyway, for Florrie, a romancer like her son, but not deliberately untruthful, it was a sight not to be missed.

Later, staying with the Thomases at Bishopston, above a glorious deep valley leading to the sea, I got to know Jack very well. He had been senior English Master at Swansea Grammar School, and was surrounded by his books, which had been a solid background for Dylan. He was a tallish, balding, dark, sad-faced man, with a somewhat bitter sense of humour. He adored his wife, and their happy sexual relations continued well into late middle-age. 'Excuse me, dear,' Florrie would say sometimes, in the afternoon, 'but Jack does like me to go up on the bed with him.'

Unfortunately, he had been a heavy drinker, and it was not getting better, though I never saw him obviously drunk. In the evenings he would walk across the Bishopston fields to the pub and return, some time later, rather red in the face, with more bottles of beer, to which he would sit me down. He had had cancer of the tongue: and would relate to me night after night, the horrible sufferings his radium treatments had caused him. Florrie used to blame me for 'encouraging him'; God knows I did not, for he was unstoppable. All I could do was drink up, and listen.

The treatments, apparently, did arrest the disease, for it was not of cancer that he died.

Dylan had a story about him. He claims that when he (Dylan) was a very young reporter on a Swansea paper, he was returning drunk on the tram to the Uplands one night, when the tram stopped, and another drunk, but flat out, was reverently laid beside him on the floor. This was Jack Thomas.

I never believed this. I tended to take nearly all Dylan's stories with a grain of salt, while not openly expressing this. But I think he knew: and that it was a strike against me.

Another story he told was of himself, while standing at the bar of a pub, being approached by a huge and minatory navvy, who said with a leer – 'Wouldn't think I was a pansy, would you, mate?' To which Dylan replied, as quick as a whistle, 'And you wouldn't think I wasn't, would you?'

Again, perhaps, *ben trovato*.

His letters reveal his great humour: both the wildest shaggy-dog humour, and genuine wit. Wherever he sat became the focal point of a roomful of people. He responded to flattery, and never minded if it was laid on with a trowel. He was essentially a life-giver, partly because it was in his nature, and partly because life was what he loved to give.

I am speaking about him only as I knew him, as a very young man. In his later days, famous, wild, distressful, drunken, anxiety-ridden days, I did not know him at all. On Proust's great cliff of time, which grows unceasingly terrible and vertiginous as we grow older, down which we dare not often look, the figure of Dylan is to me a long way below.

But we have to climb, if we want to live, and our downward glances must become, with the years, more and more infrequent.

20. The Liberal Package-Deal

I have voted Labour ever since I had a vote. Next time, I am not sure what I shall do. Not vote Tory. I shall probably abstain. Meanwhile I remain a liberal, with a small 'L'.

Now the liberals have devised a package-deal, every item of which the faithful are required to accept. Let me open the package, and examine a few items. There are some I find unacceptable.

1) 'We are all guilty.' This fatuous shibboleth, as I have said, neatly frees us from the necessity for any guilt at all. We are 'all' guilty of the death of Marilyn Monroe. Portentous essays have been written about this. But the word 'all' is signficant here. If there is one dissenter, then the proposition is wrong. I am not in the least guilty. Never a *cinéaste* after the war ended, I did not so much as see a film of hers. This does not mean that when the facts about her miserable final years emerged, I was not filled with pity. But, I was in no way responsible. We are 'all guilty' – somehow – of the Moors Murders. I am not. I have never, by speech or writing, contributed to the ambience that could make such horrors possible. Good God, have we not enough sins on our own consciences, that we have to pretend to spurious or perhaps more dramatic ones? Let us avoid sloppy metaphor.

2) (not unconnected with 1). 'The guiltlessness of the guilty.' We are induced to believe that almost no one is ever guilty as charged, or if by chance someone may be, it is never through any fault of his. It is the fault of 'society': and by that is meant absolute determination by environment and by nothing else. The mere mention of genetics fills the fashionable thinkers with horror. (Have they observed how the genes operate in children in the same family?) But modern discoveries in

genetics also fill these people with *fear*. What unpleasant truths
may we uncover? Ever since the discovery of D.N.A., some
scientific rethinking has had to be done. (Dr Jensen has been
warned not to go in a lift unguarded, for fear of the possibility
of physical attack.) There has been a call to ban genetics, in
some universities. But the essence of science is truth – and we
must not expect all truths to be agreeable. (In this respect, cast
a memory back to the adulation of Lysenko, whose influence
on Soviet biology was as bad as it could be. But he drew his
conclusions from *purely environmental sources*: and has been
pretty well rejected today; because it cannot and did not work.)

Even if the genes prove to play a larger part on our make-up
than some of us like to accept, this only means that we must
enforce an ever-improving environment for their correction,
so far as is possible. Our responsibilities will become more
serious, not less.

Suggestions for the sterilisation of the 'unfit' are revolting
to the dignity of any man. Medical science is so far advanced,
that many people considered unfit can be helped to a normal
life. I have seen mentally afflicted children coaxed, by an
infinity of patience and loving-kindness, into living a life where
happiness is possible for them.

Of course, the dread of an intensification of racialism is behind all this – and it is by no means a dishonourable dread.
England has made its assimilations pretty generously, especially
when confronted by the expulsions of General Amin. But oddly
enough, that dread tends to make some people look upon all
immigrants as the same. Some are able: some of those I know,
exceedingly so. Some are not: they are bewildered by brusque
removal from their original way of life, tend to cling together,
and so do become practically unassimilable. With all this, we
have to cope: we must and we will. Environment, here, is of
desperate importance.

The young thug who stands in the dock, charged with having beaten up an eighty-year-old woman for a few pence? It

may be his hard luck that he is unlucky both in genes and in environment. But it does not become us to assume, in a burst of bleary sentiment, that he cannot be guilty as charged: we must wait for the verdict. Even more, it doesn't become us, and with the same bleary sentiment intensified, to feel that, if he really happens to be guilty of the fact, it is no fault of his. Our judicial system may not be perfect, but it is the best we can manage now.

People here often say, 'Let us reserve our chief pity for the victim.' Well, let's.

We must have an eye to the defenceless. Some students of a Scottish university recently disgraced themselves by trying to mob the Queen, one man waving a bottle in her face. To begin with, they were insulting a woman peculiarly defenceless because of her office. She was in no position to retaliate, even by word (though the younger members of her family have recently taken to doing so). The rest of us, in her position, would have had something to say. She went on gallantly smiling, which I think Queen Victoria would not have done. And perhaps Queen Victoria would have been right. Whether the defenceless are mugged by victims of environment or not, it is absurd to weep crocodile tears over the muggers.

3) 'The abomination of censorship of any kind.' As I have said already, we have it, have we not? – and stringently – in the form of the Race Relations Act. Who would wish to see it repealed?

No liberal, I think, would dispute this. But he rarely raises a voice against films of revolting violence being offered to a society in which crimes of violence rose by 30 per cent only last year (1972). Art! They cry. Integrity! And the worst of all cant – these films are *moral*, and made for moral reasons. They are not. They are made for a certain public which revels increasingly in blood and violence, and they are good box-office. This is not to say they are necessarily devoid of art: but art can be, and has been, used for a lot of dirty work.

When I wrote my short book, *On Iniquity*, I said I was glad to see the passing of the film-censor – a wide-minded man, by the way – but that I felt things were too much for him. Nowadays I am by no means sure that I should express such enthusiasm.

Violence on cinema and television screen is probably not corrupting in the sense that viewers necessarily go out and do likewise (though some imitative crime has been observed). But they do tend to get thoroughly desensitised. They can take worse and worse displays of cruelty until they have little feeling left – not only for the creatures of fantasy, but ultimately, for human beings. And along that road lies Auschwitz.

Do not imagine that all those camp officials were enthusiastic sadists. Many were. But the majority had been conditioned to a point where they became quite devoid of feeling. Those prisoners – particularly the Jews – were not human beings any more. They were just slaughterhouse animals.

It is no use to say scornfully, 'You needn't go to the cinema, and you can turn off the T.V.' People *do* go to the cinema and find it extremely hard to turn off the television set when they see something brutal (though I think for the most part that our television companies are in the main fairly responsibly-minded – at any rate, they are, in relation to their American counterparts) because brutality is *fascinating*, so long as we ourselves are not at the receiving end. The very thing we hate seeing, so hypnotises us that the switch often isn't turned.

We should not pretend to be better, or more high-minded, than we are. Most liberals take a far more lofty and optimistic view of human nature than I do.

Films of extreme ugliness and incitement to brutality may arrive smothered with X-certificates, but most children, if not obviously infantile, will get to see them somehow. (They are very cunning in this respect.) I say quite clearly that some of these are unfit for public viewing, and should not be offered to it. I am not prepared, for one, to believe that anything contributing to the brutalising of society should be tolerated.

On the subject of books, I agree with the liberals that there should be no censorship. Books are not a part of the mass-media (more's the pity, perhaps) and reach fewer people. I do not, however, object to seizure of the worst 'hard core' pornography (I wish someone would lay down guide lines between what is soft, and what is hard) nor of the now rare desensitising 'comics' proffered to children. You may remember that we did, in fact, prohibit the import from America of 'horror comics', and that there was no outcry against that. I saw a good many of them, and they were sickening. I remember one about the villain sewing up a girl's mouth with a sewing-machine.

My only objection to our recent 'liberties' – which have been a blessing to most of us, and let us not forget, though overall the effect on literary art has been more bad than good – is that it has made many writers, however unsuited to them it is, compelled to put in the compulsory 'sex-scene', and to fulfil the fashionable demand for four-letter words. How pitiably few these are, and how they have already lost their impact! I once shocked a student audience by saying that I proposed to use none of them, but should substitute 'shog off'. This is from Shakespeare, and it merely means 'move along'. I think this gave them far more kicks than any of the more common expletives.

I would, however, say one thing further about pornography: I wonder that the Women's Liberation Movement is so silent about it. That is, a great amount of it is devoted to the degradation of women. *The Story of O.*, by someone (a man, I think) writing under the pseudonym of Pauline Réage, is devoted to this, and to this alone. The heroine is slowly, lovingly, and slaveringly reduced, by appalling cruelties, to the state of an animal: at the end she is a non-person. She seems to enjoy it, but this makes things no better. The writer has some talent: which makes them worse. Such talents are better buried under a bushel, and left there.

Of the theatre I have little to say. Take off your clothes, or don't: most of us have seen it all before, and it has become a cliché. Simulate sodomy and fellatio if you must, but don't make a habit of it. The fashion for insulting the audience seems to have worn itself out. It is a very odd kind of audience which finds this sort of infantile tomfoolery pleasing.

4) 'Blasphemy is quite O.K.'

The liberal assumption is that England, formerly a Christian country, has no Christians in it.

Well, the churches are half-empty, the clergymen ill-paid, and faith is at a discount. But it is still there. Why those of us who are still believers should be gratuitously insulted, or wounded, time and time again, is beyond me. For those of us who still think that the teachings of the Sermon on the Mount, are the finest set of rules ever given man to live by, however feeble we are in their observance, to have such teachings mocked by – forgive me – intellectual tiddlers, is intolerable. If they were not tiddlers, they would pay the same respect to a religion which has endured for centuries, as to the beliefs of the Stoics and Epicureans, which I do not imagine they have studied.

It is a remarkable fact that the most beautiful and astringent biblical film ever made – *The Gospel According to Matthew* – was made by Pasolini: a Communist. No vulgarities here, no wallowing in the bloody details of the Crucifixion: just a straight and severe story about a great man. I noticed that many clergymen, who queued at the Paris Pullman cinema, came to scoff; and remained to pray.

We must respect one another's beliefs. Charles is not a believer, but he respects my beliefs. In lowest terms, perhaps it all comes down to a question of sensitivity?

5) Non-selective education of any kind. If it means fair shares for all, I understand and sympathise, but if it means that the brightest will be forced to proceed at the pace of the dullest, then I say that this is social and human nonsense, and

will only lead to gross unfairness to a minority. And that minority any civilisation needs, if it is to survive.

So where does this leave me? I have attempted to demolish certain 'liberal' assumptions, because I believe they are not truly liberal. 'Permissiveness' has become the right to free speech *for anything some people choose to hear*: and that is not good enough. We must often listen to what we do not in the least want to hear, if we even pretend to be a free society. And after we have heard it, we can begin the debate.

I detest racialism: in revolt against the ideas of my father, I dare say, I have never felt racial prejudice. I want every child to have the best education possible for him, and in this respect, the parent should have the freest choice available. Some children are born academics: for others, the good life – if we can make it a good life – lies elsewhere. I oppose the censorship of books, mainly on the grounds that few people read them, though I reserve the right to change my mind if some really preposterous outrage should crop up. The theatre must be allowed to go its own way. Television, the greatest mass-medium of all, must be left to the social responsibility of those who run it. There should be religious freedom – and by this I mean freedom from trivial insult to the beliefs of many. To a serious play or book, in opposition to these, I should have no objection. But I mean *serious*.

I believe in the Pill: God help us, we all must – unless we are Catholics – if the flow of illegitimate children and of abortions, is to be checked. I believe in responsible sex-education, though how mankind has survived without it for so long, I find it hard to comprehend.

I do not believe that earlier menstruation means earlier emotional maturity. This is bosh, and dangerous bosh. Incidentally, the age of menstruation appears to have stabilised, and presumably won't go lower.

Lastly, I believe in the final establishment of a socialist society. But it is not with us now, and it is absurd of us to try to behave as if it were. It may be a long way off, unless the demands of the more extremist Trade Unions make life impossible for the general public, and I suspect that this could only result in a swing to the extreme Right. But which ever side took over, as an authoritarian government, they would see to it that the strike weapon would be the first to be abolished. Anyway, we must make do primarily with what we have, and make the best of that.

21. Travels II :
U.S.S.R., and a Note on
the 'Generation Gap'

Recently, at a reception at the Soviet Embassy, an *Izvestia* correspondent asked me: 'Why did you go to the Soviet Union in the first place?'

I replied, 'Because of my knowledge of, and deep interest in, Russian classical literatures. I did not believe any great upheaval could have changed *people* much. I expected to discover traces of Tolstoy, Chekhov, Dostoevsky. But I was rather surprised to find that in the field of human personality, Dostoevsky was not, as I thought, a fantasist: on the contrary, I found him a realist.'

My questioner was amused.

I am not going to write a travelogue. This has been done often enough already. I shall say little about places, unless they are fairly unfamiliar to western readers, such as Tbilisi and the river at Rostov-on-Don. I need to talk about people, and it is because I want to embarrass none of the friends, that I shall use their names seldom.

I was not altogether honest with my *Izvestia* acquaintance. I could have said that I had rejoiced in the ideals of the Revolution of 1917, and still recognised the good they had wrought. (To turn a country of a majority of illiterates into a country almost wholly literate, is no small achievement.) Of the Stalinist horrors I had not, as a girl, been aware: I am aware of them now. But I am not prepared to condemn this great country, out of hand.

It is hard to write of it. If I write of it too warmly, fanatic

Russophobes in this country will say I have been 'conned'. If I write too critically, I may cause pain and anxiety to many of my Russian friends.

So I shall try to write of precisely what happened.

And here I may say that Charles and I, having made many trips to the U.S.S.R., found no attempt by anyone to 'con' us at all. They did not think we were fools. For one thing, we refused to 'play politics', which is a trap into which western visitors often fall : so they learn nothing whatsoever. We made acquaintances both on the left and the right (I use these terms for convenience) and it was rare for either side to refuse to talk to us freely and argue late into the night.

We went first to Moscow in June 1960. That was in the springlike, early days of the 'thaw', under that wayward, Dostoevskian but essentially progressive figure (not strong on contemporary painting, though, which remains – in its official form – bad) Khrushchev. We went under the auspices of the Writers' Union, and of course, were thereby privileged. I should like that made clear. I know how desperate, uncertain, and gramophone-like some Intourist guides can be, though here, obviously, there are striking exceptions. But, poor girls, they are responsible for far too much : for the shepherding, feeding and safety of far too many people, and for attempting to keep them on the ideological rails. We only suffered once : from a guide in Leningrad, who turned to us sternly with the remark, 'Perhaps you may have heard of Lenin!'

We were met at Moscow airport by an impressive delegation, including that great and stalwart man Tvardovsky, with flowers : and by the woman who was to be our interpreter over the years, Oksana. She was the most wonderful oral interpreter I have ever met. Her English accent was not perfect : she did not care. She said the important thing was grammar and a large vocabulary. She was also a bit of an actress : when she interpreted our speeches, and we made jokes, the laughter would come readily. She was a dedicated Soviet citizen, though always ready to argue a case. She became a close friend. She is one still.

Here I must say more about Tvardovsky. He was, and is, one of the most beloved poets in the U.S.S.R. His ballad-saga, 'Vassili Tyorkin', and its sequel, 'Tyorkin in Hell', are part of everyone's luggage. He was grieved that it was not published in England in his lifetime (though a translation is appearing at last). It had, he said, been translated into English for Russian use, but that, he added ruefully, 'Is like taking your own sister to a dance.' He was best known here as the courageous editor of *Novy Mir*, from which post he was removed just before his death. It was he who first published Solzhenitsyn's *One Day in the Life of Ivan Denisovitch*, with Khruschev's consent, but was later refused permission to publish *The First Circle*. Solzhenitsyn, at his graveside, made the sign of the cross, which might have puzzled Tvardovsky himself, who was a devoted citizen of the U.S.S.R., a Communist, and a party member. But Solzhenitsyn is a devout member of the Russian Orthodox Church, which makes things even harder for him. Tvardovsky was a very big man, with piercing blue eyes, and a flat Slavic face. He was absolutely free in his speech, and could be extremely funny. Parties at his very handsome dacha were, in my husband's phrase, remarkably apolaustic. I never met a Russian of liberal tendencies who did not love and admire him: I did both. Some of the things that have happened since his time – and were happening during his later days – would bitterly have grieved him.

But to continue. This was a preliminary visit. Moscow: the smells, intermingled, of lilac, building dust, Russian cigarettes, and that at first offensive petrol which finally evokes nostalgia, individuals to meet, groups to attend. The Kremlin, red and stupefying: St Basil's, a Hansel and Gretel church made of coloured sugar sticks. Sparrow Hills, with the ugly university and the ski-slope, and at one side, a lovely church with onion domes of turquoise blue. Leningrad, a delicious night's train journey: a white night, with the sun blazing at three in the morning. Leningrad, in its faded pastel splendour: the Hermitage, through which I raced like one demented – too many marvels to take in, but one had to try. I kept it up (as I could not do now) for three hours, till even Charles and Oksana were on the point of striking. All travellers' stuff.

But I now want to go forward two years in time, and say a word or two about Yevgeny Yevtushenko, Zhenya, as everyone called him. I met him first, not in Moscow, but in London, at a luncheon given in his honour. He was then at the height of his fame: a Siberian, very tall, delicately handsome, used to giving his highly histrionic poetry readings, in his tremendous voice, to audiences of 30,000 people. He had already written the courageous *Babi Yar*, and was later to write, even more courageously, having a nose for danger, *Stalin's Heirs*. It was to be prophetic.

There were those in England who imagined that, because of the freedom of travel he was allowed, he might become a dissident. Nonsense, if one knew anything about him at all. He was Russian to the core and a splendid ambassador.

I did not know then that he knew anything about me.

But he did. He knew that Charles was in hospital in Moorfields, temporarily blinded after an eye operation (whether he would ever recover the use of one eye was doubtful) and that I was to visit him after lunch was over. Nothing would do but that he must go with me, he must meet Charles, he wanted to wish him well. So he and I went off, with interpreters, to take Charles by considerable surprise. I don't remember what Zhenya said to him, except that it was full of kindness and imaginative sympathy. No one could have got through, to a man who could not see, a greater impression of eager friendliness, and the hope that they would meet in full sunshine in the future.

I have heard criticism of Zhenya, when times grew harder: a good deal of it is prompted by envy and malice: but one does not forget such gestures.

We saw him many times between our first meeting and our most recent, in 1971. He had been to our flat in Cromwell Road, to which we had moved from Suffolk in 1957, on several occasions: once to a large party, where he recited with generous vigour to people sitting all over the floor and along the hallway: once, to read to us, privately, for the first time, *Stalin's Heirs*. I have seen him only for a short time since, and know little about his anxieties.

We went on long visits during the more relaxed times: with Philip, Lindsay and her American friend, Betty Linn Smith, who had been Beauty Queen of the College of William and Mary, Williamsburg, Virginia, where both had been educated, we went to Rostov-on-Don and spent ten days in a dacha attached to a rest home for miners, just above the river, and right on the Steppes. (We were told casually that it was all right to go for walks, since in August the wolves kept to the ravines.) Here we boated and bathed. I had told the girls they were not to wear bikinis. 'But Russians do!' 'You won't.' So they appeared on the river beach in neat little chic cover-up suits from California, and were more of a sensation than if they had appeared stark naked. Betty Linn was an expert at water-ballet, and performed feats in the middle of the Don that sent emulating miners bubbling to the bottom. (They rose again.)

On that occasion Mikhail Alexandrovich Sholokhov gave us a dinner in Rostov itself. (Charles and I had already stayed with him in his extraordinarily palatial house in Veshenskaya.) I am not going to mention all the very many writers and academics whom we met, by name: but I must say something in fairness of him. Short, back like a ramrod, with silver hair and a delicate face that seems to be made of silver also, he is a pure Don Cossack, and an Old Guard Communist. It is among his Cossacks that he most cares to live; he is rarely in Moscow, but keeps open house in Veshenskaya. He does not care to eat alone: there are seldom less than ten persons at breakfast, and often three times that amount at other meals.

When he goes abroad, his public statements can be dismaying, though I have known him speak at his own table, to his own Cossacks, about the evils of anti-semitism. 'This must never happen again.' And one morning, after I had announced at dinner the previous evening that I was a Christian, he suddenly rose to his feet at breakfast and said: 'I have been thinking all night about what our friend "Pamélla" [he always called me that] has said. Though I do not share her beliefs, I respect them. Today is Sunday. If she wishes to go to church, I will go with her.' Naturally, I did not accept this most quixotic offer. (Besides, I believe a Russian Orthodox service lasts for three hours.) But his statements for internal consumption can be dismaying also, and many of the literary young feel he has failed to support them when they needed help most.

But let there be no mistake about this. Sholokhov is a great novelist. *And Quiet Flows the Don* is a great book, a deeply tragic book, and nothing like a churned-out work of 'socialist realism'. Even young students, writers and poets who are his ideological opponents, will not deny that. His best work was concluded by the time he was thirty. Now – well, perhaps there is a novel to come, 'They Fought for their Country'. We shall have to wait for that. Perhaps for a long time.

In private, he is wildly, often bawdily humorous. At his dinner speech at St Andrews, where he received an honorary degree, he made a discourse of so racy a character that he had his interpreter frequently convulsed with laughter, and at a loss to know how to put what Sholokhov was saying into fairly decorous English.

But his remarks about the great poet Boris Pasternak (not a great novelist, I think, and had the Swedish Academy given him the Nobel Prize for his *poetry*, all would probably have been well) are not easily forgotten in the West, nor, I think, by many in the East. They were probably thrown off, half ironic-

nearly all arising out of a complete misconception of the *mores* forget that he was a kingly host. I cannot, and I will not, deny my gratitude. I think we must try to think of Mikhail Alexandrovich Sholokhov, not in the here-and-now, but in the context of history, as we think of Gogol. Was there not there, too, much to deplore? (To put it mildly.)

A final Sholokhov story. One morning, he offered to make me a present of one of the little islands in his spur of the river Don, which he seemed to own, on condition that I should cultivate it. I protested that I was a poor hand at horticulture, and that during the war, trying hard to grow vegetables, all I had successfully produced was mignonette. 'Then,' he said triumphantly, 'you shall plant *le réséda.*'

I have never achieved my island, though Charles, on receiving an honorary degree at the University of Rostov-on-Don, was made a present of a complete Cossack uniform: cap, boots, *burka* – an immense sheepskin cape, designed to cover not only oneself but one's girl-friend, when eloping with her on horseback across the Steppes.

In 1967 we went with Philip and Martin to Tbilisi, to the hospitality of a great friend of ours, an academic, and a noted Shakespearian scholar. This is an eastern city, totally different from anything I myself have ever seen in the Soviet Union. Tree-lined streets, half-obscured alluring houses, with latticed balconies – to my eyes – Moorish in influence. There is an abundance of growing fruit, so scarce in Moscow – which, incidentally, has sacrificed a good deal for the well-being of the vast Republics. We went to a fifth-century church on a hill, older than any church in England, where there was to be heard taped choral singing of ninth- and tenth-century Gregorian chants.

To lunch in a Tbilisi restaurant, if you are with anybody well known, and may even be slightly known yourself, is an experience. We went into a welcoming vault, where we were invited to an enormous meal. (I have a slender appetite, and great Russian meals are always a strain on me.) After that was more or less digested, we had to make the rounds of all the tables, at each one drinking toasts in champagne. The very hot sunlight seemed hotter by far after that. Not much vodka in Tbilisi, but Georgian wine in plenty.

We visited the studio of the sculptor Amashukeli, whose statues – daring by Moscow standards – tower over the city, and the studio of the late Piros Manishvila, a primitive painter of quite remarkable verve and delightfulness who will decently bear comparison with the Douanier Rousseau. I would love to have one of his works, but most are in museums, all highly prized.

We went to Moscow again: but this time, it was only a short trip for Charles and myself. We were there chiefly to collect our royalties (which come in notes, wrapped in large brown paper parcels – the Russians do not use cheques – and have to be paid in elaborately to the Moscow Narodny bank, being counted many times, even if a patient queue is waiting behind). We needed these roubles for the young men: we were sending them on a journey (while we went home) from one side to the other of the U.S.S.R. Khabarovsk – with China ' 'cross the bay', as Kipling would certainly have said: Bratsk and Irkutsk in Eastern Siberia, on to hot romantic lands, Samarkand, Bokhara. They spoke adequate Russian, and were somewhat annoyed that they had to go with a guide: but this kind of visit could be arranged no other way. They travelled on the Trans-Siberian railways to Novosibirsk, having infinite stolidity and endurance, and then on by air.

So far as I can judge, they were all intensely interested in what they saw, but rather as world travellers than as tourists. The young, it seems to me, are less inclined to 'gawp' than their elders. As they find, so they take. They are not constantly making futile comparisons with things in their own country. They make no attempt to equate Bokhara with Birmingham. Why should they? They eat what they are given. They listen

to what they are told. They are the last people to make instant
judgments.

I have heard some blush-provoking idiocies by English and
American tourists in the hotels of Moscow and Leningrad:
of the country in which they were travelling.

If nation should ever be able to speak peace unto nation (poor
John Reith!) then I believe it will be by the journeying young
of this generation that it will be brought about. I do not mean
the hippies on the dope-trails, looking for self-gratification. I
do not mean the drop-outs, wandering without purpose, sometimes at their parents' expense. They only bring their solipsistic
worlds with them, wherever they go.

The young have been much berated. There are those who
have no aim but exhibitionism and destruction. But there are
others who have a deeper sense of purpose, a more profound
structural sense of the way the whole world works, including
the Poor World, than any generation since this century began.

I like and admire so many young men and women that I see:
they often drop round to chat with us – I mean Charles and
myself – and we always enjoy their company. They refresh
what I have left of my own enthusiasm of youth. (I did say to
Philip that sometimes this made me feel like a vampire bat.)
But I think that if we, in our advancing years, were to put any
sort of metal drain or pressure upon them, they would cour-
teously, quietly, and ever so silently, fold their tents like the
Arabs and, like them, steal away.

I am not being masochistic. I have my own ideas, often far
removed from theirs, and I like to hear these discussed. If I
agree with my opponents, I will gladly say so, and reconsider
my position. If I do not, I remain unshaken. I have, I think,
still workable brains, a long career behind me, and greater
experience than they in the intricacies of human relationships.
(Let no one dare to speak like this before the age of sixty. It
is cheek.) I expect them to give me, which they invariably do,
a serious hearing. They, for their part, are more widely-

travelled, far better educated, and they understand their peers as I cannot.

So, if we all wish to dispose of the pernicious – even vicious – nonsense about the 'generation gap', we must meet each other in debate on terms of equality and respect.

I was often at odds with my mother. But never did I feel that we were animals of different species – she, for instance, a jaguar, I a warthog. Dissent was conducted on the terms of equality. I have felt little of it with my own children, except, perhaps, with Lindsay, when she was in her teens. Never seriously, though.

The 'generation gap' has been, then, a modern journalistic invention on a par with the non-existent 'Angry Young Men'. Family strife, rupture, misunderstanding, is ages old. Nevertheless, we are not to believe that a new gulf has been created, across which *communication is impossible*. Communication is always possible, if the will on both sides is there, if heads and tempers are kept cool, and tribute given to one of the noblest of goddesses ever conceived, though not in terms of Robespierre and the *Champs de Mars*: the goddess of Reason.

22. Migraine

I am reluctant to write about so depressing a subject. Still, I had about thirty years of it.

My first attack came when I was eleven years of age, and was then not believed in. Children didn't 'have headaches'. I was only believed when, one Sunday at lunch time, when we were having chicken (something of a luxury then, and of which I was very fond) I did not appear at the meal, but was found in the bedroom praying miserably for release from pain. From that time, till my late teens, attacks were sporadic: then, for many years, they became frequent. My worst periods of suffering were in my early thirties and early forties. (Pregnancy would release me from them for a blessed nine months at a time.) Through some of these attacks I would work: I had to. But for the most part, they were totally incapacitating.

Let nobody think these are just common 'headaches'. In my case they were the classical *hemicrania*, the 'half-headache' of the Ancient Greeks, on one half of the head only. I don't want to indulge in melodrama: but I remember several occasions when, at the height of an attack, I would bang my head frantically against a wall, less in the hope of knocking myself out than in the hope that one pain might overcome another. At those times, death would have seemed preferable to what I was going through. I mean that.

If migraine were depressing to me, it was also depressing to my family. For there is a curious thing about it: it tends not to happen at times of crisis, but afterwards, when relief should bring relaxation. It is precisely then that the horror springs (it has a great affection for weekends), having been preceded often by a strange state of euphoria. I got used to these moments of unnatural well-being, and knew with sinking heart what they meant.

Migraine would also ruin something to which one had been looking forward. A dinner. A theatre party. A visit to the cinema. I well remember, in the fifties, looking forward with eager anticipation to an evening party being given at Christ's College, Cambridge, in the garden, by our friend Jack Plumb (Professor J. H. Plumb, the historian). I had a new dress for the occasion, new shoes. I hoped to have a wonderful time. We were staying, Charles and I, at the Master's Lodge. I was quite happy until, about an hour before that party was due to begin, I knew the familiar aura which heralded trouble: series of pothooks and hangers looping up and down before my eyes wherever I turned them. I had to lie down, and to send Charles off on his own. After an hour and a half in darkness, I managed to dress myself, and went out to the party. There I wandered about holding, but not drinking, since in a migrainous attack, alcohol makes one feel infinitely worse, a glass of white wine, and trying to beam socially at the many people of whom I was fond. What should have been a delight, became a nightmare. The ironical thing was, that just as the party was dispersing, my migraine dispersed also. I was able to sit for a while talking and drinking some whisky, in Jack's rooms.

During the worst periods of my life, I would have an attack every fortnight, each one lasting for five days.

Now I think I have grown out of it. But there are records of those who continue to suffer into extreme old age.

Who, then, not having experienced it, cares? Migraine is not a killer, though I believe that years of it can bring about serious personality changes. It is not, like cancer, murderous: though it has something in common with it: the causes are multiple, so that anything in the nature of a 'cure' may be far ahead in the future. For migraine, the Greeks had their word, I believe there are even mentions of it in the archives of Ancient Egypt. It is, of course, if the industrialists cared to investigate, the cause of a great loss of man-hours. Some realise this, and do what they can to help. Others simply do not.

In the early sixties, I wrote a novel, *The Humbler Creation*, which contained a very frank account of a classical migraine attack. This attracted the attention of Peter Wilson, who had devoted every minute he could spare from his working life, to founding the Migraine Association, based on his home in Bournemouth. (He was later to receive a decoration for his pioneer work.) This was a lay body, of which he asked me to become President. Out of this little acorn sprang a sizeable oak: the Migraine Trust, at first under the chairmanship of the late Lord Brain. Our patron is H.R.H. the Princess Margaret, herself a sufferer: and if I may presume to speculate on how many official engagements she must gamely have carried out, while migraine had her in its grip – well, perhaps she would not like it if I did speculate. But I could, if only she were a Ruritanian princess and not a real one.

The Migraine Trust has been a success, though enough money is hard to raise. Nevertheless, it did establish a clinic in the City of London where sufferers could go at the beginning of an attack: and furthermore, if that attack were sufficiently advanced, would not be required to stagger there under their own steam, *but would be called for*. Here, they were treated with the best analgesics that we now know, and allowed to rest quietly in the dark, till the worst of the pain was over. Here, also, an attack could be observed from its very beginning – or almost its beginning – through its various stages: which has, of course, been greatly helpful to research. The Clinic has now moved to more spacious premises in Charterhouse Square – the Princess Margaret Clinic.

Here I know I am in a quandary. I promised to write of what has been of prime importance in my own life. And, damn it, this has been. *Suave mari magno*: but I cannot regard, from my welcome shore, all those other strugglers in that hideous sea, with equanimity. To those who have never ever had a bad headache most of the foregoing will appear meaningless, even hysterical.

By those who know something of that black spider in the brain, which grips with suddenness and infinite tenacity, I shall be understood.

And by those who have watched others suffer, such as my husband Charles, who has never had a headache in his life, and yet has supported the Migraine Trust for all he is worth, I shall be understood also.

23. A Reluctant Note on Music

At the age of about ten, I was allowed to do something very peculiar indeed. My mother's friend, who had two rooms in our house, was harpist with the orchestra at the London Coliseum, under the direction of Sir Alfred Butt. (Her name was Edith Strong.) He had no objection to my sitting beside her harp, on a stool in the orchestra pit, provided I kept quiet – which I could see no reason not to do. I must have been perfectly visible from the stalls, but my presence appeared to cause no comment. In the intervals, I was taken down the echoing corridors to refreshments in the band-room.

I was learning to play the piano myself, and one of my joys was to sit in the room next to Edith's listening to her practising. From her, I learned to love Debussy. 'En Bateau', on the harp, at a slight distance, on a still summer afternoon, falling like drops of cool water, was a magical experience.

At the Coliseum I watched, for the most part, music-hall. I best remember Du Calion ('the Loquacious Laddie on the Tottering Ladder') who used to do precisely what this description indicated: to climb an unsupported ladder of great height, and chatter blithely on the top of it. He used to swear at the Coliseum draughts – they would be the death of him, one day. I was there the night he fell. But he did not die.

Then came the season of Russian Ballet – Colonel de Basil's, I think. I saw Lopokova, Karsavina, Woizikovsky, Massine. It was entrancing. Later, something gradually dawned on me: I did not enjoy the performances of these wonderful dancers unless I liked the music. Whose *Petrouschka* did I love? My memory is vague. But here was dance, completely married to music. Who danced Falla's 'Miller's Dance', and 'La Jota'? I don't know. Perfect again. But if the music bored me, then the dance did also. This explains my present indifference to ballet: I cannot appreciate *La Fille mal gardée*, because I find Hérold's music tepid. A weakness, I suppose. But, in the whole, I get little pleasure from ballet, and less from balletomanes. You might think that such an early experience would have indoctrinated me. Not a bit of it.

I turned to music pure.

It was evident that my own skills could have no outlet. My practisings in freezing rooms before breakfast put me off. And besides, there was my difficulty with the scale of octaves. But listen, I could.

In my teens and early twenties, I regularly attended the Promenade Concerts at the old Queen's Hall, which was burned down during the war. I was never skilled enough in tactics to find myself a place near the fountain, to the borders of which one could cling if, from sheer exhaustion, one felt a little faint. I was stuck in the standing crowds. But oh, the sight of Sir Henry Wood ascending the rostrum!

The Bach nights were most intoxicating to me, as Bach is still, above all composers. But they were gruelling. If the evening was hot, there was a constant thud of fainting bodies. I never joined them: I invariably got out into corridors when the first sweats broke out.

> Ah, but a man's reach should exceed his grasp,
> Or what's a heaven for? (Browning)

But Bach's reach did exceed his grasp, and heaven was opened for all of us. The skies opened wide, the heavenly hosts descended, within full view, all blazing, all gold, wing-tip to wing-tip.

Wagner nights. I was, and am, a lover of Wagner, though he can have passages of excruciating dullness. But he won't let us endure them for long. Siegfried's horn—

> *'Le son du cor au fond des bois—'*

The leitmotivs, painstakingly picked out afterwards on the home piano.

Damn Hitler and his Wagnerian passions. Bad men can have sound tastes.

I remember Churchill's wartime statement that he had no objection to Bach, Beethoven, or German music in general: but that he might take exception to a spirited rendering of *Deutschland Über Alles*.

Bach is Paradisal, in joy or in sorrow. But for the sheer essence of the Earthly Paradise, I will nominate Sviatoslav Richter's playing of *L'Ile Joyeuse*, which reminds me of *The Departure for Cythera*, Fragonard's painting in the National Gallery. A boatload of beautiful persons, a 'jet-set' perhaps, setting out for a voyage of pure hedonism. Empty-headed, doubtless, and empty-hearted, but sailing out on the wings of ineffable pleasure.

I am sorry that Richter, as it is said, didn't like England. I remember looking out from my study window in Cromwell Road, to see him striding on, red-head lowered, through the snow. I hope he changes his mind: after all, we may not be so bad as he thinks.

Anyone who is a true musician, reading the foregoing, will gather that I am not a musician in their sense at all. I have musical freaks, I have literary freaks: I do not respond to Jane Austen, and I do not respond to Mozart. Apart from Wagner, I have no love of opera.

My son Andrew, a genuine musician, far better than I am, appears to regard music as a purely solitary activity.

I do not regard music as a solitary activity. I want to share it. In the intervals of a concert, I need to express excitement. It has been my ill-luck that Neil, though enjoying many things in an eclectic fashion, did not care to go to concerts: and Charles likes to describe himself as tone-deaf. (Not altogether true, as I have discovered.) Charles and I very rarely listen to the radio; and television, in the musical aspect, makes its offerings rarely.

So I have drifted away from music, far more than I like, and my ignorance distresses me. There is a current T.V. quiz called 'Face the Music', which gives me much pleasure: I would swop a dinner party for it any day. But I feel myself very fortunate if I can get 30 per cent of the answers right. It charms me because it sometimes brings in the most extraordinary floodings of memory. Where did I hear that? I know. I used to play that, didn't I? (Memories of numbed fingers on frozen piano-keys, in the drawing-room under Irving's chandelier.)

Singing I loved. No one who hears me now would believe that, as a schoolgirl, I had a high soprano voice: this was broken by an excess of training, or rather, by being induced to cope with a Rhinemaiden before that voice was sturdy enough. Almost overnight, I descended to a baritone range. My children, when I sang to them, did not appear to find this disagreeable. Still it is not something I should care to put upon public display.

I should not have embarked upon this subject at all, had I not promised to mention the importances of my life, and music was important. I could once read a score pretty adequately: now I am sure I could not. It has all gone, except for the occasional unexpected bonus: for instance, when a bus had just disembarked its tourists in the Grande Place of Bruges, the radio still playing, of all things, a great favourite of mine: d'Indy's *Symphonie Cévenole*. So can music spring upon all of us miserable musical drop-outs, and re-ignite us for a moment with its flame.

24. Education

'To each according to his abilities: to each according to his needs' – putting it a different way.

Children, even from earliest infancy, are obviously not all the same. Some are clever, some are average, some find school-work hard, whether as a result of the genes, the home environment, or a combination of both. The aim of education should be to raise the level of the second two groups, while not penalising the first.

Take your gifted child. Allow him to proceed only at the pace of the dullest, and his performance will certainly suffer: for he will get bored, and may soon become a drop-out. In the eyes of some educationalists, he is to become one of a penalised class. The idea is that these children should take no credit for their brains: in a sense, they can't. Their brains are not their fault. They just chance to be able. I have heard the theory that the bright child should devote his efforts to raising the mental level of the less fortunate. (Sometimes he will indeed do this, on his own initiative.) But is he not to deserve an education that stimulates *him*? Our country, like others, needs its bright men and women, if it is to be efficiently run. So, at a higher level, does the human race, if it is going to achieve any heights.

We must not overlook the achievements of the Chinese system of competitive examination. The Americans have, in the past, made every educational mistake in the book. But things are slowly changing there. Must we go back to the point at which they set out?

I believe in the importance of primary school training, and that it should have its serious side. Most children, even at four, love to learn, and take pride in the skills they are taught to acquire, all is a voyage of discovery, and their capacities for discovery are fresh and great. Plenty of play-time, yes: but to keep them messing about all day with finger-painting, basket-work, etc., is in a sense to insult those capacities. Some of the pre-preparatory schools (yes, yes, privilege I know, but we will tackle that problem later) will not take a child unless, at five and a half, he has a decent grasp of reading, and some idea of arithmetic. So it can be done.

What comes next? Secondary education. And here we come to the real quarrels. It is obvious, for practical purposes, that we must have our comprehensive schools, though here the units are often too great. But I vigorously oppose the idea of destroying our grammar schools, though this is the conventional wisdom of the day and presumably won't be resisted. Yet, with a modicum of social imagination, grammar schools could still be valuable to some of our brightest children. They have been agents of social mobility, curiously enough – much more so than comprehensive schools are likely to be. In 1969 (the last year to produce full records), 7 candidates from comprehensive schools won open awards at Oxford and Cambridge, out of just under 1,000. Grammar schools, like the comprehensives, are nowadays non-fee-paying: so there would be no monetary problems here.

There might be, as has been suggested, social ones. The perpetuation of a class system. The idea behind this is that a middle-class child is rather more likely than a working-class one – though this is by no means inevitably true – to come from a home with books in it. But are families then, to be penalised for providing their children with the tools of education, if those children care to use them? (This is usually quite voluntary on the young child's part.) It all seems pretty ridiculous. A great many children do not take to academic work, and long to go out into the world as wage-earners: sometimes they must. But others do wish to continue, with an eye on the universities. I do not believe, for the sake of the former, that the school-leaving age should compulsorily be raised to sixteen. This means that teachers (there is a shortage), will have to cope with enormous classes – as they do already – each with their quota of resentful, frustrated teenagers who are determined to learn nothing at all. At fifteen, there should be a clear choice. If the child has hated education up to then, and has had to be driven like a mule, it is highly unlikely that another year of it will reveal to him its delights.

On the question of selection, I am greatly relieved that the Eleven Plus is on its way out. This always seemed to me a rough and ready procedure which proved precisely nothing: except that the child was good at Eleven Plus examinations. Heaven knows how many children were misdirected in their educational lives by this piece of tomfoolery. (Though I know this view is disputed by a great many people, who think it has a certain selective value.) I believe the old examination, an essay, some mathematics, a general knowledge paper, was far better.

I should say that the question of 'streaming' was a vexed one, if I believed that it was a serious question at all. Yet, if there is no streaming, the class objections to grammar schools recur with exactly the same force. Further, the opponents of streaming claim that the child in a B or C stream will be humiliated because others are in the A stream. So what is the alternative? That all are to be educated on the same level, and at the same pace: which, to the more energetic and academically-endowed children, will be an intolerable process. Unfair, if any form of selection is made? What is 'fair'? And whom are we to be fair to? It is often said that one cannot expect justice in this life. But what is justice?

Obviously, there are things most of us are simply unfitted to do. If I had practised since infancy, I could not have been a gymnast on the scale of Olga Korbut. Nor could Charles ever have run a four-minute mile. It does look as though aesthetic skills of the highest order, at least, are largely ruled by the genes.

The effort should be in the direction of *mobility*, from getting the child from the C into the B stream, and hopefully from the B stream into the A stream. Here I can hear again that ghostly chorus of furious teachers. Have they, in many cases, any time to do anything but *keep order*? They have my deepest sympathy, there are many things wrong with our public education, and this is among the many. I hope it may ease itself in time, though I confess I don't know how.

There seems a lot to be said for sixth-form colleges. Nobody would be compelled to attend them. But others would jump at the chance, since these should be, by their nature, more fitted to the nascent dignity of the young adult, and a preparation for university life.

Here I would say, before passing to another aspect of education, that it seems to me as wicked to hold back a bright, enthusiastic child, as to force one who is less so, like a goose intended to provide *pâté de foie gras*.

I must now declare my own interest, and probably can't do better than by running through the education of my own children. I taught Andrew myself from 3½ to 4½ to read, and to do simple arithmetic. (The latter had to be simple if I was teaching it.) He proved very good at both. On returning from Staines to Chelsea, I followed my social principles and sent him to a local primary school with the unappetising name of Cook's Ground. This proved a complete disaster. Among the uproar of forty children in a class, he learned nothing. Indeed, he began to regress. So I took him away after two terms – and sent him to a pre-prep school in South Kensington. It was a heavy strain on my resources: but I was only paying £3 per week in rent, I had no car, and did without many other things. I suppose my heaviest personal expenditure was on cigarettes. Here his work returned to standard form: but now another problem arose. He wanted to go on where his friends went, and so, from school to school, he did. After that the strain on me eased. He won an industrial scholarship in engineering to Cambridge. He then spent two years in America, one at Harvard, one at Columbia: but returned to England to work for his Ph.D. – this time in solid state physics. He is now a lecturer in Theoretical Physics in the University of New South Wales.

Lindsay, unlike her brothers, had no real academic inclinations, though she has her own very different and varied skills. Charles and I, then in Clare, Suffolk, sent her to local private schools. When we returned to London, she went to St Paul's Girls' School, but had to leave at sixteen since we were going to California, and she could not stay behind. There she attended a private school in down-town Berkeley, and having fallen in love with the United States, would not be budged. She finally found a place at the College of William and Mary, Williamsburg, Virginia, where she spent two years.

By three, Philip was reading nicely, by four fluently. When we returned to London, we sent him first to a nursery school, then to that rigorous pre-prep school, Wagner's, which has since disappeared. I have never met, anywhere, with such intensive teaching. Not everyone enjoyed it. Far from it. But when Philip left at eight to go to California, he had an excellent grounding in Latin and French.

We were at a loss to know where to send him to school when we got there: we did not want him to lose his languages, or to be at a disadvantage when we came home. It was, oddly enough, the wife of Admiral Rickover who recommended the Three Rs, thirty miles away in Marin County, and the oddest educational establishment I have ever come across. It looked like a collection of Nissen huts. There were no games – the children could play those at home. No lunches – they took their tin boxes. But the Three Rs was determined to *teach*. No nonsense about forcing you into your age group: if you were good at a subject you went into a high form. If poor in another, into a low one. The result was that Philip found himself, for Latin, in a class of enormous Californians, some of them seventeen and eighteen, being coached for Stanford.

He liked this school well enough, even though it meant a very long bus ride and a mile's walk almost vertically uphill on the way back. California had completely cured four years of miserable bronchitis.

When he returned to England, Philip went to Cumnor House, in Sussex, a somewhat eccentric, but kindly and academically accomplished prep-school. (For American readers, this means a school for children between 8½ and 13.)

He won a scholarship to Eton, and entered College as a King's Scholar. Eton may sound a place for plutocrats. Curiously enough, for the academically skilful, it isn't. (College houses precisely seventy boys.) From now on, our educational costs *decreased*. In College you may not, even though your father is the Aga Khan, be charged more than half the normal fees. If your parents are really broke, you will be charged nothing, not for keep, food, teaching, even the very odd school uniform. (I think this attractive: and something will be lost aesthetically from the High Street of Eton if the boys go – as they eventually will – into grey flannels. Just look at Boudin, and see the use he makes of black.)

At sixteen, Philip won an exhibition to Balliol to read Classics. He did not go up till he was eighteen, but filled in the time travelling first right up East Africa, the second year spending a semester at Trinity College, Toronto, and then exploring much of Canada and the United States by Greyhound bus. At Balliol, he read for Honours Moderations, having decided to finish Classics decently before switching to Chinese.

Privilege? To an extent, certainly, though both boys, by means of scholarships and grants, and in Philip's case journalism, were able partly to pay their own way. But still, to an extent, privilege. And I am still a Socialist. Although I remain so, I am maddened by the short-sighted education policy of the Labour Party.

But one point I am going to make, not in justification of

what I have done – since to the committed nothing will justify it – because there is a freedom that remains to me. Charles never inherited a penny but won his way from grammar school, first to the University of Leicester and then to Cambridge, by scholarships and grants. I inherited a meagre sum from my mother and aunt – a few hundred pounds. The money I have consists purely of my earnings: and I reserve the right to use my earnings as I please. Pop-stars use their (often astronomical) earnings, as they please. Why should I be more frowned upon than they? I don't want lavish country houses, I don't want Rolls-Royces, Jaguars, or whatever is the 'in' car now. I am ignorant on this subject.

Before I married for the second time, and before more help came to me, I spent that money on giving my children the best I could afford. Strangely, if the boys had been potential tennis champions instead of good academics no one would have raised a whisper if I had spent thousands on having them coached in California. Believe me, money, however strained it may at one time have been, did buy one privilege: in the main, *the privilege of small classes*, which I wish profoundly could be the heritage of every child.

Eton? I can speak only of College. Here no class distinctions were recognised, no snobbery paid to money, no racialism tolerated of any kind. It has changed very much since Cyril Connolly's day. No one beat Philip within an inch of his life, or, indeed, beat him at all. Rotten at games, he played the very minimum he had to: and a blind eye was turned to his lack of prowess. At one time, he was encouraged to go and dig an old lady's garden once a week – just to give him some fresh air. I shudder to think of that poor old lady, and what happened to her bulbs.

Here, I must make a point upon which Philip insists. Eton, as a whole, is an aristocracy. College, a meritocracy. Both may sound equally dirty to some ears. But I believe we must have merit, if we are to survive. Life is becoming increasingly com-

plicated, and people with various definite skills have to cope
with it. Imagine that our education, as is probable, goes wholly
comprehensive, we shall still, as with the Soviet Union in their
special schools, have to make proper provision for the very
bright.

I want, practically speaking, to see *more* opportunities for all
children, not less; for the bright as well as the not-so-bright.
Of course we must try to raise the level all round. But not at
the cost of any one section, even if that section has the impudence to be exceptionally able.

I do not want to abolish the public schools, but I should like
them, if they can, *to make far more scholarships available*.
Actually, to survive, they'd have to go much farther than this.
There has been a quiet revolution, that has practically passed
unnoticed. Some of the scholarship examinations for the great
public schools have abolished Latin and Greek as compulsory
subjects, and have offered a far wider range. The real 'privilege' has always lain rather deeper. Hitherto, the only boys
who could hope to compete *must* have had a classical grounding: which means, with the exception of a few grammar
schools, that the children must first have attended private
schools. And this, of course, means a sizeable parental income.
I do not know whether the change-over is yet having its effect,
but if it does, it will open some of the best teaching to more
of our academically gifted, no matter what their parents' income.

I daresay my own brief education has had its effect upon me.
Any scholarship I could have won, at that time, would have
carried derisory assistance. I have wanted my children to have
better luck than I. I have no sympathy with parents who fear
that a higher education than they had, will alienate their
children from them. It is the height of selfishness. For parents
are likely to die, and the young are likely to go on: with the
responsibility of improving this deplorable world laid upon
their narrow shoulders.

We need the best children we can possibly get: and so long as the child in the 'C' stream has an honourable and *full* fighting chance of making his way upwards, we shall get them.

25. The Pursuit of Happiness

'Life, liberty, and the pursuit of happiness.' From the *Declaration of Independence*. (It read originally 'life, liberty and property', but perhaps this was felt to be tactless.) A noble statement if ever there was one, but like many noble statements, with an element of nonsense in it. We cannot pursue happiness: the thought of it has been a chimera that has deluded Americans ever since the Declaration was penned. Happiness comes to one unpursued.

It comes suddenly, and may not even be for our own good: but it comes irresistibly.

What is happiness? Someone said it was the absence of pain, and I think he may be right in essence: but it is a drab and incomplete conception. Happiness must have its element of pure excitement. I think only the mystic poets, Crashaw certainly, and George Herbert, really understood it. But, so much the worse, most of us are far from being mystic poets.

The happinesses of a good childhood are manifold. Buttercups on a common, blazing, lubricated yellow, to the height of a child's breast-bone. The discovery of little, transparent green crabs in sea-pools, of sea-anemones, seeking to absorb – fear in this, but there is often fear in happiness – the timid touch of a finger-tip; a field of bean-flowers, black and white, and strong-scented, near a Dorset village. Rarely is childish happiness associated with the social event, the birthday party: this can bring apprehension, and even misery. Childhood enjoys its wildest happiness in solitude.

In adolescence, and into maturity, happiness may show itself in reciprocated love. Calf-love, or grown-up love: it is all the same. 'Love' is, I suppose, now a four-letter word in the most suspect sense. But anyone who denigrates it, is ignorant of how life works. If he has not experienced love himself, he has the greatest part of world literature to explain to him what it is. Did Dante write nonsense? Did Shakespeare? Did Robert Burns, or Robert Browning? Love is the *holding-process* of happiness. It is, of course, rooted in sex; but it can outlast the sexual function. *It is as powerful as that.*

In love, it is almost incredible that one can be loved in return. For in that way, one cannot love oneself, or see one's reflection as it would appear in a lover's eyes. What does he see in me? What does she see in me? These are the perpetual questions. Very vain women, and very vain men, the narcissists, may be able to answer by a glance in the mirror. For most of us, the process is mysterious.

To be in love is to lose self utterly: at least, in the beginning. It is the desire to serve utterly: on both sides. It is a departure of the soul from its clay, and may never again be experienced until death.

Sexual indulgence is simply not enough. Taken casually, it can be as agreeable, though no more satisfying an amusement, as masturbation. For sexual experience to be worth anything more than a night out, heart and mind and tenderness must be involved.

So much for sexual happiness in love, which is by far the most important happiness we fellows, crawling between heaven and earth, will ever know.

There are, however, other sources of happiness. The scientist devoted to his work: the musician, to his: the painter: the theologian: the priest: the nun. I except the writer: he must have a great experience of all things good and evil available to him, and sex, in whatever form, heterosexual or homosexual, must have its sizeable part.

Soldiers often take great joy in war, and its disciplines. (I make no judgments anywhere here.) I have sometimes met civilians, exposed to danger from the air, who will say that *their* war, with its comradeship, was the happiest time in their lives. They have meant it.

> The good are always the merry,
> Save by an evil chance,

wrote Yeats, in a euphoric mood. This is by no means always true. I have met some merry people who concealed malice in merriment. Goering, so far as I can judge, seemed to be a man of high-spirits. It is a remarkable fact that when this evil fat man cheated the gallows by means of a cyanide pill, most of us could scarce forbear to cheer.

Happiness cannot be pursued. What can be pursued, is a certain freedom from discomfort. This lies at the bottom of all the social work ever attempted. Those who give their lives – many of them young lives – to the derelicts, the drop-outs, the drug-ridden, are attempting to free them from a degree of discomfort. And when this happens, the social worker knows happiness, and his unfortunates perhaps a degree of it. I have seen Skid Row, in New York: the drunks propped up in doorways, or lying on the pavements and in the gutters. What happiness for them? I suspect the brief one, of another bottle of Red Biddy, or whatever their pathetic tipple is. I have heard people say (though not so often, in these socially-conscious times), 'I'm not giving to that beggar. He will only drink it.' Precisely: if that is what he chooses to do, make your donation. We do not make a gift with the proviso that only a certain use shall be made of it.

Let me describe a moment of intense childish bliss. The family were having a 'musical evening', I had been put to bed. My mother, guessing that I might sneak out and sit on the stairs, had left the drawing-room door open. I heard the first performers through 'The Wolf', 'The Moon has raised her Lamp above', 'Maire, my Girl'. No pleasure there. And then arose a glorious voice. (One of the professionals who sometimes came to us.)

Ah, Moon of my Delight, who know'st no wane,
The Moon of Heav'n is rising once again;
How oft hereafter rising shall she look
Through this same Garden after me – in vain!

For the first time, I retreated to bed voluntarily, without having to be chased there. After that, I wanted to hear nothing
else. An underrated poet, Fitzgerald. But that voice! A tenor,
perfectly controlled, upsoaring with the ease of a lark. I never
found out who the singer was.

Happiness is found by many in religion. Sometimes, I find
it: more often not. I am too bad at it, too lax. I have found it
in a single psalm. But isn't this partly the delusion by art?
For the psalms are art. The musical setting makes all the
difference. Some settings are superb, others the apogee of
tedium. So what am I worshipping, God or Art? (Though He
has a great deal to do with the latter.) All seems the same, when
delight rises.

He who bends to himself a Joy
Doth the winged life destroy;
But he who kisses the Joy as it flies
Lives in Eternity's sunrise.

Blake: much quoted. But what does it mean? That joy, though
transient, may be captured for ever – that is, transformed into
happiness, a more steady state – if no attempt is made to hold
it? If this is true, how can we know when the moment of joy
has come?

Of course I know that the Declaration of Independence does
not mean the 'pursuit of happiness' for the individual man and
woman. There are countless personal tragedies for each which
are unavoidable. It means, in its final form – the unending
effort to build the Just Society.

26. I. Compton-Burnett

It is fair to say, and I must say it at the beginning, that she never liked me. Nor did I really like her very much, though I had for her an intense admiration. I used to say that if her books appeared every Monday, like *The Magnet* (with Billy Bunter), in my youth, I should relish each as much.

The fault for getting off on the wrong foot, was certainly mine. I wrote to her, saying that I had been asked to write an essay for *Writers and their Work*, for the British Council and Longmans Press, on her novels. In reply, she sent me a postcard, in her pellucid handwriting, inviting me to dinner. I gladly accepted.

The point here, if I may make excuses, is that I am by nature pathologically punctual. At seven-thirty, I was outside her flat, in Cornwall Mansions, in a freezing Sherlock Holmes fog: to the best of my belief, half an hour early. This, I thought, simply wouldn't do. I was, I believed, expected at eight. So I went for a perfectly horrible walk, round and round that Gothic square, and at last, at five to eight, presented myself. Miss Compton-Burnett's maid greeted me, if greeting it could be called. She said: 'Madam has been at dinner this past half-hour.'

I had mistaken the time.

I was led over what seemed like acres of parquet into a big, lofty-ceilinged room. At a table in the corner were Miss Compton-Burnett, her friend Miss Margaret Jourdain, both small, and a lady who seemed to me equally small – though this may have been the result of my trauma in the fog – whose name I did not catch. I made my apologies as best I could.

Miss Compton-Burnett, ivorine, sharp-featured, with eyes

green as peeled grapes, interrogated me. Was her handwriting illegible? No, I replied, but in fact when I received the card I had been in the midst of a domestic crisis, and had misread it. The questioning continued. Yes. No. I'm awfully sorry. No. But. How—?

At last I was permitted to sit. I do not think the dinner could have been utterly spoiled since the main course was corned beef. And during the next three-quarters of an hour, nobody spoke a word to me. There was a good deal of gossip about displeasing creatures the three of them met, in some place or another. I was silent: though not as a result of rebuke. In fact, I was furious. She did address one sentence to me. This was: 'Do you know a *person* called Cyril Connolly? I call him a person.' (In some way, he must have affronted her.)

At last we rose, and went into another Gothic room, very cold, where someone had set light to a fire of little twigs. No smoking, of course: no appropriate apparatus. (I was luckier, on the next occasion when I met Miss Compton-Burnett. 'Some of my best friends smoke.')

At first, whenever I attempted, at some decent hour, to take my departure, a tiny but firm hand – my hostess's, put me down. As I eventually fought my way to the hall door, I was accompanied by Miss Jourdain. She said to me kindly, 'You mustn't mind. Ivy isn't at her best tonight.' Outside, I sat on the steps of Cornwall Mansions – still in the fog – and smoked and smoked. I was thoroughly unnerved.

Nevertheless, I had to persist with the work I was doing. This time Ivy – I'm afraid we all thought of her like that, though I myself never addressed her by her first name – asked me to tea. It was an incredibly formal tea – a meal I do not like – with sandwiches, scones, two or three kinds of jam (and God help you if your spoon went in the wrong one), and various cakes. I ate all I could of these carbohydrates. Then I asked her directly about *Dolores*, her first novel. 'It is only juvenilia,' she said, 'you may forget about it.'

I explained that if I were to write a remotely scholarly essay, I could not forget about it.

'If I had a copy,' Miss Compton-Burnett said, with surprising airiness, 'I would lend it to you.' (I later learned that she had several.) 'I would not', she added, 'like to see you go round to the British Museum.'

This, of course, I did: next day.

My third meeting with her was not only happier, but a source of excitement. I had come to ask her how, over the years, her books had been received. She retired for a moment, then came back with a large cardboard box. 'Here are all my reviews. You may borrow them. You may take them away with you.' This was an act of generosity, and I appreciated it.

She had begun, by then, to talk to herself. As I leafed roughly through them, I heard her talking busily away above my head, but not to me. It was an uncanny experience.

I returned home with my trophy, and I spent half the night sorting them out all over the floor. Arnold Bennett, writing on *Brothers and Sisters*, had been the first to discover her great gift. But the final literary accolade did not come till many years later: when the *New Statesman*, reviewing, I think, *Manservant and Maidservant*, headed the review: 'Château Burnett, 1947'.

These were purely personal experiences. I grated on her, she grated on me. But very many of my friends, Francis King, Kay Dick, Kathleen Farrell, Olivia Manning, and many others she loved: and was loved by them. They were all on her wavelength, which I was not. When she died, she left to each of them a mirror.

Whatever Dame Ivy's personal relations with myself (and I think she would have disdained admitting to have had any whatsoever), I admired her as an artist inordinately. She was a great original. I do not go along with those who think she had strong links with Jane Austen. As an aphorist, she had far more in common with Oscar Wilde. Listen to *An Ideal*

Husband, and see if similarities, especially in speech-rhythms, do not arise.

She was one of the most impressive people I have met. But I have come to the conclusion that impressive people have a compulsion to impress. Look at Queen Victoria. Dame Ivy, unlike Dame Edith Sitwell, would not meet people quite on their own level. No satisfactory life of her is going to be written as yet, though a memoir has been, recently.* Frank Birch, a friend of her young brother's, told me a great deal about the strange life of the Compton-Burnett family in Hove. But Frank is dead, and his statements remain unsupported.

What remains is her work, and its astounding *aperçus*. Who, entranced by her, can resist the shock of laughter when she hits the nail bang on the head?

Yet it was in part this masterly nail-hitting which added to my unease in her presence. It was not really the subtlety of her character-drawing, as a whole, which was disquieting. What was disquieting was her habit of exposing the hypocrisies of speech in normal social intercourse. Of course, we all use emollients, and are none of us strictly truthful, as we might be if we were fools enough to play some horrible 'truth game'. But whenever these hypocrisies arose, Dame Ivy was down on them like a ton of bricks. I found myself not so much watching my step – obviously she did not spread trip-wires across her carpets – but my speech: and that I do not care to do, more than is normal. I am not much given to profanity, but on leaving Dame Ivy's flat, I tended to mutter profanities to myself as a form of relief.

People, of course, she knew about: but a peculiarly circumscribed number of them. She had no idea, for example, of how most people made a living; when it is suggested that one man runs another's estate, there is never any insight into him when he is doing it. Her servants have been much praised, and de-

* I was wrong. Mrs. Hilary Spurling has given us the splendid first part of a two-volume biography.

lightful they are: but to me few of them ring true. They are
far too articulate in a literary sense – or some of them are:
one suspects that they are concealing their schooling and the
fact that they have come dramatically down in the world. I am
sure Bullivant never existed.

Young and adolescent children, she *did* know about; and
her portraits of them are tender. Aubrey, in *A Family and a
Fortune*, which I rank among her very finest novels, is a most
moving and beautiful creation. It was the adolescent boys who
touched her heart the most. I often wondered, had I brought
my sons – young then – to see her, whether we shouldn't have
got on much better.

But her knowledge of people as such? Sometimes profound,
sometimes *voulu*. What she did know about was human nature,
in the broadest possible sense, and the fact made me uncomfortable. I suppose few of us like to suspect that we are seen
through. Our hypocrisies may be – and usually are – kind:
like good manners, they oil the wheels of society, and Lord
knows it needs oiling, perhaps more than it ever did.

Oddly enough, I do not think that had I known Marcel
Proust he would have made me uncomfortable – irritated at
times, perhaps, because I like to sleep at night and not to be
summoned (had I been male) for iced beer and conversation
at some ungodly time in the small hours – but no, not uncomfortable. And Heaven knows, he knew about people, if
ever a man did. But his world is one we are invited to enter
as into the Arabian Nights, while the world into which Dame
Ivy invited us was her actual drawing-room. One had a grue-
some feeling that, for the moment, one had *become* one of her
characters, and not a favourite one at that.

Yet I have a feeling that had I known her well enough to
come to her with some troubling personal problem, she would
have been kind and, within her own range, wise. But there
were some things she would not have understood at all.

Thinking back on her, it strikes me as possible that she

would have made a very good reigning monarch in Victoria's day, if Victoria hadn't got there first. Presence Dame Ivy had: courage and determination: and, I believe, the absolute conviction that she could never have gone far wrong. Empress of India? She would have made a splendid show. Any attempt at assassination she would have met with the scorn it deserved. Anyway, she was absolutely unforgettable: as Victoria is, to those of us who could not possibly have seen her. Dame Edith Sitwell, whom I did know pretty well, and loved, would have made a good job of it: but her sense of ridicule – of herself – would have got in the way. She might have laughed at all the wrong moments. Dame Ivy, at *no* wrong moments. She was extremely witty, in her writings: but I could never detect a real sense of fun in herself. Those who really knew her, may feel quite differently. I am pleading a rather brief acquaintance. Well, let us at least say this: I don't think she would have appreciated a 'shaggy dog' story. Dame Edith certainly would, and she made many a practical 'shaggy dog' joke of her own. That 'comparisons are odious' is one of the most absurd tags ever invented. Many comparisons can be revelatory, and even flattering to the two persons compared. I hope mine are this, because they are meant to be.

However, to return to her work. Some of her novels are quite amoral. The wicked *do*, like Anna Donne, in *Elders and Betters*, flourish like the green bay tree. Dame Ivy appears to pass no judgments: but she does so, like a cat passing judgment on some mouse whom it intends to allow, eventually, to escape. There is one oddity that I noted in my British Council pamphlet (since superseded by one by R. Glyn-Grylls, who has brought the novels up to date). In *Dolores* (1911) the pervasive idea is that of the moral obligation of duty to others, no matter what the sacrifice. In her next novels (she re-started writing after eleven years), all that has changed. The same idea recurs again and again: that to be useful to others is nice for them but not for yourself.

Something had happened, during those long intervening years, to make her change her mind: radically. What?

She once asked me why her novels had such small sales here, and vestigial in the U.S.A. I replied, 'Because they are so difficult to read without a major degree of concentration, and only a small number of people do read in that way. If one misses a single line of your books, one can get completely lost.' She remained puzzled and unconvinced, and her publisher bore the brunt of her doubts.

For me, they are endlessly re-readable. If I was not on her wavelength as a person, I am certainly on it with her novels.

I believe her posthumous novel, *The Last and the First*, is incomplete. She must have had another trick up her sleeve, another reversal of fortune. One can almost hear it coming – the sound of its rustling. But not quite. And now we shall never know what that trick was.

Her physical description of people (descriptions of place were few and perfunctory) were remarkable, though she never refreshed one's memory after that first portrait. She rarely verges on the lyrical: but her lovely description of the death of Blanche, in *A Family and a Fortune*, for me the most attractive of all her novels, approaches to that. Improbabilities abound in them, as when a man and wife, presumably lost at sea, return separately home; he to his family, she ill in the next village, secretly succoured by the familiar friend-housekeeper, leaving him free to commit bigamy – almost – he is saved by his wife's return in the nick of time. In cold blood it seems, and is, ridiculous. But to read it is enthralling.

Murder, incest, the forging of wills, drivings to suicide – under the close mesh of her prose are all these things. And she did appear, from interviews she gave, to believe, most extraordinarily, that they were pretty common in the staunch old English family, *circa* 1910. Homosexuality, male and female, often appears in the books. It might seem that this would have shocked a less sophisticated public than we, at the time they

were written : except that so few of that public had the patience
or understanding to unravel her complicated pieces of literary
crochet.

She was, of course, a cult writer. Though I know she is now
established in the literature of the twentieth century, I cannot
be sure what her place will be in the whole of English literary
history. I used to think she might find rest in that perimeter,
about which stand Firbank, Peacock, Beddoes. Now I am not
so certain that she will not edge her way further in. Having
been a 'cult-figure', however, has its disadvantages : it means
that one's admirers, generation after generation, have to keep
up the pressures. If they do, they may bring about an improvement of those elusive sales figures that puzzled, and troubled,
Dame Ivy so much in her lifetime.

27. Family Cricket

In 1951, a year after Charles and I were married, we went to Tilbury to meet his brother Philip, his beautiful wife Anne, and his daughter Stefanie – then four years old. I had heard little about them, except that Philip Sr had been Assistant Commissioner in Fiji, for fourteen years.

Not so long after, our Philip was born. What should we call him, which would distinguish him from his uncle? We decided that Philip Sr should be known, Fijian-style, as Philip Levu, the large, and Philip Jr, Philip Lai-Lai – the small. (This could not last for ever, since Philip Lai-Lai rapidly outgrew Philip Levu, but that was years ahead.)

They all came to see us from time to time – we were then living in Clare – and family cricket emerged. At eighteen months, Philip Lai-Lai liked to watch it from his pram (on the top of which sat Buzz, one of our many Siamese cats). Bored on occasions – as who wouldn't be – he would burst into the song learned (not accurately) from me—

> Oh Minnie Mine

[He tells me now that he actually used to think that 'Mine' was her surname.]

> Where are thou roving?
> O stay and hear
> Your true love's coming
> That can sing both high and low.

The terrain was pleasing. A smooth lawn, flanked by rose-bushes and beds of pansies : to the left, a summer-house, spidery and not particularly attractive, from which led a long path, shrub-bordered (we were rich in exotic shrubs, since the former owner had been a horticulturist) and passing by two little ponds, which I found a dead loss, since whenever I put gold-fish into them, I discovered they had disappeared by the follow-ing morning: to the left the greenhouse: and then two parallel paths, charmingly flowered, leading down to an arm of the river Stour. Here – though we had wired it off for fear of Philip falling in – were moorhens, and our familiar swans, who would come from a quarter of a mile at call.

As Philip Lai-Lai grew a little older, he had a small cricket-bat of his own: Charles was enthralled. Himself, he had been a useful cricketer: but Philip Levu had captained the Fijian cricket team round the Antipodes. It was Charles's dream that his son should one day play at Lord's: but alas, after the first infant enthusiasms, Philip proved as inept – and as gloriously uninterested in any form of games-playing – as I had been myself.

Still, it was fun while it lasted. I always had to take my turn, and on one occasion – a catching match – contrived to beat Philip Levu. I shall never understand this freak of fortune. He was, of course, an excellent athlete, and so was Anne. Stefanie was showing great promise. Charles, despite the weak-ness of his eyes, was pretty good. It was too early for us to judge Philip Lai-Lai. But Lindsay, Andrew and myself – well, I suppose we did our best, though Andrew would often sidle off and go fishing.

Meanwhile, Philip Sr had become Bursar of Rugby: he had a pleasant house, and a garden well-adapted for family cricket. (To send the ball over the wall into the road was six, and out.) Some time later I met my other brother-in-law, Eric, who was at one time Secretary of the Leicestershire County Cricket Club. His wife Jess was also a considerable athlete: I think she was once Ladies' Bowls Champion. They, too, had a long garden. So, more cricket.

I didn't mind, though it was a slight humiliation to be given a *bat*, when the others operated with a stick.

I had learned a certain amount about the game through

Charles, during the early years of our marriage, and I was fascinated. I was not afraid of asking silly questions: indeed, if one is to learn anything, one must. I think he was pleased with me on the day he discovered me watching a Test Match on T.V. *by myself.*

But it is no use pretending that any form of games really absorbed me. I could always think of something better to do. 'Games' – this being a generic term – seem to me so much a matter of the specialist skill that no one who does not possess it comes within touching distance. So why pretend? No one wants to find a place persistently within the second-rate – in my case, it would be the fifth or sixth.

It would not break my heart if nobody ever played a game again. But it would break the hearts of millions. So let us be fair: let us be appreciative of the inordinate joys which to some of us are incomprehensible.

When my elder son left Uppingham, he told me he had conducted a ceremonial incineration of all his games equipment. His sister Lindsay, so far as I can gather, made no such grandiose gesture, but simply walked away. No, we are no good at it, not myself, nor my heirs. We miss much, I know: but how would it have profited us if we had been of any use at these skills? I do seriously believe that at schools organised games should not be compulsory: though they should be available, for many derive great pleasure from them. The others, the non-games-players, should have a decent amount of exercise and fresh air, whether in the form of long walks or anything else that occurs to the imagination.

But oh, those horrible hours in the freezing cold at Clapham Common, at hockey – if I were lucky, in goal – for I might have a feeble team against me, in which case, the ball would not come my way. (I had a decent eye, and was sometimes able to poke the ball in the other direction.) 'Bully off!' Could anything sound more inconceivably silly? Such bogus overtones

of masculinity. What conceivable good, healthwise or otherwise, could this do the reluctant?

Yet I am not altogether happy. If I could have played an
adequate – and not merely a rabbity – game of tennis, it would
have given me pleasure. God knows I tried. But to fail – and
fail – and fail—

28. Marcel Proust

Some time in mid-war, a friend of mine whose family, living in Staines, had showed me much kindness, called upon me. He was Royston Morley, a drama producer for the B.B.C., who seemed to have read everything, and retained it all in his head. It appeared to bother him somewhat that, though a vast amount of English poetry was stored there, and could be poured out at any moment, crevices of his brain would stuff themselves with the words of almost all the popular songs he had ever heard. He thought that the mind has its limitations, which seems to me quite untrue. That day, he spoke of something which was to be of great importance in my life. He spoke of Marcel Proust. Had I ever read him? I said no, and he lent me Part 1 of *Swann's Way*.

From the beginning, I was enthralled. Having earned rather more than usual from one of my books, I bought the entire set. For a fortnight I was, as Stalky's Beetle might have said, 'drunk with it'. I read it in every possible spare minute, not lagging over the philosophical disquisitions, not tying myself up in Bergsonian thought, but getting the feel of the book, the flow of it: the narrative – for there is a solid one there – the marvellous characters, the fun, the tragedy, the grotesquerie, the final glory. I have read it ever since, yearly, though not at such a pace, for the rest of my life, both in English and in French.

When I was giving introductory lectures on Proust to students in America, many years after, I uttered the following heresies. One. Unless you are *completely bilingual*, and no faking, you must read it for the first time in English: Scott-Moncrieff's translation is one of the most wonderful in the whole history of translation, despite some slips, some inaccuracies, some confusions that make the chronology – about which

Proust didn't seem to mind much – more muddled than it actually is. Andreas Mayor's conclusion, a new translation of *Le Temps retrouvé*, is far more accurate than Stephen Hudson's (who took over after Scott-Moncrieff's death) but it is not as beautiful. Two. You must read it for the first time *quickly*, or you will become bogged down. Then, you have all the years before you in which to savour, ponder and re-read. Read it in French, if you can. But the English do incline to adopt Proust as an English writer, and his genius is not much obscured by translation, if your French simply isn't up to the original. I have been criticised for these divagations from stern scholarship. *Ou phrontis?* Or, 'I don't care'.

For me, *Remembrance of Things Past* (it should be translated *In Search of Lost Time*), opened an entirely new world. I remember writing rather flippantly to the drama critic, the late James Agate, who had said something disparaging about Proust, that when I died, I hoped to go to Heaven and become a Guermantes. This letter he duly printed in one of his *Ego* books – I forget which.

Youth in Combray: the young Marcel made a wonder of it all. He could even draw a certain beauty from the picture of himself masturbating in the lavatory – the only door he was allowed to lock – with the lilacs blooming outside the window. Aunt Léonie, in her hermetic bedroom. M. Swann, who almost caused Mamma to fail in giving Marcel his goodnight kiss – but not quite: the child enforced it, and, his plea surprisingly backed by a mood of indulgence from his father, kept his mother by his bedside all night: and from that point, he subsequently dated the decline of his will.

I am not going to retrace the course of *A la Recherche du temps perdu*. This essay is meant for those who have read Proust.

Here I should like to tell a story. When I was staying in Cambridge (Mass.) I was invited to give a lecture at Brandeis to students of French. It was very sparsely attended, though most of the French faculty had done their stern duty and had turned up. Mine was not intended as an introductory lecture, and I realised, with a sinking heart, that the students were not really with me. However, I carried on.

About twenty minutes' later, two elderly ladies tiptoed in, and sat in the front row. To my extreme gratification, they appeared to be hanging on my every word. Question time came. I was sure one or the other of them would speak first. I carried on to the end of the lecture, about forty-five minutes in all.

I was right. One of them did. And the question was – 'Miss Johnson, what was that book you were talking about?'

I often wonder what Proust taught me. Nothing, I believe, in style and in surface presentation. But he did teach me how to look at, and round, characters. He taught me the trick of false presentation – no one was as he seemed – but I had already learned some of that from Dostoevsky. No, what I learned from him was to study – or try to study (I don't wish to be presumptuous) character in the round. I no longer looked at my people as if they were paintings, two-dimensional. I tried to regard them more in the light of sculptures, with a door at either end of the gallery. According to the door at which one presented oneself, each piece of sculpture would seem different: it was the reconciling of these different aspects that was all-important.

Proust has given me more *joy* than any other writer – Shakespeare excepted: but then, one has the rather disturbing sense that the latter is not only the greatest writer who has ever lived, but who ever will live. The thought may be daunting to great ambition. I cannot even agree with the criticism that Proust has his *longueurs* (though to make a concession, I think it would be bearable if the disquisition on military strategy at Doncières were omitted). Some complain that there is far too much about Albertine. I can only say that if two more volumes about her were discovered tomorrow, I should be the first to seize upon them.

I have written and lectured about him. But judging from George Painter's peerless biography, I doubt whether I should have liked him as a man. Those nocturnal visits, those summonings in the small hours! Those difficult, over-heated friendships. Yet he must have been an enchanting talker, making all tiredness drop away. Might we meet our great writers in Heaven? I can envisage an interminable queue for Shakespeare, and a very sizeable one for Proust. But who would mind queueing in eternity? After all, there might be nothing else to do.

About 1947, Rayner Heppenstall, poet, novelist, and features producer for the B.B.C. Third Programme, suggested to me that I might contribute an 'Imaginary Conversation'. I liked the thought, and soon came up with an idea. It seemed to me that the characters of Proust were so 'immersed in Time' that they could be moved about upon Time's chessboard, setting them down in other places, and in other years. I would let them all talk together, and they should do it in 1941, during the German occupation of Paris. I would call it *The Duchess at Sunset*. This was broadcast, beautifully produced by Heppenstall and magnificently acted, several times; and was in general so successful that I was asked to write five other Proust programmes, using a similar technique. I should add that, to some purists, these were anathema, but I think they had forgotten what Proust said himself, that in *pastiche* lay a profound form of criticism. 'Je ne saurais trop recommandé aux écrivains la vertu purgative, exorcisante, du pastiche. Quand on vient de finir un livre, non seulement on voudrait contínuer à vivre avec ses personnages ... mais encore notre voix intérieure qui a été disciplinée pendant toute la durée de la lecture à suivre le rhythme d'un Balzac, d'un Flaubert, voudrait continuer à parler comme eux.'

Proust: *A Propos du 'style' de Flaubert*.

The second programme, *Swann in Love*, was more or less straightforward: but taken back to the first meeting with

Odette (in 1872, I believed) when the Guermantes were young. This raised the vexed question of chronology, into which I shall not go now : but I calculated that the Baron de Charlus must have been about twenty-nine. This had, over the years, about six repeats. The third was called *Madame de Charlus* and tried to recreate his marriage. I set it in the Siege of Paris and the Commune. The fourth, *Albertine Regained*, was something of a *jeu d'esprit* : it told her story from her own point of view – somewhat different from Marcel's – and had a surprise ending. It was meant to be fun, and also to be criticism. *Saint-Loup* was the fifth : it attempted to follow the reasons for the strange change in his personality, and it used Bloch as a catalyst. The last was *A Window at Montjouvain*, a summing-up so far as was possible, of the main themes of the book and the final exhilarating triumph of Art over Time.

These programmes were, as I have said, magnificently acted : notably by the late Max Adrian, a perfect Baron de Charlus, and by Anthony Jacobs, who was both Marcel as narrator and Marcel in the action of the plays. Nearly all the music was authentic – the *petite phrase* was from the Saint-Saëns piano and violin sonata in D minor : the music of Odette's *Pauvre Fou* and Albertini's *Le Biniou* came out of the air from an unknown friend in Paris. The '*Vinteuil Septuor*' was a most imaginative piece of pastiche composed by Michael Head.

The programmes were not originally in the order I have given, but were at last broadcast in that order, over a period of six weeks. I don't know when any work has been so blissful to me as this one. I loved the rehearsals, the producer. I loved all my actors.

But here, a sour note – or perhaps just a sad one – must intervene. I had had tape recordings privately made of the programmes played in sequence : unhappily, only two of them really came out well. So, as I had been asked by several American colleges for the loan of recordings, I asked the B.B.C.

whether I might have their tapes professionally copied by
the H.M.V. Company. (I had, of course, no idea of making a
commercial business out of this.)

I was met with a flat refusal – or rather, was made to understand that if consent were given, it would be only as the result
of a set of conditions with which they must have been aware
I could not possibly comply. They might as well have asked me
to spin flax into gold, as in the fairy story.

Several years later, I enquired again (vicariously) about the
B.B.C. tapes. So far as I could gather from an informant, they
had all – with the possible exception of *The Duchess at Sunset*
– been scrubbed. If this should prove to be untrue, I am prepared to make my apologies, for my relations with the B.B.C.,
on 'Critics', the television 'Brain's Trust', with talks, features
and drama departments, have been a source of much happiness.

But to destroy that superb acting, that music! (Neither of
these, of course, to my own credit.) I can't altogether forgive
that.

Something was salvaged from the wreck. The programmes,
under the title *Six Proust Reconstructions*, with prefaces, cast-
lists, and fragments of the music, were published in England
by Macmillan (1958) and later, but without the music, and
under the title, which I don't like and think pretentious,
Proust Regained, by the Chicago University Press.

These books, and my one good tape 'A Window at Montjouvain', remain. I can still hear the Baron de Charlus's scato-
logical tirades, rasped out in Max Adrian's unique voice. He
was the perfect Charlus. And now he is dead.

29. *Depressions*

For the past ten years or so, I have suffered from periodic bouts of depression. Sometimes I can put these down to spells of indifferent health: more often, they appear quite causeless. I am at my worst on waking – getting out of bed is always a torment, just as getting into it a joy – and also at my worst doldrums during the hours of the afternoon. I may be deluding myself, but I don't think I often make this apparent to my family, though everybody knows that I am invariably far from good at breakfast. Certainly my housekeeper, who is often wounded by my taciturnity.

These bouts are seldom of long duration though sometimes they may continue for days. Once, some years ago, they did become bad enough for me to consult my doctor, who gave me some anti-depressant pills: but these merely produced a state of mindless calm, in which work became impossible. No, I have not consulted a psychiatrist, and I shan't. I am not bad enough for that. And I have to confess that I am afraid they might do me no good. I think I might behave like George Best, the footballer, who, when forced to consult a psychiatrist and asked afterwards what the latter said, replied, 'I don't know. I wasn't listening.'

Winston Churchill spoke of having a black dog on his shoulder. Somewhere, recently, I came across a reference to a black dog on one's *foot*. Shoulder or foot, it doesn't make much difference. I know at once that it is there. (I have seen it in a dream.)

It is apparent the moment that I open my eyes and look at the cross made by the window frame. No help is coming from there. For I can hear a tune in my head, and it is going to persist, tormenting me for hours. Sometimes it is soothing, perhaps 'Speed, Bonny Boat', or Debussy's 'En Bateau': sometimes purely ridiculous, such as 'There was I, Waiting at the Church'. What it is is not significant: it is simply, through the bad hours, going to be impossible to dispel. I did try to explain to my doctor what this was like: I did not actually *hear* the music, or in any way externally hallucinate it; it was simply in my silent head.

I would try to think of all the most comforting poetry I knew: George Herbert, Manley Hopkins—

> And I have asked to be
> Where no storms come,
> Where the green swell is in the havens dumb,
> And out of the swing of the sea,

and sometimes the most bracing: Browning – 'Waring', or

One who never turned his back but marched breast forward.

But all to no good.

Sometimes these depressions would be filled with nagging guilts, usually almost formless; some with the irrational fear of sudden death. I don't think that particular fear is at all usual with me at any other times. But during these fits it will be bound up, ludicrously, with rat-racing thoughts of the mess I should leave behind me. Nobody, they say, is indispensable, and in my clearest moments, I believe this. But the thoughts go on. Are all my affairs in order? Am I leaving behind me anything I should wish destroyed? Who would find me, and what shock should I cause?

I am, to all intents and purposes, insulated during these periods, from normal life. I am practically immobilised. Writing, if I can force myself to it, is often the best palliative: but not fresh air. I can find horror in the streets.

To what these states are due, I do not know: they are possibly genetic, since my mother's temperament was, in her later years, markedly depressive. I am extremely happy with my husband, who is by nature well-balanced, serene and high-spirited, though he can be plunged into deepest gloom when something is genuinely wrong, or he fears it is. My son Philip gives me joy and an abiding interest, and my elder children have both given me my full share of interest and pleasure. My household is as well-ordered as it can be, considering Conchita's Latin temperament: she does love a good 'scene', and if she gets it, feels infinitely better afterwards. But I do not, and if I sense the storm rising, ungenerously deny her this therapy and rush up to my study. But she has been a wonderful support to me for twelve years, and is the friend of us all. My books are passably successful, and when things are going really well, the writing of them brings me to a state of elation.

So, with all the suffering in this tormented world, who am I to have these depressive bouts? But that is an idiotic question, and I dare say I simply put it in to make myself look less callous, and more 'aware'. Those of us who do have to endure these things, know perfectly well that with all our mental strivings and wrenchings, we cannot help them.

During these phases, how I loathe Pippa, leaping out of bed and chirruping about. The prospect of a day's bliss, going about moralising in song to all and sundry! A smug little girl, I think. Tears are no release to me, because I can cry very rarely. This shocks Conchita, who thought I displayed a stony heart when one of our three beloved cats, and her special favourite, died.

The worst thing, is when I think that God has no further use for me. My Calvinist side then comes uppermost. I search for all the words of comfort – 'Who am I, that man cannot trust Me?' – but they do not appear to apply to myself. Not then.

I am writing of this, partly as a form of catharsis, and partly because it may reassure others like me that they are not alone. The sudden sense of desolation is no rarity. I remember, in Southern Russia, walking with Charles, Philip, and Oksana, how I dropped behind: sat down on the Steppes, and wept. For God's sake, why? I don't know. (But it did seem a very Russian thing to do.)

John Betjeman, that fine and still underrated poet, knows all about this. He has never said so – or not to me, since I have never had the fortune to be an intimate friend – but just you read certain of his poetry, and feel the fear and horror behind it.

Still, my deeply depressive moods are comparatively rare. 'What a piece of work is man! The beauty of the world, the paragon of animals!' At Stratford-on-Avon, when I am not being maddened by some director's gimmickry, I am always happy. I was always happy in Venice – except, one night, when a fit of depression coincided with a reading of that most depressing of all novels, *Madame Bovary*.

With Charles, I am always happy, if he is free from professional worries, or when any of the children are causing serious anxiety – which is uncommon. But when I am alone, I am always afraid the dog will spring, on foot, or shoulder, where he pleases. So – Shakespeare, Proust, or detective stories: or crossword puzzles, the great panaceas. I do not know what I should do without *The Times*.

Spring, however, is coming. I dread the winter; I suffer abnormally from the cold; I have a deplorable circulation. I feel rather like Proserpine, though it is plain that she fell for Pluto when he abducted her. I expect it was warm down there, in any case.

This winter has, up till now, been pretty mild. (February 1973.) But still, it is winter. With the first outbreak of almond blossom, my spirits rise. A. E. Housman says I have about ten years to go if I am lucky – to see the cherry-tree in bloom. So I shall endeavour to do so, the first crocuses, the dwarf iris, the forsythia over someone else's wall – these give me a tremendous lift. For ever, generations will be able to rejoice in them, unless dust and destruction descends all over the earth: which I do not think it will do. The daffodils will begin to peer, and the doxy will be patiently waiting over the dale, skirts raised in joyful anticipation. There is only one thing to threaten both her and the daffodils: pollution. But I do not propose to write an essay on this. Let others get on with it.

Postscript. During the past year these depressions have largely disappeared. When I do get depressed there is a reason for it: it is no longer illogical. I mention this since it may bring comfort to others.

30. A Happening in Los Angeles

During our time in California, Charles and I were invited to take part in a two-night public discussion, upon some more or less benevolent subject, with Aldous Huxley and Harold Urey. If I could remember what that subject was, this story might make more sense: but whatever does make sense in Los Angeles?

If I could also remember whether it was to be televised, this would also help. But this I do remember, and it is important, that we on the platform were almost totally blinded by arc-lights – and Aldous was, totally. Charles's sight has never been of the best, but I could only clearly see the front row: and not the space between this and the platform.

In the morning papers, there was a private advertisement of the fact that Jesus Christ II was coming to disrupt our meeting. When we arrived at the hall, which was packed, there was a leaflet on each seat to confirm this interesting fact. It didn't bother us much, though we did notice an abnormal number of campus police. This time, the Pretender's name was given, but I don't recall what it was.

From the beginning, I think we all sensed an atmosphere of tension, but it did not worry us, since we were all experienced at this particular kind of public utterance.

Charles spoke. I spoke. Dr Urey spoke. Aldous spoke. And then came the drama.

From a seat in the front row – I could, as I say, see this pretty clearly – there arose a broad-faced, flat-faced young man, somewhat above middle height, sturdily built and formally dressed. He announced himself, with complete conviction, as

Jesus Christ the Second. He could understand Snow and Urey
– he had expected no more – but Aldous and I, professing to
be Christians – (I am not sure that Aldous did) that was too
much. If he might be permitted ...

He was not permitted. The campus police descended. At
this point the scuffle began to appear general: several people,
students, I suppose, joining in. Now, I could see little, but a
sort of brown and dusty rumpus. Urey, nothing. Charles nothing. Aldous nothing. I took it that something pretty rough
was taking place, and that the audience was excited, but so
far as we on the platform were concerned, we just had to sit
it out.

There was a brief interval to clear up this brouhaha, and
then we were requested to continue.

But when we did, a good third of the audience left, in
obvious dudgeon. What on earth had we done? We watched
them trooping out, and drearily we went on to the end.

Afterwards, however, Aldous and I were united on one
thing: Charles and Urey definitely were not, but they were
not listened to. We had found out that Jesus Christ II had been
taken to a police station. There had been a pretty fierce struggle
and ejection. Aldous and I were convinced that injustice might
have been done, and that we must find out to which police
station the young man had been taken, see him, and offer him
what help we could.

Charles and Urey shrugged wearily, but let us have our way.
(How could we be *quite* sure – this was in the forefront of
Aldous's thoughts and mine – that the young man was not
just conceivably who he said he was?)

Then began the long drive through the night. Nick after
nick – he might have been to any one of them, but he had been
passed on. It was very late. Harold Urey tried to while away
the time by saying that he, at least, could explain to me the
Second Law of Thermodynamics. So, for a time, he seemed
able to: he was a marvellous expositor. But eventually he lost

me. He had begun to talk about the 'engine' – what engine? My lost and exhausted soul past any sense, I could only think of a puff-puff. Mrs Urey said, 'Oh stop it, Harold. Can't you see she isn't with you?'

At last we came to a police station where the young man seemed to be held, and where his supporters were milling around. On seeing Aldous and myself, they rounded upon us. I suppose there were thirty of them, but there seemed to be hundreds. Amid their denunciations, I heard just one thing: Jesus Christ II had come to denounce the Atom Bomb. We had, at least by not supporting him, all spoken in its favour.

Against such nonsense, reason seems powerless: but a certain degree of nonsense will expel fear. I got silence somehow – Aldous could hardly see anyone, and was completely bewildered – and announced the following: that under the arc-lights, not one of us had been able to see what had happened. So, we had come to interview the young man if possible, and help if we could. With regard to the Bomb, the boy was no serious protester, but a religious crank. This quietened some of them somewhat, but others continued to clamour.

I approached the station captain. I told him who the platform party were. If Jesus Christ II was available, we should like to see him. The captain replied, with, I think, a hint of relish, that he was no longer there: he had been conveyed to another police-station, a good long way away.

That broke me, and I think it broke Aldous. Charles and Urey, with what strength they could summon, were both smiling like Cheshire cats. The protesting students announced that we should all be subpoenaed for something or other. I found this worrying, as I needed to get back to Berkeley and the children.

However, we were so tired that an exploration of more police-stations was out of the question. We all went back to bed, and slept the sleep of the just – for no one could possibly be juster than we were.

In the morning, a sober body of students came to make their
apologies. They realised that we were at fault in no way. They
had made enquiries through their lawyers. They appreciated
what we had done in an attempt to help. They now realised
that Jesus Christ II was a crank, a by no means unfamiliar
phenomenon in Californian society.

The second evening of our discussion passed off quietly.
After the adventures of the night before, it was incredibly
tame.

The sequel came a year or so later, when Charles and I were
at the University of Michigan at Ann Arbor.

It was a misty blue day, warm and quiet, and we were
having tea, when a visitor was announced. The name seemed
only vaguely familiar, but the flat, cordial face was, to me,
very much so.

He advanced cheerfully, 'I don't suppose you remember me!'

'Oh, yes, I do,' I replied, none too pleasantly. 'You are Jesus
Christ II and you bust up our discussion at Los Angeles.'

He nodded, beamed, and simply shrugged the whole thing
off. It had been kind of us all to come and look for him: but in
fact no charges had been brought, and the police – some time
in the small hours, I gather – had let him go. All that was old
history.

He accepted a cup of tea. He wanted to tell us what was
happening to him now. Decorously dressed, as usual, well
scrubbed, shoes well shone, he seemed as rational a young man
as one could wish to meet. He was, in fact, in Ann Arbor itself,
not as an undergraduate but under the guidance of a theologian
on the faculty.

He was happy: all was right, nothing was wrong. He did
not stay for more than fifteen minutes. He had just come to
pay a courtesy call. He went off into the radiant afternoon, out
into the Earthly Paradise. We never saw him again.

This was nearly thirteen years ago. I have often wondered
what happened to him since. I think he had even then given

up being Jesus Christ. Did his bliss persist? Dotty or not, I am sure he was harmless and good. I hope the Earthly Paradise did not fade or grow sour for him, and I think that, if Aldous were still alive, he would feel the same as I do. But then Aldous and I were not altogether devoid of a sentimental streak.

31. Two Eye Operations

These, endured by Charles, have been described so poignantly in *The Sleep of Reason* and *Last Things*, that I have nothing to add from his point of view. But I should be omitting one of the great importances of my life if I did not add something of my own.

One morning, early in March 1962, Charles woke me up. He was in distress. He said he had a dark veil covering one half of his left eye – never, in any case, a good one. We got to an ophthalmologist, as quickly as we could, our minds filled with the fears we dared not express. Brain tumour? He saw us at once. What was wrong was a detached retina: he urged an immediate operation to pin it back into place.

Here Charles was in a quandary. He was due in three days to travel to Scotland, to be installed as Rector of Saint Andrews. He argued this with Lorimer Fison. If he went, what risk would he be taking with the success of an operation afterwards? The answer, after much hesitation, was this. If the operation were done at once, there might be an 80 per cent chance of success. If it were delayed, perhaps 60 or 70 per cent. Charles decided to fulfil his obligation, and to go into Moorfields Eye Hospital immediately upon his return.

We had difficulty in blacking out the afflicted eye: this was to have a certain repercussion later. He could not wear an ordinary black patch, since it so depressed his glasses that it was impossible for him to see out of the lens over the good eye. So I contrived a black bandage that covered the eye afflicted, this going right round his head, and slanting over one side. It looked odd, but it worked.

The journey to St Andrews was agonising. Lindsay, Philip and I went too: it was our task to see that he did not make the least stumble, let alone fall. The children were anxious, and very sedulous. Somehow we got through the ceremonies, sometimes uproarious, for the Rector is the representative of the student body, and at last were able to return to London, where Charles went straight into hospital.

Now, to replace a detached retina is an extremely tricky, but not obviously a dangerous, operation. But the aftermath was miserable. He had to lie for days in darkness, motionless, both eyes covered. He refused to allow anyone to feed him, but insisted on being given sandwiches, which he could put into his own mouth. He has described the wretchedness of his hallucinations, and to this I will not add.

Every morning his secretary helped me to deal with his mass of correspondence. Then I got to the hospital as quickly as I could, to talk to him, tell him all the news, read him the newspapers and the novels he fancied. (You cannot read Jane Austen successfully aloud, but both Dickens and Trollope are splendid for this purpose.) In the evenings I stayed as late as I could, arranging for a series of visitors to take my place. But his nights were dreadful.

At last the day of final inspection came. Lorimer Fison said at once, 'I'm sorry. We've failed.' It was a terrible blow: it meant that the sight of the left eye had completely gone. 'But,' he added, 'you may as well have the comfort of seeing with the good one.' And he removed the bandages.

In the meantime, when Charles was still totally blinded, a cartoon appeared in *Private Eye*, never one of the kindest of periodicals. It was a malicious cartoon by someone whom I shall not name, depicting Charles, cavorting naked, wearing the black bandage I had made for him to wear during his quixotic journey to St Andrews. Underneath was the caption, 'In the country of the blind, the one-eyed man is King.' Not just insensitivity: staggering cruelty. Naturally, Charles was not told about this until a long while afterwards. (One of *Private Eye*'s regular contributors resigned in disgust.) I have never met this cartoonist: I hope I never shall. We are told to forgive our enemies. I can usually forgive mine (as I cannot forgive myself for many things) because I tend to forget even who they are: but I cannot forgive Charles's.

Only a few days after his discharge from Moorfields, something miraculous happened – or it seemed so at the time. It was straight out of *Jane Eyre*, where the blinded Mr Rochester *sees* that Jane has on a blue dress and is wearing something glittering round her neck. I was at the dressing-table. Charles said suddenly, and I saw that he was covering his good eye, 'I can see your shape against the window.'

Lorimer Fison came, and agreed that this was indeed an extraordinary phenomenon: somehow the retina had floated back into place.

In June, Charles and I paid one of our periodic visits to the United States. He was recommended to go by sea, where the risk of jolting would be less than in the air. This pleased me, as I am fond of ships. We had, in fact, a very pleasant trip. Charles still was unable to read without undue strain, so I took up again my habit of reading to him. We both became so absorbed in Trollope's *The Duke's Children*, the most charming, probably the most perfect of his books since it contains little tiresome extraneous matter (though it lacks the sombre, rather dotty grandeur of Mr Crawley, in *The Last Chronicle of Barset*) that we could hardly wait to finish our lunch, go down to our room, and take it up again.

Things went well until October, when again the retina became displaced. Lorimer Fison insisted that Charles go back to Moorfields, without delay this time, for a second operation.

On the day it was to be performed, I was due for a 'Critics' recording. I did not wish to go. 'Oh, don't be silly,' Charles said, 'you know it's quite a trivial thing. You go to "Critics" and come straight on to me when you're through there.'

I never made that recording. Towards the end of lunch, the telephone rang: it was Lorimer Fison. Charles's heart had

stopped for three and three-quarter minutes on the operating-
table. It was going again now, though external massage had
failed and he had had to be 'opened up'. (I later learned that
the emergency was so great, that Fison had done this himself.)
He seemed quite all right, but perhaps I could get along
straight away?

The shock was blinding. I explained as best I might what
had happened and someone put me into a taxi. Of the ride, I
can remember nothing at all. But I remember waiting for five
minutes – was it more, or less? – it seemed like half an hour –
by the hospital lift, waiting for someone to fetch me. I dreaded
to hear that Charles was dead. I was taken at last into the
anteroom of the operating theatre. Charles was still on the
table, just conscious. He recognised me, and smiled. I sat for
a long while holding his hand. I realised that his chest was
bandaged, and that there were tubes in his ankles. 'What are
you doing here?' he said at last. He was already suspicious. I
said that 'Critics' had finished very early. He frowned. Something didn't seem to fit.

At last they were able to wheel him back to his room and
put him to bed. Outside the door, Lorimer Fison and the
heart surgeon spoke to me. Should they tell him what had
happened, or should they not? I said, 'Of course you must tell
him. He's not a fool. He knows something's up already. And
he will soon find out that he's covered in plasters.'

They went to break the news. A few minutes after, I was
able to see him. He was perfectly conscious now.

I said, 'Well, old boy. You've given us a time of it.'

He replied, 'Listen, my girl. I'll tell you what happens on the
other side. *Nothing*.'

I said this was no time to discuss theology.

He has written himself of what that shock meant to him.
It is, to me, almost unbearable reading.

Eventually I went home. I slept little that night. The sister
had told me that I might telephone as often as I chose. I did.

At midnight. Two o'clock. Four o'clock. Five o'clock. I was at the hospital in the morning, as soon as I could get there.

I will pass over those horrible days. It was wonderful when, one day, I went to his room, and saw that all the equipment necessary, in case of a relapse, had been removed.

But he made an excellent recovery, and the operation on the retina was this time successful. He has only peripheral vision in the left eye now, but that is better than monocular vision only. At least it restores the sense of balance. He is now able to read and write easily, go to the theatre and cinema, and watch television.

It was about a month after his cardiac arrest, that reaction set in really violently for me. I found myself crying uncontrollably, at the most inconvenient times. I managed to conceal it, because Charles was markedly cheerful, more so than he had been, I think, for months, and this wouldn't have been much fun for him.

But the real nightmare, of course, was his alone, and in *Last Things* he has made it imaginable – or nearly.

32. Detective Stories

Unlike Edmund Wilson, I really do care who killed Roger Ackroyd. So does Professor Jacques Barzun, a scholarly expert on the subject of the detective story.

This form of literature has really meant an enormous amount to me.

'La chaire est triste, helas, et j'ai lu tous les livres.' These moments come upon one. Glutted with literary glories, and tired with writing, I often want the kind of book not in Mallarmé's mind: a book with an absorbing mystery, *and absorbing characters*. (I must write off the puzzle pure and simple, basing itself on railway time-tables or the ebb and flow of the tides.) In hospital, for instance, what better books are there to kill time?

Admittedly, for the hundred one reads, only one may seat itself in the memory. But this means that of the remaining ninety-nine, a good few can be re-read with pleasure.

It is an absurd mistake to think that the 'classical' detective story was ever read for morbid reasons. The murder was brief (in the Sherlock Holmes stories we have, indeed, very few murders at all) and usually pretty bloodless. The charm of the 'classical' was the atmosphere: and the hunt among credible and well-differentiated characters for the villain. I am afraid that Raymond Chandler, for all his gifts, began the great change. Our own English expert, Julian Symons, himself a most distinguished practitioner of the crime story, does not regret this. But I do. I detest the squalor of the 'private eye', the kick in the teeth or belly, the unmitigated violence. I don't want it.

But can that Body in the Library lie there for ever?

Dr A. L. Rowse invited me one day to lunch at All Souls

where I was to meet Agatha Christie. I said, 'If I do, I shall genuflect.'

I did meet Dame Agatha. 'You said you would genuflect,' said Rowse. Certainly I had said so. And I did.

In our own day, she has been the most eminent of detective story writers. In her early and middle periods, especially, she had a unique gift of psychological subtlety, which more 'serious' writers might well have envied. She almost always tricked one, of course, into hitting on the wrong suspect: but when the right one was found, there could have been no conceivable doubt that he – or she – was the *only person* psychologically capable of having 'done it'. This is her great secret. Nobody else has come within touching distance of it.

She has given much joy. She is well-on in years now, and I hope – she seemed in fine fettle when I met her – that she has many more years ahead of her. But when her time does come, I think she deserves a turn-out similar to that of Anatole France.

There was a very curious figure indeed in the field of the detective story, the late H. C. Bailey, who seems to have been forgotten by all but myself and Jacques Barzun. His detective, Reggie Fortune, was a forensic surgeon, uxorious, given to the stuffing of carbohydrates (especially crumpets and cream cakes). His mind and his method were both obscure: Bailey needs reading with care as no other detective writer does at all. His long-short tales are difficult, in one way that Ivy Compton-Burnett's novels are difficult: miss a single word, and you have lost the whole point. I have had to read certain stories of his two and three times before I have really got the point myself.

Two women remain as practitioners of the classic *genre*: the pair calling themselves Emma Lathen. Their interests lie in Wall Street: their detective is the urbane banker, John Putham Thatcher. Their stories are practically bloodless, and full of wit: they know all about financial matters, and on this side, I admit, they are sometimes too much for me. But they are infinitely superior to many straight fiction writers whom I could name, but won't.

Now the whole thing is splitting up: into 'thick ear' novels, with a maximum of violence: and pure suspense stories, by many English and American women – Celia Fremlin comes first to my mind – which are written with the minimum of detective interest. The best of these, I love. But as violence grows more and more in society, so the 'detective' novel of violence grows in popularity. I do not think I shrink excessively from violence as such, though I will avoid it if I can. But much of this crime-story violence is so very, very cheap: it has become so formulated as to become, at the same time, garbage. I would guarantee to write, if required, a description of violence to match any of the devoted practitioners: but I would do so with my tongue in my cheek.

The Russians are very short of light literature: that is why they devour the works of Agatha Christie ('Agta', they call her) whenever they can get hold of them. To serialise 'Agta' may save a magazine from collapse. For what they like is the background of an English country house, with the vicar, the doctor and, of course, the butler, on hand: and the body, if possible, in the library. Dame Agatha's royalties must be stacked up for her there to a degree I can hardly imagine: but they are, of course, frozen, and if she wants them she may go – as we do – and collect.

I should mention at this point, that a volume consisting of three crime stories, by C. P. Snow, John le Carré and Dick Francis (a superb practitioner), sold out an edition of 150,000 copies in three days.

Other women I have admired are Ngaio Marsh (though her hero, Roderick Alleyn, is a figure as personally and privately adored by his creator as Lord Peter Wimsey), and the late Dorothy Sayers, in particular her books *Gaudy Night* and *Busman's Honeymoon*: these not for their detection, but for their over-heated romantic and sexual imagination, which, I confess, I relish: thought there was an awful moment when Harriet, Lord Peter's bride, leaned out of the window on the morning after the wedding-night, tying her tie. What the devil was she doing with a tie? She might as well have been waxing her moustache.

I must not forget the late Margery Allingham, an excellent writer of the detective story, of whom I have a strange tale to tell. Meeting her at a cocktail party and finding her surpassingly amiable, I dared to ask her why her stock detective, Mr Albert Campion, seemed so ineffably grand, and what happened to him.

She answered, simply, 'Oh, he came to the Throne.'

Stupefied, I asked her, 'But who was he?' To get the staggering reply: 'George VI.'

It is wonderful how the idealising imagination works.

Of the men, I usually enjoy John Dickson Carr, for his atmosphere as thick as black treacle: but as for his locked-room mysteries, I confess that I haven't been able to work out a single one of them, even when the solution was painstakingly explained to me.

Time-wasting, all this? No more than going to the cinema, and this doesn't involve moving from one place to another. I once met a young man who told me that he never read anything that was not first-rate. How, I wondered, did he know it was, having no standards of comparison? I am in favour of eclectic reading. Certainly, much of the fourth and fifth rate is intolerable, and never gets more than a glance. But it is equally silly to say that, in literature, you can't sort the pornographic chaff from the erotic wheat, so you can make no value-judgments at all. I am always suspicious of those whose certainties are absolute. A young friend of mine, then a student, proposed to write her thesis on Trollope. This her tutor shrugged off in derision, and no more was heard of it. What an ass the man must have been!

I remember well when even Dickens had to be put back on the map as an academic subject. Humphry House began it, and Edmund Wilson made the final breakthrough; just as Kipling was put back there by, of all people – and all honour to him – T. S. Eliot.

In the twenties, I might have been as much derided for rejoicing in Dickens and Kipling (in fact, I was refused a volume of the latter's poetry for the only prize I ever won at school, but was, blessedly, compensated by Browning) as I sometimes am for rejoicing in detective stories now.

Of course, very few of these can be classed as 'literature', in the sense that literature is something which outlasts, or overbears, fashion. Conan Doyle can. Chesterton can. The vast majority of detective writers would never survive the rigour of a 'thesis' – nor do they aim to offer themselves for such an attention. They are entertainers, and that is no mean thing to be. I have read many a contemporary straight novel that made no attempt to entertain at all – whether by intellect, insight, wit, or the simple skill of carrying the reader's interest onwards from one page to the next. (Purely aesthetic 'entertainment', perhaps? But this is very much in the eye of the beholder.) I say these novels are no good.

We all need our rest-periods. We may play bridge, or chess: we may be games-players, cinema-goers, or television watchers. Or we may need detective stories: in at one side of the head and out the other, most of these. But what pleasure they give us during their passing through!

The detective story does fulfil one need that should be filled by all prose literature: *the need to arouse, and to satisfy curiosity*. Oh, what will happen next? For this purpose, it is ideally fitted. A quick-roused curiosity, a quick satisfaction. There are people who insist that *A la Recherche du temps perdu* is without narrative. This is nonsense. The book has a strong narrative line, though taking its time about it: and

Proust had an excellent narrative gift. James Joyce's gift is more slender but it is there: otherwise *Ulysses* might be intolerable, and for me, *Finnegans Wake* simply *is* intolerable.

33. 'The Way We Live Now'

'Uglification': the word, coined by Lewis Carroll, ought now to be in common usage. It is all about us, actually and metaphorically.

London is being destroyed. It was, in its very essence, a low, and not a tall, town. Now the property-developers are at work, and hideous high blocks are arising everywhere. The rot set in with the Park Lane Hilton. After that, great useless towers sprang up everywhere, defacing the skylines, insulting the graces that are left, out of scale with the rest of the town. High-rise flats, in their inanity and inhumanity, continue to proliferate. I say they were conceived and erected by soulless men. What people want when they are resettled are *homes* – no more than four storeys high at most, and damn the cost of the ground – grouped around community centres: by which I mean, to each one a decent pub, a good general shop or supermarket, a youth centre. I do not want any longer to see already rich men making pots of money out of erecting hell-holes for people to live in. I don't care if they do lose money. I don't care if we all do. I don't care who does. We must stop the uglification, fling to the depths of ridicule these empty office blocks: derisive objects for people desperate even for a roof over their head.

Not suitable for homes? I suppose *anything* will do for a home, when you have no home at all, even an appalling tower block. I am a rotten economist – in fact, I do not understand the subject at all. But I know that something will have to be done about land values, unless we are going to make a disgrace of our city.

Who cares? Which Party cares? Does any Party care?

London is a mild city compared with New York, which has

become pretty well detestable. Nevertheless, crimes of violence in our metropolis are increasing at a ferocious rate. Don't tell me there has been no encouragement from the mass media, because I don't believe it. I don't want to dwell on this further, since I have discussed it before. But let us try not to be totally permissive cretins, and remember our social responsibilities, not to intellectuals genuinely incapable of going out with knife, cosh or gun themselves, but to those people in a vast society whose excitements are likely – in a few cases, but some – to be stimulated to action. We are most of us such horrible snobs: we feel that anything which can be resisted by ourselves, can be resisted by the violent, the potential criminal, the drop-out, the man hard-up for a few pence. Uglification? It is all around us.

When I wrote my book, *On Iniquity*, based on the Moors murders, which was an attempt to explore the social forces which may have lain behind them, I was sometimes accused of 'hysteria'. (This is a recognised cliché of abuse). If I had been accused of anger, I should have admitted it. It makes me angry to see the squalid contents of so many newspaper-shop-windows, and I am angry when I read reports of vapid persons exposing themselves before classes of children. What on earth do they think they are teaching? What on earth good are they doing? To teach the distinction between the sexes? I think the children are less silly than they.

March 1973 saw a series of strikes, threatened and real. I am familiar with the history of the Trade Union movement, and appreciative of all the sacrifices it has made in the past for fair wages for fair work. Last year (1972), when the miners and power-workers struck, public opinion on the whole was behind them: because theirs was a rotten job, and they had had a rotten deal. So that the public had to put up with the miseries and did so with good grace.

But this March (1973) we had a go-slow from the gas-workers, which closed down schools, hospitals and industrial plant. We were all afraid that if it attacked the domestic consumer seriously, it might be dangerous to human life. For old people, it would mean the fear of hypothermia: for the merely incompetent, the dread of having to close down, in a panic, complicated (or rusted) appliances.

The hospital ancillary workers, many of them, struck. This meant a heavy burden on the remainder, such as nurses, whose job is regarded as vocational. On them, and on such outside help as they could get, fell the burden of getting meals, sufficient clean linen, and general sterilisation. They, in the name of common humanity, *could* not strike, no more than the doctor or the priest.

It is over now. But if strikes spread again this autumn, brought about by the appalling rise in prices, there is a danger that the whole country may be brought to a standstill. (This may be an exaggeration, but it is in the minds of a good many people.)

Yet, unless I misinterpret them, this is what some of the militants actively appear to want. To whose good would this be? To the satisfaction, perhaps, of a good many, who believe in the *tabula rasa*, but to the good of no one. Just a wholesale destruction of the good, as well as the bad. Out of anarchy, nothing has ever arisen except tyranny, which finds itself in perfect conditions for the spring.

Osbert Lancaster had a splendid cartoon quite recently. It depicted an entry of choirboys singing, to the stupefaction of the Vicar:

> Fair waved the golden corn
> In England's pleasant land,
> When full of joy, one shining morn
> Walked out the reapers' band.

The English are not happy. Too many things are going wrong. The news is consistently disagreeable. In 1940, when the news was worse, we at least had the comfort of having an active part to play. Now – and I revert to the pursuit of happiness – where is happiness to be found?

For the young it may still be within reach. For those of us who have only a limited number of years to go, the prospect is bleak. An uglification of our towns. A moratorium on our moral structure – if any exists, a kind of mindless hedonism, politically destitute. A kind of ghastly introspection, which ignores those parts of the world, which greatly need our help. We are becoming solipsistic.

The glory of the Welfare State has lost some – but let's not exaggerate, not all – of its brightness. The National Health Service is still functioning, much to the fury of the American Medical Association. The poor do not seem to resent conspicuous over-consumption, provided this is confined to pop-singers, film-stars and soccer-players: it would be dull to find glitter nowhere. The golden ceremonial of the Queen – on State occasions – appears to be very little resented. We don't, on the whole, want to see a monarchy on bicycles. As a nation, we are superbly good at putting on a show – and for God's sake, we need something to brighten us up. We need a fairy on top of our wilting Christmas tree.

American guests continue to assure us that they admire the still-existent politeness of our public servants. Well – compared with some of theirs – it remains roughly true. This springs partly from the fact that the English are a patient people, and have to be very hard tried before they lose their tempers. Hence the threat of ever-increasing strike-action, because it is difficult to force them into a state of panic.

Many civilians did panic, during the worst of the wartime bombing: but most of them, sustained by the general atmosphere of public stoicism (one of the most effective of our doctrines) managed to drive panic down. People have their attachments to public symbols, such as John Bull – whom I always regard as looking ripe for coronary thrombosis; Uncle Sam, a not particularly healthy-looking figure; Marianne –

well, I don't think the French have ever paid much attention to her. (She is so very bulky.) But as our public symbols are, on these we do tend to model ourselves, in a vestigial, certainly an unconscious, degree.

No one has a monopoly of bravery: the Russians and the Germans had at least as much power of endurance as we had; no one could have had greater than theirs. That is what makes modern bombing policies designed to 'bring people to their knees', look so ridiculous – and so contemptible. Not because the assaulted peoples are, by nature, heroic. They have got to be. There is all too frequently nowhere they can run to. Then we can see how the whole of their care and ingenuity is directed to the safety of their families, chiefly to their children. They must simply do their best. This is called courage.

The war in South East Asia – so we are told – has 'ended', if it can be ended. The conflict in Northern Ireland – how Hotspur would have rebuked my Finsbury terms – is beyond solution, so far as I can see. Anyway, I am not going to wade in. How do we show our courage now? In saying Boo to militant strikers who may appear to run riot? There is no courage in this. It is simply a huddling together in acute discomfort. But there is nothing else we can do, is there? So we huddle.

But do not forget that it is in our temperament – as the war showed – to huddle indefinitely. And so long as some of us suspect that many of these wage claims, in their haste, are not industrially but politically based, we can go right on huddling.

On the whole, this country seems to be behind the most responsible strikers. But the strikers who reduce to the lowest danger level the hospital and gas services, services for the old and for the schoolchildren, have forfeited a great deal of public sympathy.

I felt warmly towards those hospital ancillary workers, some of whom, appalled by what they saw, went back to work. This is not blacklegging. It is a feeling for human beings. Their pay is contemptible, and they must have an increase. My own daughter worked for several months as a low-paid nurse (un-qualified) at a mental hospital. Her hours were long, her wages pitiful. But she said, 'Do you think I could strike?' I think we must treat our nurses and our ancillary workers as special cases, and not take advantage of the moral difficulties of their position.

Clothes, food, and elegance in general.

I have not cared much, for some years past, about clothes. So long as I had two decent suits, without cigarette burns or moth-holes, they would do. But I did love them greatly, and only became befuddled when my juniors began to array them-selves in peculiar tat from antique supermarkets. In my view, they looked absolutely dreadful: because they allied themselves to nothing, and nothingness in clothes is as awful as nothing-ness in architecture.

Elegance is, in the main, only a supreme form of neatness, a precision of choice in accessories, and is not essentially some-thing one has to buy with very much money. I like to wear hats occasionally but hate gloves – however, I can always, on formal occasions, carry the latter.

Food. The war taught the English how to cook. Materials were so scarce that it became necessary for the greatest possible inventiveness in their use. I know I could make a very credit-able 'cheese soufflé' out of powdered egg. Now, with restric-tions lifted, we can provide some of the best – and cheapest – cooking in the Western world. Of course, it would be absurd to claim that the 'little' Italian and French restaurants in London are really cheap, by ordinary eating standards: but they are still cheaper than they would be in France or in New York.

All the foregoing is fribble, of course. It is simply an attempt to see how the world goes by through a certain window. Some of us are comfortably housed, or have comfortable flats: many have country residences as well (though we don't) and nearly all have cars – which we don't, except for my daughter's Mini which is actually growing a *lining of moss*.

Some are comfortable in the suburbs – in Betjeman land: much nicer for the residents than most people suppose. Some are living in poverty, with the final descent to the lower slopes of Notting Hill Gate, where the chimneys arising above the house where John Christie murdered so many women, still arise. The street has another name now. How can one possibly pretend to provide a panorama of living? Half of us do not know – with the best will in the world – how the other half lives: though organisations such as Shelter attempt to bridge the gap. Some of us, through the accidents of life, have a fair idea.

But 'the way we live now' cannot help but be in a state of siege. Only yesterday (8 March, 1973) bombs exploded outside the Old Bailey, the Ministry of Agriculture, one in Dean Stanley Street – from Ireland, of course, though no blame has yet been apportioned to any particular element; utterly pointless violence. I do not suppose London will see much bombing, but it has seen something. (A demoniac voice echoes in my ear, '*You* do not suppose? Just wait for a while, and see.' Well, perhaps I had better.)

So I make my way through the quiet streets of Central London, among the harmonies of Cubitt's buildings, and I wonder how long this will be peaceful. I walk down sometimes to the stately elegance of the Royal Hospital, Chelsea, and its surrounding gardens. How long, O Lord? I am inclined to think, since we are doing nobody any harm, that it will be for quite a bit.

34. Children and Parents

'For better for worse, for richer for poorer, in sickness and in health –' These are the promises made by men and women in the marriage service of the Church of England. I also like to think they are made, silently, secularly, in many a register office, with its refulgent registrar and its display of flowers to cheer the whole business up.

But there are times when I wonder whether the same lines do not apply where children are concerned, *vis-à-vis* their parents.

I have said elsewhere that we must breed children primarily for *their* benefit, though obviously they profoundly elevate our own happiness or, equally, bring us unhappiness and anxiety. They are not to be used as a form of therapy: we must never *use* them, either in this way or in any other.

How often does the cry arise from the child, in moments of frustration – 'I didn't ask to be born!' No, you didn't, but unless you have had singularly bad luck in life – battering parents or no apparent parents at all, you have had some fun, haven't you? Remember, your parents often have guilt-feelings towards you. A smack on the leg or bottom when you were intolerable and had to be brought out of hysteria – these parents don't forget. They could always, they feel, have done much better than they did. Well, when it comes to your turn, just see if you can improve on what they did for, or to, you.

It is my experience that, during the period of adolescence, the reproaches heaped upon parents – if the child is given to verbal expression – are preposterous, but never mind about that. The time is approaching when the children are fretting to leave home – far earlier than once they did. What is one to do? Take risks, and go along with the main stream? With the boys,

I think one must, if their instinct is to strike out on their own. Usually, and perhaps surprisingly, they are up to no mischief: sometimes they are bent purely on travel, on seeing the world on a shoe-string. One can let them go when they leave school, with however dubious a heart. Girls are different, whatever Women's Lib say about the matter. They are more vulnerable – if nothing else, their relative lack of physical strength would make them so. They would be ill-advised at, say seventeen or eighteen, to make the trip to Africa or to India alone. (I do not refer to the drug-trail to Katmandhu, in search of 'mystic experience': this seems to me self-regarding in the last degree.

But the young want to get away from what is ironically described as 'the nest'; however comfortable we, the parents, try to make it for them, *we always do it wrong*. This is largely because our energies have begun to flag, and we can't keep up with them – and would look idiotic if we tried to. So the girls particularly (some of the boys at the universities like somewhere to come back to, when they are not on their travels) share flats with other girls, live untrammelled lives. They are adept at giving one another bad advice, but what can one do about that?

The point at issue is not whether one lets them go (unless one is Mr Moulton Barrett one has no option, and even he had one conspicuous failure) but how one feels when they do it. At adolescence, or earlier, one tends to find that the overt expression of affection becomes impossible, apart from the hail or farewell brushing of a cheek, one becomes acclimatised, and when the break comes, is ready for it. It is different, of course, for the widower or the widow, who have lost all they had. But if both parents survive, and remain fond of each other, there is no particular problem. Deep interest in their children remains: they feel it is not too much to ask for one occasional visit, the telephone call, the postcard. *But how damned humble they have become!*

I say, I hope bracingly, that our children do owe us something, unless we have given them a wretched deal. All those nights, sitting up, watching with dread the course of infantile diseases. The effort to give pleasure. The business of clothing and educating, so far as our inclinations – or our necessities – move us. Those patches of adolescence, in which we may observe that our children are feeling pain, but are able to do little about it. Anyway, no adolescent is going to listen to us.

None of us wishes to become a burden upon our children: indeed, the whole idea is peculiarly abhorrent. (We have no tradition of ancestor-worship in this country, which might help things along.) Yet a part of the burden of our age, unless we are as fit as fighting-cocks, will probably have to be accepted. We shall die, all in good time, and if we are fortunate, our children will mourn for us for a while: but soon, they will know a perceptible lightening of the spirits. They will breathe new air. They will really know the full meaning of liberty.

There is no doubt that as some of us grow old, so we become more crotchety, more demanding. We try consciously to plan *against* this, to take a strong line against bedevilling our children's lives in any way. But by then of course, we shall not be so strong, and resolutions may be hard to put into effect. Very fortunate are the married couples who take joy in each other – by which I mean the avid sharing of common interests – when their children have left them. Alas, there are too many grumbling and helpless widowers, too many creaking (and wappend widows.

One of the bad things about growing old – there are many, and Wordsworth's 'Old age, serene and bright, and lovely as a Lapland night' seems to me the most abysmal slop – is that we become suddenly afraid, before our children, of saying the wrong thing. For, in reasonably good health, we do not *feel* old: we feel as intellectually alive as we felt at twenty or thirty

– but any attempt to behave as though we did gets an embarrassed stare. So, to an extent, we are always acting. Acting our real age.

To any woman, there comes an awful moment when she realises that the dress she is trying on is *too young for her*. Her looks are more important to her than any man's (the narcissist excepted) to himself, and so, when she perceives herself in her mirror very, very slowly rotting (because that is what she is doing), she feels it keenly.

Oddly enough, I have longed on occasion, for great wealth for one purpose only: so that I could buy a dressmaker who could keep me in self-confidence and cover up the ravages of time. How petty it seems! But there is no good pretending you are not capable of pettiness when, in the teeth of world chaos, famine, misery, you know you can be.

I have been speaking of parents and children in general, not wishing to violate my own privacies. But in this I have been lucky: my own children do not snub me. I have heard other parents brutally and publicly snubbed by their offspring: which is quite as painful as hearing a married couple squabble in public; in fact, worse. Making fun of me is a different thing, and quite acceptable.

There is no hope for it. For richer, for poorer: for better, for worse: in sickness and in health. These are the responsibilities our children may have, in some part, to undertake for us. Pray they don't. Pray God we don't put a foot neatly across their threshold. We never mean to.

Families with shared interests – literature, music, theatre, cinema, painting, even television – what have you – are likely to come off luckiest. Does this smell of élitism? It may smell of what it please: it is a hard fact. For it takes social intercourse, at all age levels, out of the purely personal. Nothing is more boring than endless *personalia*. A family devoted entirely to soccer, may, for instance, have the same advantages, so we are not being so *élite* as all that. Just so long as a family recognises that there is a world elsewhere, there is every hope for its solidarity.

There are vast, umbrageous shadows thrown across the whole question of parents and children. To begin with, the young child cannot give love: but he can accept it. Little by little, genuine affection creeps in – not merely as a reward for parental endeavour – and may in time become powerful. Then there is likely to come a period of distrust. The child's will is strong. How far are his parents proposing to fight it? I suggest that more parents than do, should be prepared to fight damned nonsense when they see it: but if what is proposed is thoughtfully considered and not nonsense at all, then they should give the child all reasonable support.

Then comes the period when the child reaches full adulthood, and must live his life with as few claims from his parents as life allows. For it is a somewhat painful fact that the passionate interest in the child bestowed by his parents is not reciprocated. It can't be. He is a creature unbudding, with infinite potentiality: how exciting! His parents aren't exciting, unless they go in for political or other public activities, liable to keep them in the path of the storm. But they have budded and flowered, and now their leaves have fallen.

35. Literary Style

'Le style est l'homme même.' (Buffon)

'The style is the man.' This has been quoted often enough. It means that what a man *is* determines his style: so that true literary style can never be a deliberate act of will.

The style of the later works of Henry James became more convoluted as his mind became so. Proust's is intricate, though in quite a different way, because of the intricate workings of his fine intellect. The style of Robert Louis Stevenson, in the formal sense one of the most beautiful of all English, or Scotch, writing stylists, arose out of his own perfect and natural clarity. It is, in its simplicity, almost impossible to imitate, though a gallant attempt has been made recently, in a television version to conclude *Weir of Hermiston*. On the screen, it looks well: but to read it in paperback shows the impossibility of matching up the new with the old.

To have 'style' does not inevitably mean possessing grammatical perfection enough to satisfy Fowler. I have often grinned a little wryly when I have seen a young writer grappling with Fowler's precisions. After all, unless he is really illiterate, he does not need to try. It is we who make the language. I believe we are now officially permitted to indulge in split infinitives: though I dislike them myself, and usually go a long way round to avoid them.

Style can take quite a different form from purely literary perfection. I am told by Russians that Dostoevsky wrote a sort of journalese: his style lies in his *power*, as did Dreiser's, a lesser but still very formidable writer. Dreiser can, and does, often write quite horribly from a technical point of view: but with what force! It stamped itself over his entire work, so that I think, if one found a page of his manuscript drifting along a windy pavement, one would know that it was his. This would be true of all the most *powerful* of writers. Tolstoy? A page bearing no mention of Anna, of Pierre or Natasha, might have been harder to identify. His writing is pure, but it is in his infinite truth that his style resides.

Flaubert, I think (I am swimming against the tide) fussed too much. I always get from his novels a sense of strain, which for me usually prevents a full emotional response. So it is with the later Henry James.

Dickens, one of the most natural writers who ever lived, poured out his manic and depressive moods all over the paper, with the ease of someone emptying a bucket. If ever the man was the style, he was. Of course, he made heavy corrections: most writers do. But the first instinctual setting down of what he wanted to say was the best part of himself.

'I remember the players have often mentioned it as an honour to Shakespeare that in his writing ... he never blotted out a line. My answer hath been "would he had blotted a thousand."' This could only have come from Ben Jonson who, except when he was writing lyrics or letting his dramatic vein run freely, was something of a classical pedant.

No one can deny James Joyce style, especially in the fine early books, like *Dubliners* and *Portrait of the Artist as a Young Man*, but in *Ulysses* and above all in *Finnegan's Wake*, he has gone all out for the deliberate creation of a 'style' like a greyhound after an electric hare. The results of this immense struggle (the hare was caught in *Ulysses*, anyway) are often exciting and beautiful: but they make rather for music, or poetry, or sometimes grand opera, than they do for the creation of a novel. Joyce, like Jonson, was a pedant and there all resemblance ceases.

Trollope is a far better stylist than is generally thought. His human understanding and compassion, his splendid dialogue, all make for a style of his own: though he wrote sloppily at times, and I personally would he had blotted a thousand subplots. But then, poor chap, he gave the game away when, in his *Autobiography*, he admitted the speed and the discipline with which he wrote. Many writers are given to both speed and discipline, but they tend to conceal the fact. In Trollope's day, more than perhaps in ours, the stereotype of the romantic writer, with exophthalmic eyes wildly rolling in search of something called 'inspiration'; working in sudden bursts and pardonably drunk (or tubercular) between times, was dear to the heart of the public. Trollope actually worked most industriously in the Post Office and took his pleasure in the hunting-field: and had the lack of tact to say so. His finest work lies, perhaps, in his great set-scenes: Mr Crawley confronting Mrs Proudie at the Bishop's Palace: the Duke of Omnium rebuking Lady Glencora for her electoral indiscretions: the same Duke, delighted to find that his two wild sons had, for once, joined him at breakfast just to give him pleasure, trying to repay them by kind little jokes and well-meant homilies. Many others. Here is the true 'style', if it is looked for.

We are still living in an age of 'experiment' in art, though this has all too often meant pure stylistic experiment, and no experiment at all in the extension of human understanding. That is why so many 'experimental' novelists in this narrow sense, find that very few people read them, and the ordinary cultivated reader has been driven back to history, biography, or the memoirs of soldiers and politicians. As I remarked many years ago, criticism (which tends to admire and to concentrate solely upon 'experiment' in style, as style is commonly understood), has been driving art steadily underground. Only a handful of English and American novelists can make a living out of this work alone (without the additions of broadcasting, journalism, or 'sitting' on campuses engaged in the hopeful but impossible task of teaching creative writing): and when they do, it is almost always because they care about those outmoded things – as some see it – character, narrative, atmosphere.

Style should only be complex in strict relation to the complexity of the subject: and deliberate obscurity should be checked. *The Brothers Karamazov* is, in parts, a very difficult book indeed, because it has great intellectual complexities: but Dostoevsky has done nothing to make this worse. In *The Devils* (usually called *The Possessed*) I do think he has raised some unnecessary barriers. I once calculated that it was only when I got to p. 247 of my copy that the whole pattern began, en-thrallingly, to emerge: but his method in this book is to bemuse for far too long.

The style of Proust is so iridescent that it seems (until one is used to the enormous lengths of his paragraphs and his unique rhythms) difficult to the beginner: which it really is not. No *Oxen of the Sun*-like parodies here, and singularly little, during the entire long work, which is truly extraneous. If the essence of Proust's style could be expressed in painting, the result would be rather like one of Monet's great *Nymphéas*.

I have deliberately refrained from speaking here of living writers because I think we lack the perspective to do real justice to our contemporaries, and may fall into grave errors which we might recognise in twenty or thirty years' time. God knows it was hard enough, as a weekly reviewer of fiction (I was one, for seventeen years) to make snap judgments. It was necessary, of course, but it always left me with an underlying sense of unease. How far did I overrate Lagerquist? Underrate the later Thomas Mann? I did try not to let my claws show very often and think that, except in one or two cases, I succeeded. The novelist-reviewer has often been criticised, but at least he, or she, knows something of the *intentions* of the work under re-view, and understands the difficulties that have gone into achieving it.

The highly self-conscious style is usually, to me, an irritant: unless, like Wilde's, it serves the cause of wit. *The Importance of Being Earnest* is highly-stylised, and remains one of the great English comedies. But prose is different. I have always been maddened by Walter Pater. 'Hard, gem-like flame', indeed! What bosh. And what on earth does it mean?

I think my perpetual urge to know what things mean adds to my suspicion of formal 'styles', as an end in itself.

To sum up. The difficulty of style should only be consonant with the difficulty of the work. There is no need to create difficulties, even if they make the writer seem profound. *Finnegan's Wake* is an unjustifiable complication of a subject matter insufficient to bear so much weight.

Complication is one of the manias of our era. If you are saying something really complex, you should do your best to spell it out for the reader in so far as is possible. *Sense and Sensibility* is by no means an 'easy' book, but Jane Austen did not try to make it more difficult than it actually was. *The Wings of a Dove* is a difficult book, and James did wrong, stylistically, to obfuscate it. The Parables of Jesus are not at all easy, though he used the form that they might be more so. (Though I have never yet understood The Unjust Steward.)

In fine, it is no use showing off. You will only, when the chips are down, have produced the effect of having done so. The nineteenth-century novelists were wiser than we.

36. Endings. (1) A Partial Conclusion

This may be the last book I shall write. If I should follow it up with half a dozen more, I shall look a fool for saying so. But what could I conceivably care? Self-concern is a prerequisite of youth. To my old confrères, the critics, I tip my cap in respect, because we have shared the same profession, and I shall read with interest what they say – and may on occasion, perhaps, be gratified: but on the whole, I shall not care.

In writing this book, the one thing that has caused me some pain is the need for reticence on some subjects. I should have wanted to say much of Charles: something more about my children than I have done. But I am revolted by any idea of a moral strip-tease. My house is mine. If my children care to make it theirs, then it is theirs. We shall all talk as much, and as seldom, as we please.

I have called this book, *Important to Me*: and now realise that there is no end to that. To begin with, I wish to say that sexual-plus-emotional love is all important. It is at the deepest foundations of life and joy. Take my word for that. (You may not, but so much the worse for you.)

It does not, of course, remain at that peak of excitement for ever. But something else then intervenes: a kind of exquisite friendship. An absorbing unity of interests.

To children: fall into love, before you fall into sex, otherwise you are going to get horribly let down.

This is my final homily, to you, or to everyone else. And I know of what I speak.

Last week I went to Max Adrian's memorial service at St Paul's Church, Covent Garden. It struck me that, for so ebullient a man, it was a trifle overweighted. I kept on thinking of his ditties, 'Jolly, jolly Customs men are we', and 'I'm in love with a wonderful ghoul!' I am not suggesting that an amalgam of these should have formed an organ voluntary. But I think I did want to say goodbye to him more gaily.

I don't know whether anyone will give me a Memorial Service, or not. On the whole better not: I have a terrible feeling that nobody might turn up. But if this did take place, I should like it to begin with the First Movement of the Third Brandenburg, and end with Widor's Toccata in F – usually, nowadays, a wedding voluntary, but remorselessly cheerful. I should like someone to read the final paragraph of *A la Recherche du temps perdu*, in Stephen Hudson's translation.

All very quick – it is bound to be a very hot or a very cold day, transport may be tricky, and people will be wanting their luncheons. This will serve to write me off completely, and so much the better. *Taxi! Taxi!* I can hear the rushing feet, see the upstretched arms.

How awful if no one came! Perhaps better forget the whole idea, no more than the fantasy of a moment.

I don't know what has forced me into such a fit of morbidity, except that, at the moment, I am suffering from a beastly complaint called bronchial spasm (through eating my fill of that stranded whale) and sometimes it is hard to breathe. I shall pick up all right, I suppose, and in a fortnight may be playing my favourite game of miniature golf at Coq-sur-Mer (de Haan) – which has long been a favourite place of mine on the Belgian coast. Though I must add rapidly that no such tragedy as occurred in my novel, to which De Haan partially provided a background, has ever darkened this delightful place, and the dunes are bare of menace.

I am much looking forward to the future. Philip says I must go to Tanzania – well, I will get there somehow. Raymond Burr, of Ironside and Perry Mason fame, a good actor and a great philanthropist, once offered to take Charles and me to

Kyoto – though this, I feel, might be too much of a strain on me. Who on earth wants a travelling companion who constantly needs to retire to bed? I have to say that even in my girlhood, two in the morning was the latest hour I could endure. But there are great parts of Italy and France that I have not visited! What do I know even of England? Not the Derbyshire Dales, nor the Lake District. What I know of Scotland, is cold, cold. The rocks are beautiful and precipitate down to the foaming sea, and the fulmars beautiful as they fly: but everyone seems *to want to open windows*. The Scotch are a hardy people. I do not much, in fact, care for places which have not the artefacts of man. Scenery is not enough. Delphi, now – but Delphi has everything, including circulating flights of miraculous doves, and at the end of it all, the Castalian spring, and the eager Bronze Charioteer, whose guardian loves him like a son. 'Look at the callouses on his poor heels!'

Where should I like to make an end? Well, not on the Steppes. I had an irrational dread of that. I should have been so far away – *from what?* I do not know. But far away. Very far away.

Not that I should wish, wherever my ashes were, to be ceremonially visited. I just want to lie in English earth – or, more precisely, to be scattered somewhere around it. (Not put in some wretched urn in a hole in the wall.)

Am I afraid of death? Honestly, I do not know. I will know when the time comes. But I hope I have much to look forward to before that happens. As I have said, I have still not seen Piero's *Resurrection* at Borgo di San Sepolchro. I wonder if I ever shall? I have not seen Hugo Van der Goes's *Adoration of the Shepherds*, because when I went to Uffizi, it was away being cleaned. My luck. I have seen my fill of my beloved Flemings. And I have seen most of the great Museums – and some private collections – in the United States. But there is so much more, so much more!

Time runs out like the bath-water. In the bath, one can

always put the plug back in. But then it grows cold. Time is like that.

For me, no madeleine dipped in tea, no stumble on a paving-stone in the Baptistry of St Mark's. I have had fleeting experiences of this kind, of course: most people have. But I have never been able to grasp them as they flew. They have never spurred me on to creation. Dear Proust: even if all his 'experiences' brought back only one thing – his childhood – and the later ones in the drawing-room of the Princesse de Guermantes were a little suspect, he deserved them. He had worked long in silence, solitude and sickness, long before he began to write *A la Recherche du temps perdu*. His was a heroic life.

In 1971, the centenary of his birth, the name of Illiers was changed to Illiers-Combray. This was a gesture so graceful, so absolutely right, so exquisitely French – in the most classical French manner – that it is beyond praise. I can't think of another writer who has ever had such a tribute paid to him.

No madeleine for me. But I hope mine comes to me from some other source. (Why should it? Still, one can always hope: and trust.) In the time that remains to me, I hope to tell, in my writing, the absolute truth. Of course, since I write novels, they must of necessity be largely fabrications: but I want to tell the psychological truth as stringently and as clearly as I can see it. It is an odd thing that after a lifetime of adoring Shakespeare, Proust, Dostoevsky, it is Tolstoy who finally gives me an ideal. I care for *Anna Karenina* – which is sometimes dreadful in its truthfulness – I have read, re-read, and am, I confess, largely untouched by *War and Peace*. Yet it is the truth of Tolstoy that I reverence.

I should like, in my fiction, if I write any more, never to tell a psychological lie to make a situation more easy, or to make it fit. Many of the novels I read today seem to me full of the most preposterous psychological shenanigans. We may be in the grip of a contemporary desire for fantasy, which I confess I do not share. I am left cold.

At least, I am left cold by this kind of fantasy, which far too often purports to represent life. Books of fantasy read in my childhood hold for me a permanent joy: later, I have been enthralled by some – not all – of the C. S. Lewis's *Narnia* stories. Tolkien does not move me, and I don't know why: this is something of a chagrin to my son Philip. In my childhood, the Brothers Grimm were far more important to me than Hans Andersen, who seemed to me either slightly cruel, or soppy. The Brothers Grimm were frightfully cruel, when they wanted to be – but soppy, no. My edition had all those brutal-looking German woodcuts. I think they enriched my youth, never gave me a vestige of a nightmare, and added up to the wonderful accretions of the creative imagination.

So I come towards the end of this book. It has been a selfish book: it has been about the things that were important to *me*. Now I think nothing is so important, as what happens to Charles and to my children.

I think I can fairly say that I have no hates, unless it were for bullying girls, much larger than I, who made a part of my school-days a misery. I don't care now, of course.

As it happens, our living-room looks on to an open road, with the fine black and white spire of St Mary's at the end. No one can build us in, so we shall have the sunshine through our windows to the end of our days. On fine nights, it is a perpetually marvellous spectacle. Aeroplanes, helicopters, slip across an infinity of Tiepolo sunsets. So we ourselves sweep across that expanse of sky from time to time. So, I imagine, metaphorically from life to death. One day – the end? Well, there must be an end, mustn't there? The more luminous the better.

I like the image of a life as a swallow flying in from the darkness into the great hall, and, after its moment of light, out into the darkness again. But if it is to be acceptable to me, the swallow, after the second darkness, must come into the light once more.

'*Timor mortis conturbat me.*'

Few intellectuals have been undisturbed by this. It has a ring to it that is almost a jingle. It could be a song for skipping to:

> Eenie, meenie, miney mo,
> *Timor mortis conturbat me.*

I don't know why we all regard death as so peculiarly special. It is the great commonplace. Birth seems much more extraordinary.

Meanwhile, it would be as well if I started thinking about writing another novel.

37. Endings. (2) The Sea

I was sitting at a café window, on the promenade at De Haan, watching a stormy sea. The great rollers, dung-coloured, charcoal and black, breaking into dirty white crests, thundered up the beach, exploding but never reaching the sea wall. The sky above was leaden, the gales moaned and the rain cracked against the windows. Even inside, in the warmth of the room, I could feel the inner chill: it had been a terrible beginning to April, and bitterly cold during the days we had been in Belgium.

At that moment there appeared, in the sky, not a ray of sunshine, but something like a tremor of light: which at once lent a less dirty touch to the breakers, but left the rollers unchanged. Then, simultaneously, the rain came down harder and there grew, high up, a patch of Poussin blue. A pale rainbow glimmered over the dunes to the right. The blue spread, the sun poured down and the rain ceased. The rainbow faded. The water was now changed to a lighter grey, a purer yellow, with blue hardly perceptible but full of promise. Within a few minutes, the promenade was alive with children on their hired bicycles, the frames bright red and yellow and green, fighting joyously against the gale, all of them a danger to life and limb. It was filled, too, with adults in leather coats and anoraks, determined to be in a holiday mood at all costs.

I felt a considerable uplift in my spirits, which had been lowered by the icy and blustering walk to the café. From the window now, it really was possible to delude oneself that it was spring.

Soon, Philip's friend, another Philip – Philip Mansel – joined us for a few days. He drove us over one morning to Ghent. The weather was as horrible as ever, the wind worse: even

Charles, who seems to have a remarkable inner thermostat, was
glad to get out of the cold. St Bavon was closed till 2.30, so we
had a drink at a café and then a leisurely lunch. I was excited
at the thought of seeing again, for the third time, Van Eyck's
The Mystic Lamb, for me the most beautiful of all paintings.
The chapel was freezing; even the custodian, huddling by his
little electric fire, was shivering. On chairs set along the wall
there were the usual tourists, but no crowds this time.

Then the painting, the first impression like an enormous
display of incomparable jewels, dazzling, mind-shaking. The
falling into place of the marvellous panels: the martyrs passing
by their hedge of roses. St Christopher leading his pilgrims,
angels with faces of ineffable purity raised in song, Saint Cecilia
absorbed at the organ, sad Adam and Eve, all hope gone:
the Immaculate Lamb, so mild on his altar, blood spouting in
a slender fountain from his breast, angels worshipping about
him: and above all, the three great figures: the Virgin Mary,
crowned with lilies and roses, rubies and pearls, St John the
Baptist in a green cloak, and in the middle, Christ in Glory.
He is a young man, with only a delicate growth of beard: but
so fatherly, He seems not only the Son but the Father himself.
I think of him as God. Max Friedländer, does indeed call him
'God the Father'. His face is serene, stern, but promising
mercy. He is wonderfully attired, in triple tiara and robes
richly embroidered: a glittering, blazing, vermilion robe at
His feet; almost a blinding crown, the golden filigree set with
a multiplicity of emeralds, rubies, diamonds and sapphires. But
it is this thing above all that gives the painting such majesty
and peace: it is God's beautiful hand raised in benediction
above us all.

Most of my friends are, I suppose, agnostics: yet I myself
find it impossible to believe that they are not moved even for
a fleeting moment, by a mystery outside of themselves, if only
by the involuntary realisation of the accretion of the passionate
faith of five hundred years ago.

If there are not too many people about, it is best to get as near to the painting as possible, so as to study the detail of landscape and flora: sometimes it seems like a complete herbarium. It is necessary to look away from it time and time again, whenever the glory begins to dim, and then to catch it again, suddenly, the peace of its wonder; all its colours restored by the momentary resting of the eyes.

When I left the chapel, I felt, on that bitter winter's day in mid-April, that something extraordinary had happened to me: not in an exaggerated fashion, not as a revelation, not, I suspect, in any sense of mystical experience. But for some time I had been rather ill – not very – with a respiratory complaint, and was making a somewhat slow recovery. As I said, or implied somewhere else, this would plunge me suddenly into fits of depression or of inner turmoil – not long-lasting, but distressing at the time. Suddenly I felt that I had only to fix my mind on that hand upraised in benediction to become peaceful again at once: peaceful, and still. Is it presumption to use a great painting as a sort of icon? Icons themselves have, for centuries, been peace-giving.

We drove around Ghent after that, passing but not entering the Gravensteen, seeing beautiful houses that we had missed before, and willow-hung canals: Philip Mansel found the house where Louis XVIII had lived (a monarch for whom he has a singular fondness), now a smart antique shop: he was able to go in and photograph it. We came home in excellent spirits, discussing just *what* news had been brought from Ghent to Aix. We were all tired, but we had had a happy day. Happiness. 'The absence of pain?' Only someone who had never experienced the earthly paradise could have reduced it to that.

I am a natural worrier, as my mother was. If I have nothing to worry about, I invent something. If Charles or the children do not come in about the time I expect them, I foresee atrocious accidents – the consequences, the In Memoriam notices, the funerals, the unthinkable grief. But above all, these imaginings

are disgustingly *practical*. I have to have my plans worked out
to the last detail. Needless to say, all this would be a terrible
bore to my husband and children if I said very much about it.
When they do come in, with perfectly reasonable explanations
for their lateness, I greet them with casual pleasure and return
to *The Times* crossword puzzle.

But when I am not indulging in this sort of nonsense, I can
be very happy: like Rimbaud, I can have my *Illuminations*,
sudden and unexpected. The charm of a group of young people
seriously discussing the world they will have to cope with.
The magnificent face of some stranger, glimpsed perhaps only
for a moment. The joy when something I am writing is going
right, is flowing, as from some involuntary source. This does
not often happen. Joy in some triumph of Charles's or of the
children's. The Backs at Cambridge on a winter morning
under snow, every bough bearing its delicate loading like
blossom.

Like Proust, I think I am recovering something of the fresh-
ness of the inward eye, though I am not sure (as Wordsworth
was) that too much solitude is good for me.

From the bitingly cold short holiday on the Belgian coast,
I have learned much. The eternal uplifting transformations of
the sea, the benediction of Van Eyck. I hope they may stay
with me.